# THE GROWTH
# OF UNDERSTANDING
# IN MATHEMATICS

# THE GROWTH OF UNDERSTANDING IN MATHEMATICS

Kindergarten through Grade Three

**KENNETH LOVELL**

University of Leeds

**HOLT, RINEHART AND WINSTON, INC.**
New York   Chicago   San Francisco   Atlanta
Dallas   Montreal   Toronto   London   Sydney

Copyright © 1971 by Holt, Rinehart and Winston, Inc.
All rights reserved
Library of Congress Catalog Card Number: 79-135129
**SBN: 03-083599-2**
Printed in the United States of America
1 2 3 4    090    1 2 3 4 5 6 7 8 9

To
JEAN PIAGET
and
BÄRBEL INHELDER

# Introduction

## Early Childhood Education Series

More than any other decade in American history, the sixties might be called the Decade of Early Childhood Education. Interest in and activity concerning the young child were sparked by the exciting idea that early human development is plastic and can be altered in significant ways. In particular, the notion that mental growth is cumulative and that later development of intelligence depends in part upon early intellectual stimulation led to the emergence of a cognitive emphasis in early education, an emphasis that attracted educational psychologists to the scene. The educational psychologists attacked the "child-development"-based type of nursery-school program with its strong emphasis on social–emotional development through play and the creative arts, and argued instead for a systematic, structural approach to cognitive development. The child-development school drew upon the newer theoretical framework to defend its programs; its advocates pointed out the value of play and the creative arts for cognitive growth. They also began to search for ways to use play more explicitly for development of concepts of number, space, time, matter, and causality, in line with development as described by Piaget.

The controversy is still far from being resolved, but it is safe to predict for the seventies that some of the very extreme, even bizarre programs on both sides of the continuum will disappear. Educational psychologists will discover that "learning is child's play," as one writer has phrased it, and child developmentalists will recognize the need for some structuring for maximum cognitive effectiveness. Hopefully, both schools will recognize the affective and social determinants of learning, often lost sight of while controversy between different schools of thought raged. Hopefully, too, the tight, rigidly scheduled programs of the traditional kindergarten and primary grades with their emphasis upon workbooks, seat-work, show-and-tell, and other teacher-dominated activities will also be modified.

If progress is made in this decade, it will be due in large part to the extraordinary amount of recent research to determine which environmental correlates, including special educational programs, accelerate or retard development. Teachers and teachers-in-training need to be aware of the antecedent conditions of a given state of development. One still hears all too often the argument in justification of a program, "But the children love it," as if children instinctively like that which is good for them and dislike that which is bad. Only as teachers can evaluate the theory and research findings in early childhood education will they be able to protect children against inevitable faddists.

The Holt, Rinehart and Winston Series in Early Childhood Education is designed to present in readable fashion what the state of the art is with respect to some of the continuing problems in early childhood education.

The treatments will be scholarly and practical. Each book will review pertinent research findings and present practices and describe promising trends in the field. In my opinion, it should make a uniquely positive contribution to early childhood education for years to come.

*Urbana, Illinois*  Celia Lavatelli
*October 1970*

# Preface

This book has three aims: first, to give readers a better understanding of the mathematical ideas that one wishes to introduce to children, from the point of view of the thinking skills involved; second, to indicate some of the kinds of activities which might help pupils to understand and use these ideas; third—and this aim is intimately linked with the first—to give insight into the relative difficulty of these ideas for children at various broad age levels.

In order to attain these aims, considerable use will be made of the views of Jean Piaget of Geneva. For well over forty years he and his associates have published books that deal with many aspects of the growth of children's thinking, and they have provided us with more information on this important topic than any other group. At the same time it must also be clearly stated that their views do not explain all the facts confronting us in our day-to-day encounters with pupils' thinking; one day these views will no doubt be subsumed under a theory that will account for more of the facts.

Throughout this work the term *thinking* will be used to indicate a flow of mental actions or ideas directed to some end or purpose, thus contrasting with the thinking in which we are concerned with autistic thinking and fantasy. Indeed, it is important to accept at the outset that mathematics primarily involves mental activity directed to some clear aim, and writing on paper is only an aid.

While this book deals essentially with children's understanding of mathematical concepts, it is important to emphasize that children must also learn to compute quickly and accurately. In order to accomplish this, they will need to work exercises given in a text or otherwise provided by the teacher. As for the activities suggested here to foster pupils' comprehension of mathematics, teachers are encouraged to modify them in the light of their own situation. They can omit those which they think unnecessary for particular pupils. Even more important is the need for teachers to develop further activities to reinforce those presented here.

Finally it is important to stress that our knowledge of the growth of thinking in children is not yet sufficient or exact enough to serve as a basis for a scientific pedagogy. An intuitive understanding of children on the part of the teacher is still essential. But Piaget's work provides the best conceptual framework we yet have, inside which we can discuss the growth of children's understanding of mathematics.

The manuscript was read by Charles Reynolds of the University of Leeds, who made many suggestions for improving the text. For these the author is extremely grateful. Whatever errors or misunderstandings remain are solely the author's responsibility.

*Leeds, England*  K. Lovell
*October 1970*

# Contents

Introduction — vii

Preface — ix

**1**
The Growth of Thinking in Children — 1

**2**
Set, Number, and Numeration — 23

**3**
Operations and Mathematical Sentences — 45

**4**
Space — 69

**5**
Geometry — 95

## 6
Relationships and Mappings                                121

## 7
Further Work on Number                                    133

## 8
Pictorial Representation                                  153

## 9
Weight, Mass, Time, and Volume                            167

## 10
Classroom Organization and Children Learning Mathematics  181

Bibliography                                              193

Index                                                     201

# THE GROWTH
OF UNDERSTANDING
IN MATHEMATICS

# 1
# The Growth of Thinking in Children

In the 1950s changes began to take place in the teaching of mathematics. From that time children were increasingly expected to look at familiar mathematical ideas in new ways and to learn about new ideas. Unfortunately those who were responsible for suggesting these changes often failed to realize, sufficiently, that the development of children's thinking must also be considered at the same time. In other words, they overlooked the fact that there must be some kind of match between the quality of the thinking skills of the child and the complexity of the mathematical ideas to which he is introduced.

## PIAGET'S CONCEPTUAL FRAMEWORK FOR THE GROWTH OF CHILDREN'S THINKING

Let us now turn to Jean Piaget's views on the growth of children's thinking, bearing in mind the relevance of such growth to mathematical understanding. Two preliminary points must be made. First, only an outline sketch of his views can be given here, and interested readers should refer to other works for further details (Piaget, 1950; Flavell, 1963). Second, Piaget's work cannot tell us which mathematical ideas should be introduced to children; only mathematicians and teachers can do that. But his findings do throw much light on the stages through which pupils pass in the growth of these ideas and on some of the difficulties likely to arise at various age levels.

In essence the observations of Piaget suggest that the child comes into the world with only a few reflex-like activities available to himself. For example, he cries, sucks, and moves his tongue. These activities seem to have been pre-programmed, in the sense that the tendency to carry them out is innately given. The infant does not "know" as we adults know. Slowly, over the early months of life, he puts an organization or structure on what he does and on the sensations he receives through his sensory organs. Thus *he* is the agent that creates his mind, for he builds reality into the structure that he imposes on his actions and sensations.[1] Before he can think, he has to be able to do things as in grasping, moving, touching; and thought is evoked directly out of these skills by rehearsing them to himself. In short, thought is internalized action.

The process of acting on his environment and of organizing his experience results in the child building up sequences of physical action in infancy, and of mental actions later on, which have definite structure. Thus the infant builds a series of physical actions, which have both sequence and structure, involved in, say, the use of a stick to push an object otherwise beyond reach; in adolescence he elaborates a series of actions in his mind which enables him to understand, say, proportion. It has been with the growth of the structure underlying the development of the child's thinking skills that Piaget and his associates have been concerned. Important changes in the thinking of children take place around twenty-one months of age, around five years, at seven to eight years of age, and around fourteen to fifteen. These landmarks come earlier in able children, while dull subjects may never attain the level of thinking reached by average pupils around adolescence. Indeed there are considerable individual differences in respect of these ages.

### The First Twenty-one Months of Life

Although this is a vital period in the growth of the child's thinking, only a little will be said about it here. Readers who are interested in the details of this age range, or in the likely long-term effects of sensory and linguistic deprivation during this period, should consult appropriate texts. For the present study, it is sufficient to say that when ordinary children aged eighteen to twenty-one months are faced with a new situation, overt trial and error is no longer as necessary as it was a few months earlier in order to attain a desired end. As long as the situation is a simple one, the child's awareness of relationships is now sufficient

---

[1] This process of structuring reality is continuous throughout life.

for him to invent new behavior and see which actions will succeed and which will not, without actually trying them out. This invention comes through a covert process; there must now be some kind of inner or mental experimentation, for the infant can represent to himself how the various possible lines of action will have to be combined to attain the desired goal. His actions are now carried out in inward form—that is, they have become internalized. There is now a flow of ideas to some end or purpose. In short, he is beginning to think. The period from birth to around twenty-one months or so is called by Piaget the period of sensori-motor intelligence, since before the child can think he needs the direct support of information obtained through motor action and through the senses.

During the same time there occurs the growth of more specialized intellectual achievements such as the sensori-motor construction of the object, of causality, space, and time. These achievements are also of consequence for the later development of mathematical ideas. For example, the child's first basic notions of space are elaborated as he adjusts his actions to reach near and distant objects, and of time when he adjusts his movements to catch a swinging toy.

**From Twenty-one Months to Five Years of Age**

From the first birthday or soon after, one can see the child beginning to imitate the actions of others, to utter his first words, and to engage in symbolic play. In essence the child is forging the instruments which will enable him a little later to differentiate between a signifier (image, word) and a significate, that is, what the signifier stands for, and use the one to represent the other. The capacity to make this differentiation, and to be able to make an act of reference, is termed the *semiotic* function by Piaget.

By twenty-one months of age the child has been able to use imagery (this is internalized imitation in Piaget's view) for a short period to represent the world to himself. From this age onward, however, he can increasingly use two- and three-word utterances. For example, he can use the word "dog" to refer to the animal and talk about it in its absence. Whereas imagery is personal to the individual and is much like the object, person, or event in its representation, language is socially shared, and the sounds uttered bear no concrete resemblance to their referents. Moreover language provides the child with a more mobile and less transient model of the outside world, for the child's thoughts can travel outside the present environment in space and time since language acts as a symbolic vehicle which carries his thoughts.

Between two and four years of age no great increase in problem-solving ability takes place except for that due to physical maturation, and the growth of thinking consists to some extent in the building up of this representational ability. The child has to rework all he did earlier, using language. In reasoning he tends to display transductive thought, that is, he argues from particular to particular. For example, he may say that because Mummy is cleaning her shoes, she is going out (since previously when she cleaned her shoes she left the house). Obviously such reasoning brings the child into grievous error at times. The notions which the child builds up are termed pre-concepts by Piaget, for they lie somewhere between the notion of an object and the concept of a class of objects. Walking around the garden, he will say "snail" every time he sees a snail, without being able to decide if the same snail keeps reappearing or whether he sees instances of the same class of animals. He cannot yet elaborate the concept of a class as he will from seven to eight years of age. Thus he distinguishes a soccer ball from a tennis ball on the basis of size, texture, and the situations in which they are used; he cannot subsume them under the class of balls. He is at the first level of abstraction or dissociation from reality, for he distinguishes objects and their properties on the basis of their behavior.

In his more recent writings Piaget (1968, 1969a) has characterized the thinking of a child between two and five years of age as a semilogic,

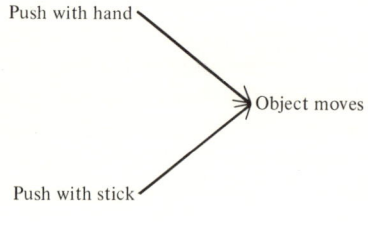

FIGURE 1

whose mathematical expression can be thought of as a number of one-way mappings or functions. This can be explained as follows. As early as the sensori-motor period, the child learns that certain action patterns on his part give certain results. He may push an object with his hand and move it, or push it with a stick and move it similarly. These action patterns are the common source of both knowledge of the physical world and of later logic. Provided the functional relationships are close to his own actions, he can well understand the former, which are expressed in the accompanying diagram (Figure 1) as a many-to-one mapping.

The child can, of course, also appreciate a functional relationship which may be expressed as a one-to-one mapping as, for example, when the object is out of reach and he has to employ a stick to move it. In Piaget's view this simple dependency between his push and the movement of the object is at the very origin of the child's later grasp of two other functions: first, that of real physical dependency, in the sense that movement of $a$ depends upon a force $b$ due to another agent—here $a = f(b)$; and second, there is a conceptual dependency in the sense that knowledge of $a$ depends upon knowledge of $b$.

Yet even at four or five years of age the child's thinking remains a semilogical structure. This is neatly illustrated by an experiment by Van den Bogaerts (1966). A number of dolls are arranged on a table in a fixed pattern which is neither a circle nor a straight line. Each doll has a different colored dress, and in front of each doll is a counter of the same color. A toy truck moves along the dolls, the driver picking up the counters which are in front of the dolls and placing them in the truck in the same order in which they were picked up. From four to five years of age children could correctly answer questions of the type, "Why is the blue counter first?" "Why is the green counter next to the yellow one?" In the second part of the experiment the child has to retrace the journey made by the truck and deduce the latter's itinerary from the sequence of the counters. The four- and five-year-olds fail on this task. In other words, children of this age can grasp that the order of the counters is a function of the itinerary (one-way mapping), but they cannot grasp a two-way mapping and understand that the order of the counters determines the itinerary.

At this age, too, the child understands qualitative identity, but he does not conserve, say, length. For example, a four-year-old knows that if a piece of wire is taken and twisted into a different shape, "it's the same piece of wire, the same thing." But he will be seven or eight years of age, as we shall see later, before he will agree that the piece of wire remains the same length when twisted into certain shapes, such as that of spectacles.

### From Five to Fourteen Years

As has just been seen, the child enters this period with thinking skills which may be characterized as a semilogic whose mathematical expression can be thought of as a number of one-way mappings. Soon after the fifth birthday changes set in which allow him to give, more frequently, what adults call sound reasons for his actions and beliefs. However, even up to seven to eight years of age the child remains in what Piaget terms the period of intuitive thought—the term *intuition* here meaning, or indicating, sporadic and isolated actions in the mind that do not yet coalesce into the tighter integrated structures yielding systematized thought, as will be the case at around seven years.

Children in the age range from five to seven or eight years cannot consistently keep in mind more than one relationship at a time. The child may well say, "This car is black, this one is yellow," but he is far less likely to say, "This sausage is long but thin." In the latter example the child has to consider two dimensions at the same time. This inability to handle two relations at a time and make a sound judgment suggests that what judgments are made at this age are likely to be affected by their perceptions, as we shall see later. This inability to hold in mind more than one relationship at a time also results in the following:

1. Children do not stick to one opinion even over short periods of time. They do not necessarily believe contradictions when they change their opinion, but they forget the earlier point of view expressed and hence they cannot compare them.
2. Thinking lacks a proper sequence or direction. The cause of an event will be given in terms of successive unrelated explanations. And since there is an inability to imagine an ordered sequence of events, there may be a reversal in the actual order of happenings. For example, the child may say, "I am not well because I am not going to school."
3. For the most part, the child is unable to see a situation from another's viewpoint, and his thinking remains egocentric. Again while his thinking is largely inaccessible to reason, it is subject to suggestion and unconscious imitation. While the thinking of adults is similarly affected, in the case of most grown-ups their thinking is more susceptible to reason.
4. The inability to hold more than one relationship in the mind at a time makes it difficult or impossible to make a comparison of relationships or a judgment. A child will tell you how many brothers he has, but he finds it very hard to say how many brothers his sister has. Similarly the relationship between the whole and its parts is difficult. For example, Piaget quotes a reply from a child, which on using American instead of Swiss names runs like this: "Chicago is in Illinois, and Illinois is bigger than Chicago, but you cannot be in both at the same time." Again, if two similar bottles of soda have their respective contents poured into two glasses of very differing shape, so that the heights of the soda are very different, the five-year-old may

## The Growth of Thinking in Children

deny that the amounts of soda are now the same. He seems unable to take into account contrasting heights and widths which could compensate for the distortion brought about by concentrating on height. It is this inability to hold in mind more than one relationship at a time, and the tendency to "center" on one dimension, which underlies the performance of children at this age on conservation and whole/parts relationship problems.

But around seven years of age the child's thinking changes again. When given a task involving conservation of continuous quantity, he will maintain the equality of the liquids regardless of the size and shape of the recipient vessels. He will reply, "You haven't added any or taken any away" or "You've only poured it." Now two relationships can be held in mind at the same time, and he realizes that, say, "short-wide" can be changed into "tall-narrow" and vice versa. That is to say, he can now envisage complete and reversible compensations, and his thinking has now become what adults call logical, systematized, or internally consistent. In essence the child can look in on his own thinking and monitor it; he is *aware* of the sequence of actions in his mind. It is now possible for him to distinguish between his experiences and the organization that *he* imposes on them. He can impose an organization on collections which contain the same number of members, thereby elaborating the concept of the natural numbers. In short, his thinking now permits second-level abstractions from reality.

For any action in his mind he can now appreciate that there are other actions which will give the same result. In other words, he can appreciate equivalences between transformations that come as a result of the anticipation of virtual actions and their effects. Thus the child understands that 2 and 3, under the mathematical operation of addition, yield the same result as 4 subtracted from 9.

Children are now ready to enter the domain of classes, relations (seriations), and numbers. Only the first of these will be dealt with here; relations and numbers will come in a later chapter. To study the growth of classificatory systems the child is given (Inhelder and Piaget, 1964; Lovell, Mitchell, and Everett, 1962) a collection of geometrical figures, letters of the alphabet, and so forth, made of differing materials and of different colors. He is told to "put together the things that belong together" or some suitable variation of this. From about two and a half to five years of age the child makes what Piaget calls graphic collections. No kind of plan can be observed in the sorting, and the end product is a complex visual figure which may or may not have meaning for the child. For example, he may start by putting together letters. If the last one is blue, he may then add a blue circle. Or, he may line up squares horizontally and then continue vertically with other geometrical figures which are mixed in respect to shape and size. Groupings of objects made on the basis of any kind of similarity of property are unstable. This is because the child's thinking remains unsystematized, and he is unable to coordinate the exact qualities which define the membership of a particular logical class—class intension—with all the objects which possess these qualities—class extension.

Between five and seven years of age one observes a change. Objects are now grouped on the basis of similar properties, and a child can often divide a group or set into appropriate subsets. For example, he may put all the shapes on one side and letters on the other side, then divide the former into, say, circles, rectangles, and squares. Yet this may not be a true classification, for at this stage children tend to be inconsistent in the way in which they sort. The circles may be divided into large and small and then further subdivided by color. On the other hand, the rectangles and squares may be divided by color and then further subdivided by size (Figure 2). This inconsistency suggests an inadequate grasp of the inclusion relationship, so that the subject deals with the various sortings as they crop up instead of applying a classificatory plan from the beginning.

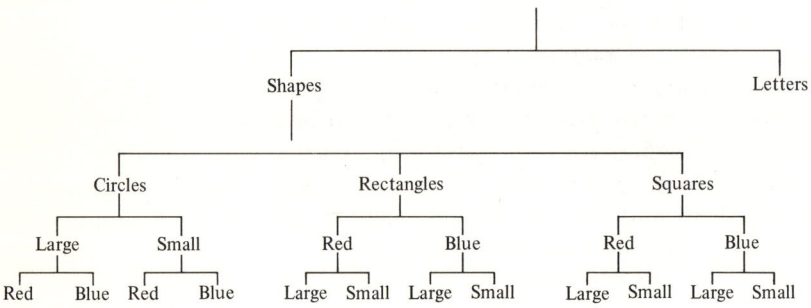

FIGURE 2

Then from around seven to eight years of age the child is increasingly able to coordinate intension and extension, thus making way for true classification. Classification is recognized by the child as a set of systematic interrelations so that $A + A^1 = B$ implies $A = B - A^1$, where $A^1$ is defined as *not A*.

In Piaget's system the term "action" is a generic one. In infancy actions are physical and observable. Later actions become increasingly internalized, as we indicated earlier, and they become more mobile and increasingly cohere to form complex and integrated systems of actions. Moreover any mental action which is part of an organized network of related actions is an *operation* in the Piagetian sense (note that the term "operation" is used differently by mathematicians). When the child's thinking has become systematized in the sense that we have indicated, his thinking is said to have reached the stage of concrete operational thought or first-order operations. Note that the child's logical thought extends only to intuitable (that is, perceptible or imageable) data although he need not have actual physical objects in front of him. Thus at the elementary school stage the child can reason about, say, mermaids, for such creatures are intuitable.

Now for Piaget, concrete operation thinking (systems of operations) must possess certain properties, for thinking that does not have these properties will show inconsistencies. These characteristics are:

1. Closure. Any two operations[2] can be combined to form a third operation: $3 + 4 = 7$; all boys plus all girls equals all children.
2. Reversibility. For any operation there is an opposite operation which cancels it. Thus $4 + 3 = 7$ and $7 - 3 = 4$: all boys plus all girls equals all children, but all children except boys equals all girls.
3. Associativity. When these operations are combined, it does not matter which two are combined first; or the same goal may be reached by different routes. Thus $(4 + 3) + 2 = 4 + (3 + 2)$.
4. Identity. There is a "null operation" when any operation is combined with its opposite. Thus $3 - 3 = 0$; all boys except those that are boys equals nobody.
5. The fifth property has two versions, one for classes and relations, the other for numbers:
    a. Tautology. Repeating a class or relation does not change it. All men plus all men equals all men.
    b. Iteration. A number combined with itself produces a new number. Thus $4 + 4 = 8$; $4 \times 4 = 16$.

With the onset of systematized thought the child shows greater flexibility in handling the materials of the sorting experiment (Figure 2). This is shown in respect both of his mental perspective and in his sorting and resorting of the materials. He will notice some property he ne-

---

[2] The term *operation* is used in the Piagetian sense: operations are concepts which are internalized responses. Of particular importance are the concepts of class, relation, and number. See Chapter 2.

glected when he commenced sorting and so change the criterion he is using, or he will change the criterion when the experimenter brings in fresh pieces to add to an existing classification. In either of these instances he shows flexibility in hindsight. On the other hand he will also show greater flexibility in foresight, because he can both anticipate a classification before making it and select a particular classification from a number of possible classifications without overt trial and error.

At this point it is worth looking more closely at the terms *retroaction* and *anticipation* as used by Piaget. Retroaction or hindsight refers to the process whereby an individual revises earlier actions in the light of those that follow—that is to say, he corrects his errors. On the other hand, anticipation or foresight refers to the apparent process whereby the mental representation of events reverses the order of their actual performance: thus in the resultant behavior, actions which occur earlier are modified by those that are to follow. Piaget and Inhelder (1964) have provided evidence that it is the increasing ability of the child to coordinate retroaction and anticipation which underpins his ability to systematize his thinking.

To illustrate this point, consider again the sorting experiment illustrated in Figure 2 (the argument can be used equally well in respect to experiments involving conservation). The child has first to answer the question "Shall I use size or color?" As soon as he has made his decision —say, size—and he has classified by this criterion, he can return to the one he has laid aside (color), for materials can now be resorted on the basis of immediate retroaction. Thus the growth of logical or systematized thought is said to be due to the movement from retroaction to anticipation, and from the latter to the recognition of systematic interdependencies and hence of transformations. A set of objects which are so rearranged that what are classes in one arrangement are subclasses in another arrangement, and vice versa, is a logical transformation in respect to the alternative arrangements. Thus the growth of systematized thought is greatly dependent upon the emergence of auto- or self-regulation through the effects of feedback.

Following the remarks about auto-regulation made in the last paragraph, we must look at Piaget's views on the value of experience, for they help us to understand why children should do experiments rather than sit and have them done by the teacher. There is, for Piaget, physical experience in which the child acts on objects to find out something about the objects themselves. For example, he finds that the weight of an object is not always what one might expect from its size, or that some small objects sink in water while other ones, much larger, float. Here there is a physical experience that abstracts, or "takes from," physical things to which the child's knowing is directed. But there is also logico-mathematical experience.

Here knowledge is not derived from the objects themselves, but from the actions performed on objects as, for example, when the child learns that four groups of three objects yields the same total as three groups of four objects. In this type of experience he has to keep a constant check on the coordination of his actions to avoid contradictions. Once again the auto- or self-regulating factor is fundamental. Put rather differently, the child reflects on his coordinating activity in an auto-regulatory sense. It is this kind of abstraction from the knowing activity itself and not from the objects of knowing (as in physical experience) which leads to systematized thought.

Also relevant at this juncture in our discussion is the distinction which Piaget makes between the *operative* and *figurative* aspects of knowing. Consider, for example, the operation of addition performed on certain symbols. The *symbols,* say, $3 + 4 = 7$ represent the figurative aspects of knowing for they are linked to the representation of specific states. But the transforming operation of combining, as such, comprises the operative aspects of knowing, for it is as real when it is done on symbols as when it is done on things. So the operative aspects of knowing, involving actions or operations, are those that transform reality for the child from one reality state to another. For example, it is the operative aspects of knowing which permit classifications and seriations, for the child can act on and transform reality. On the other hand, the figurative aspects of knowing (perception, imitation, image) confine the child to representing to himself end states, without any reference to the transformations that brought about the end state. In other words, these aspects of knowing permit the child to know only the end state of an operational transformation, that is, he may know the end state of the classification or seriation. It will be obvious from this that to understand a state, in the Piagetian sense, is to be aware of the transformations which brought the state into being and not merely to be aware of the end state itself. Very often in mathematics the child is, unfortunately, bound to that aspect of knowing which is designated as figurative.

As the pupil moves up through the elementary school and enters junior high school, his systematized or logical thinking shows increasing flexibility or mobility. Reasoning can be extended to greater and greater areas of experience with time. But his systematized thinking can still deal only with data that is intuitable; his ability to use hypothetico-deductive thinking will come at the next stage in the development of his thinking skills. Thus the pupil is able to build for himself the basic concepts of mathematics, although they cannot be elaborated all at the same time. These powers of reasoning are, of course, reflected in his greater understanding and performance in other areas of the curriculum as well. And with the elaboration of the concepts of number, weight, area, time, and so forth, the world becomes a more meaningful and significant place for him, for he now has the ability to codify his experience. Bearing these facts in mind, the mathematician and teacher decides on the mathmatical concepts to be introduced in Kindergarten through Grade 3.

**Adolescent Thinking**

This book is concerned with the mathematical thinking of pupils up to the third grade. Nevertheless a short treatment will be accorded to adolescent thinking in order to bring out the difference between the mathematical ideas which a nine-year-old and an adolescent can grasp.

From eleven to twelve years of age in the very brightest pupils and from thirteen to fourteen in ordinary children, new thinking skills begin to emerge. As the pupil becomes better at organizing and structuring data with the methods of concrete operational thought, he slowly realizes that such methods do not always yield a logically exhaustive solution to his problems. For example, he may find from his physical experiences that most light objects float. But sometimes the rule is transgressed, as when he finds that some heavy objects (which he cannot even lift) will float and yet some light objects sink. So the adolescent gropes for new methods of attack, often in the view of Inhelder and Piaget (1958) as he commits himself to possibilities. Naturally the maturation of the central nervous system plays some role in the emergence of the new thinking skills in that it permits, but does not ensure, their elaboration. More important is the continued interaction of the pupil with the cultural and social milieu (particularly in developed societies) and the resultant feedback.

While the elementary school child can make some extension of the actual in the direction of the possible, the adolescent can set up a number of hypotheses and establish which are compatible with the facts in front of him. In short, he can invert reality and possibility and look upon the facts in front of him as that subset of a set of possible transformations that have actually come to pass. Consider, for example, the case of the simple pendulum. The pupil is given a number of weights which can be attached to the lower end of a piece of string suspended from a hook. He can vary the length of string used, the weight used for the bob, the impetus he gives to the bob, and the height from which the bob is released. The subject is asked to find out which variable or variables determines the length of time of the swing. To establish this he must reason that if a particular variable, such as the length of the string, determines the period of swing, then the expected effect will occur if he makes changes in only the variable he is considering and holds all the others constant. On the other hand, if he does this and finds the period of swing remains the same, he has to infer that the length of string is not a relevant variable. Up to thirteen or fourteen years of age pupils do not understand the "method of all other things equal," although sometimes younger ones can be led to see its value while not adopting it spontaneously.

By fourteen or fifteen years of age (earlier in the very ablest pupils) new thinking skills emerge. The adolescent has now reached the stage of formal operational thought, for now verbal statements can take the place of intuitable data. A new variety of thinking—propositional logic —is imposed on the logic of classes and relations of the elementary school child. So faced with certain situations, the adolescent can invoke disfunction,[3] implication, and so forth, since formal thought begins with possibilities rather than with the organization of perceived data.

From the point of view of mathematics, formal thought is perhaps best regarded as second-order or second-degree operations. It will be remembered that the elementary school child, by seven or eight years of age, can monitor his thought processes and distinguish between reality and the order he imposes on it; these first-order operations result from the coordination of his actions upon reality. But at the level of formal operational thought the subject is able to structure relations between relations; that is, he can structure and coordinate actions upon first-order relations which themselves resulted from the coordination of actions upon objects. The recognition of the equality of two ratios constitutes the elaboration of a second-order relation, and this suggests right away why the ability to handle proportion is a fairly late acquisition. For example, an analogy of the form "3 is to 12 as 5 is to 20" involves a certain relationship between the first two terms, a certain relationship between the third and fourth terms, and the establishment of an identity relationship between these two relationships.

Thus looking at formal thought as second-degree operations helps us to understand why certain concepts are not available, except in an intuitive sense, until adolescence. Whereas the basic concepts of mathematics and science such as number, length, weight, time, and so forth,

---

[3] Disfunction involves the assertion of the truth of either or both of two separate propositions. For example: "I will go swimming tonight or I will play tennis tomorrow."

are available to the elementary school child because they are derived directly out of first hand reality, concepts such as proportion, equivalence relation, mathematical group, momentum, energy, heat, photosynthesis require formal operational thought for their full understanding, since these cannot be derived from immediate experience. The work of Lovell and Butterworth (1966), Lunzer (1965), Steffe and Parr (1968) on proportion, of Thomas (1969) on mathematical function, and of Taback (1969) on limit has shown how difficult these concepts are for most pupils in the elementary school.

It must, however, be stressed that familiarity with the content of a task seems likely to facilitate the use of formal thought in its solution. Again, when initial belief, or credibility, and logical necessity go together, the emergence of formal thought in that situation is likely to be aided; when they oppose one another, the elaboration of formal thought is likely to be retarded.

## FACTORS AFFECTING THE GROWTH OF THINKING

In Piaget's view there are four major influences affecting the growth of thinking. The first three listed below are all subsumed, as it were, under the fourth.

1. Biological factors. It is the maturation of the central nervous system which probably is responsible for the stages in the growth of thinking, which are unfolded in fixed sequence.
2. Factors which result from the process of socialization. In all cultures and societies there arise, to a greater or lesser extent, social exchanges, discussions, agreements, and oppositions, both between children and between adults and children. These factors are closely linked with the last one on this list, since the general coordination of actions concerns the inter-individual as well as the intra-individual.
3. Factors which relate to schooling and education, and to cultural transmission generally. Such factors differ very greatly from one society to another.
4. Factors of self- or auto-regulation which were discussed earlier. It is the reflection of the child on his own coordinating activities in 2 and 3, made possible also by 1, which is so important in the advancement of thinking skills.

## SOME POINTS TO NOTE IN USING PIAGET'S DEVELOPMENTAL SYSTEM AS A CONCEPTUAL FRAMEWORK

The account of the growth of thinking given here is oversimplified, but the main points have been indicated, especially as they relate to the increase in growth of understanding mathematical ideas. In practice the development of thinking proceeds less smoothly. The following points should be noted:

1. At the level of concrete operational thought, transitivity[4] and conservation do not necessarily arise at the same time; nor necessarily do the growth of the concepts of, say, number and length. For example, conservation of quantity comes a little before transitivity; conservation of length comes rather earlier than conservation of weight. A child may display operational thinking in one area but not in a closely related one. This is known as the problem of "horizontal differentials"; at the present time no completely satisfactory explanation can be given for it. Even at the level of formal operational thought, these horizontal differentials remain. For example, formal thought seems to come rather earlier in mathematics and science than in history. This matter must be taken seriously by the teacher.

2. All experience with intellectually able children shows that once a new stage of thinking is in evidence, it spreads rapidly across all areas of experience compared with the average child. Thus in very able pupils conservation of weight follows rapidly the conservation of quantity. On the other hand, in the case of the dull child, the new stage of thinking can be elaborated in specific situations for considerably longer periods. Thus the abler the child the more flexible or mobile do his thinking skills appear to be: they possess, in effect, greater capability for transfer. It should be noted that in the case of some school educable retarded pupils, the onset of concrete operational thought may be delayed until fourteen or fifteen years of age, and then it may be available only in rather specific situations.

3. Inhelder and Piaget (1958) have made it clear that the age of onset of formal operational thought is in part determined by the social and cultural milieu, and education. All cross-cultural studies have confirmed this. To this list must be added knowledge of subject matter, interest,

---

[4] For the set of natural numbers the relation "equals" is transitive, for since $a = b$, and $b = c$, then $a = c$. But for the set of natural numbers the relation "is one more than" is not transitive; 8 is one more than 7, and 7 is one more than 6, but 8 is not one more than 6.

and credibility. Likewise the age of onset of concrete operational thought in a particular situation may be determined to some extent by prior experience in and familiarity with that situation. In some less well developed societies, children are a little behind Western children on conservation tasks, but they fall much further behind on tasks which involve more flexible concrete, or formal, operational thought.

In general the picture of the growth of thinking that has been outlined in this chapter is most true of able children from favored homes. The growth of thinking and the elaboration of mathematical concepts is more irregular and patchy in less able and deprived pupils.

## THE ROLE OF LANGUAGE

It is necessary to say something about the relationship between language and thought, especially in respect to the growth of the latter. The views expressed here are those of the Geneva school (Piaget and Inhelder, 1964; Inhelder and others, 1966; Sinclair, 1969). In its view, language plays a role but not a central role in the growth of thinking. Verbal training may lead subjects without conservation or classification to direct their attention to pertinent aspects of the situation, but it does not, in itself, bring about the coordinations that emerge as concrete operational thought. Again, the acquisition of syntactic structures is much more closely linked to the growth of thinking skills than is lexical acquisition, while terms like "less," "more," "less than," "as much as" (which imply comparison and relationship) are more closely linked to the level of thought than are words like "high," "long," "short," "thin."

In short, language is structured by logical thought and is not the source of the latter: further, language helps in the storage and retrieval of information and acts as the symbolic vehicle for thought, but it does not greatly aid in the coordination of the input information. Even at the level of formal operational thought, Piaget would argue that while proposition thinking needs the inner support of language, the power of propositional thinking ultimately stems from the individual's ability to invert reality and possibility. The Geneva view of the relationship between language and thought would not be acceptable to many American psychologists nor to Russian psychologists; for these, language plays a far greater role in the growth of thinking. In my judgment, however, the weight of evidence currently available tends to support the Genevan standpoint.

From the point of view of the classroom, the work of Piaget and his associates indicates that language and action must go together in the elementary school, for language plays some role in the growth of thinking, and it certainly is the symbolic vehicle which carries thought. In other words, good concrete experience involving action on the part of the child, active teacher participation, and stimulation of discussion must all go together. Language helps the child to organize his experience and carry his thoughts with precision, and this can only be brought about by dialogue and discussion alongside action. Not until a highly flexible and developed formal operational thought is present can mathematics be taught with words and symbols alone, with no reference to concrete or intuitable data. We may, of course, be able to teach some logic to older and abler elementary school pupils, especially if the content is intuitable.

## HOW CHILDREN LOOK UPON MATHEMATICS

There appears to be a danger that some mathematical ideas are introduced too early to children, or that there is insufficient appreciation on the part of professional mathematicians that many of the ideas they would like to introduce to elementary school pupils are understood only in an intuitive and not in an analytic sense by the children. In some mathematical curricula it would seem that there is an attempt to force abstraction in pupils. Actually, this is not possible. But there is a danger that if mathematical ideas too advanced for their thinking skills and experience are forced on children, they will either assimilate them with distortion or turn away from them in distaste. It is not in any sense suggested that the child must always be "ready" for a particular idea before the teacher introduces it. The job of the teacher is to use his professional skill and provide learning situations for the child which demand thinking skills just ahead of those which are available to him. It is a question of keeping the carrot just ahead of the donkey's nose. When a child is almost ready for an idea, the learning situation provided by the teacher may well "precipitate" the child's understanding of that idea.

It must be remembered that children look upon mathematics as an instrument with which to explore the world and not as a game with arbitrary rules. The point is of such importance that there will be some further discussion of it. Mathematics can be regarded as a medium of exploration and a means of solving real life problems. We can also say that mathematics begins with a set of undefined terms such as *point, line,* and *between.* All other mathematical words are then defined in terms of such undefined words plus a few more like "the," "and," and so forth, which have no particular meaning in mathematics. It may also be said that mathematics starts with an initial set of axioms or postulates whose truth is taken for granted. Provided that we have a set of meaningful statements that do not contradict one another, we can take a subset of the statements, base further propositions or theorems on it, and prove the latter on the basis of the truth of the axiom and the laws of logic. In this sense we may regard mathematics as a game in which we make the rules and play accordingly. It is in the former sense that children look upon mathematics, and not as a game with arbitrary rules.

The writer is not alone in emphasizing this issue. Curricular changes in mathematics were first introduced into the United States around 1956, and these changes were accelerated by the advent of the first Sputnik. Criticisms of these developments also occurred; in 1962 there appeared a paper in the *American Mathematical Monthly* over the signatures of seventy-five distinguished American mathematicians voicing some of these complaints. While they welcomed the climate of opinion which was ready for change, they argued that it would be a tragedy if curricular reform in mathematics were left to university mathematicians who tended to think that young people liked what present-day mathematicians liked. Moreover university mathematicians had a tendency to think that the only pupils worth teaching were those likely to become professional mathematicians.

The seventy-five pointed out that the purpose of studying mathematics is to be able to *do* mathematics, to solve problems, to criticize arguments, and to be able to recognize a mathematical concept in—or abstract it from—a concrete situation. They deplored premature abstraction and asked for closer links with science. Naturally they agreed that a proper use of the concepts and language of abstract algebra could bring coherence and unity in the work, but they argued strongly that the spirit of the current way of looking at mathematics cannot be taught merely by repeating its terminology. In conclusion they stressed that children wished to use mathematics as a tool with which to explore the world about them and not to play a game with arbitrary rules. It is, of course, more than likely that it was in this spirit that such scholars as Archimedes and Newton were interested in mathematics.

## PIAGET AND EDUCATION

Piaget has spoken rarely and in only general terms about what the teacher or adult should actually do in the classroom, home, or other situation to further children's intellectual growth. Some of his thinking on this topic is reported in Almy (1966), Ripple and Rockcastle (1964), and Siegel (1968).

We may begin by stressing that for Piaget social interaction—giving interchange of thought and cooperation—is essential from the point of view of the child coordinating and grouping his thinking into a coherent structure or whole. This point of view argues strongly for much adult or teacher interaction with the child, and much interaction between children themselves. Such a position is at variance with children being taught as a whole class, as a single homogeneous unit, with little opportunity for teacher/child or child/child interaction. This does not, of course, suggest that a class of children will never be treated as a whole—indeed they will at times in, say, storytelling or music. But Piaget (1964) is equally certain that valuable information can only be given to the child via language if the child's thinking skills and background experience are such that he can assimilate the information. In other words, the mere fact that a child is "told" does not ensure that he understands. Hence earlier in this chapter we strongly suggested that action on the part of the child and discussion with others must go together.

Again, according to Duckworth (1964)—who is interpreting Piaget's views—good teaching involves the child experimenting for himself, trying things out to see what happens, manipulating objects and symbols, comparing the findings he obtains on one occasion with those he obtains on another and with those of other children, asking his own questions and finding his own answers. It is certainly fair to say that for Piaget children must be allowed a maximum of activity on their part, for in the development of logical-mathematical thinking skills children understand only that which they have found for themselves. This necessitates children working in small groups (see Chapter 10). Moreover, he points out that if the teacher attempts to teach too quickly, the child may be prevented from finding out for himself (Almy, 1966, page vi) and concludes that there is no point in attempting to accelerate intellectual development too quickly.

Many studies have been made of the effects of short-term training programs on the growth of thinking especially as related to the child's ability to handle conservation and classification problems. On the whole the results suggest that these attempts are not particularly successful. At best they bring about thinking skills which are available in a rather narrow setting with very limited transfer effects to related situations unless the child has already shown some evidence of concrete operational thought. Long-term studies have also been carried out to see if the use of particular curricula or materials in mathematics or science are beneficial in accelerating children's understanding in these areas.

Perhaps the best long-term studies are those of Almy (1969) and Dodwell (1969). In neither study were the findings clear that pupils who had used the newer curricula and materials had benefited over equivalent children who had not. Unfortunately both studies are bedeviled by the teacher variable, in the sense that the effects of new approaches and materials can be nullified by an ineffective teacher and/or the use of class teaching as against individual and small-group work.

This book is not written with the intention of accelerating *per se* children's understanding of mathematics. Rather the hope is that if teacher and children work hard and consistently, the latter will come to understand and like mathematics, and that teachers will have an understanding of both their teaching strategies and of the difficulties that children have.

## THREE NEW IDEAS

Before we proceed further, there are three ideas which we must consider, for they frequently occur in connection with mathematics and other areas of subject matter and will often be used in this book. The ideas are those of *abstraction, concept,* and *intuitive versus analytic thinking.*

## ABSTRACTION

In any number of objects or events that can be put into categories or classes, there is often some property that can be singled out as common to each class. For example, there could be present an equal number of chairs, tables, and children, and the property of, say, "five" could be attributed to each class of objects to indicate its numerousness. The common property of five is said to be abstracted or dissociated from each class of objects: it is an abstract property because the dissociation is carried out by the mind. Likewise there could be an equal number of blasts on a whistle, taps on a drum, and peals of thunder, and the common property of, say, three could be abstracted from the situation to indicate the numerousness of the members of each class of sound.

Abstraction is not confined to mathematical situations. For example, a person may behave in a certain manner in the home, at business, in the supermarket, and at the drug store, so that he displays in each circumstance a property to which we give the term "honest." Honesty is an abstract property; it is an abstraction or dissociation from the concrete situation and is made by the mind. It will be seen later on that abstraction or dissociation from reality can take place at different levels. Nevertheless, at all levels, abstraction indicates a way of organizing objects, events, qualities, and so forth.

## CONCEPT AND MATHEMATICAL CONCEPT

By *concept* is meant any term that can be recognized as a recurrent feature of an individual's thinking which stands for, or represents, a class of experiences, provided he can go back over the mental actions from which the term was derived and anchor it in first-hand experience or reality. Thus a piece of verbal behavior on the part of the child, as when he uses the word "number" in the utterance "number five," does not necessarily indicate that he has a well developed concept of number. He may be uttering a pair of words which he has heard others use. This is not, of course, to imply that concepts develop in an "all or none" fashion. As the writer has indicated elsewhere (Lovell, 1966), concepts may at first be rather vague and hazy, but they grow in clarity, in width, and in depth with maturation and experience. It will be realized at once that concept formation is greatly dependent upon the child's ability to abstract or "take from" his environment. Moreover it is through concept formation that the child codifies his experiences and makes his environment a more meaningful and significant place to live in.

So far the discussion has dealt with concepts generally. We must now look at mathematical concepts a little more closely. When we turn to that area of knowledge known as mathematics, we can do no better than to follow the Bourbaki group of mathematicians' interpretation of mathematics as the study of structures or the study of systematic patterns of relationships. Hence it may be suggested that mathematical concepts are but one class of concept: they are terms that exist in thought indicating generalizations about systematic patterns of relationship. Note carefully, however, that not all mathematical and scientific concepts or concepts employed in other fields of knowledge are at the same level of abstraction or dissociation from reality. Some concepts such as number and temperature arise out of the child's first-hand experience of reality. Later, other concepts develop through reflection on those concepts derived directly from reality, and entirely new concepts such as integer, proportion, equivalence class, and mathematical group arise. In this book we shall be dealing only with concepts of the first kind—namely those that arise directly from the child's interactions with the real world. Indeed because of the very nature of mathematics, its understanding is closely determined by the growth of children's thinking.

## INTUITIVE AND ANALYTIC THINKING

Very often in mathematics or in science it is said that a child has an intuitive grasp of an idea but not a formal or analytic understanding of it. In the former case, thinking is greatly dependent on the total perception of the situation, and the child is largely unaware of the processes by which he arrived at his ideas. There is, as it were, a basic awareness, not yet formalized. Usually intuitive thinking depends upon considerable familiarity with the ideas involved, and almost always such thought is unable to detach itself completely from physical reality. For example, a pupil in the elementary school may have an intuitive grasp of negative numbers, but they will be embodied in concrete situations such as "temperature below freezing" or "number of feet below sea-level." Analytic thinking, on the other hand, is able to divorce itself from physical reality. Further, it requires even greater awareness of the information used, and employs a careful step-by-step process with concepts being formulated and defined. Intuitive or constructive thought takes place before analytic thinking; both are required for mathematical studies.

Thus the notion of the natural numbers (that is, 1, 2, 3, 4, and so on) seems to arise intuitively, at a given level of intellectual development and as a result of the necessary experience, to indicate the relative sizes of collections of objects, events, and so forth. Even so it is clear that before long, analytic thinking will have to be applied to the idea of the natural numbers derived intuitively through perception and action. While 2, 3, 4 have their origins in action and impression and are the symbols given to certain properties of collections, the higher cardinal numbers (such as 529) are a substitute in a conceptual way for the properties of collections which cannot be known by action or simultaneous apprehension of the constituent members. Thus even if mathematical ideas often arise intuitively, conceptualization will not get very far without the application of analytic, logical, or systematized thought to them. Once again it can be seen that the growth of the child's understanding of mathematics is dependent upon the development of his thinking skills.

The chapter ends with a warning already given in the preface. Our knowledge of the growth of human thinking is as yet insufficient to provide a basis for scientific pedagogy, and an intuitive understanding of children on the part of the teacher must complement what we know of them in a scientific sense.

# 2
# Set, Number, and Numeration

Much of this chapter is devoted to the kinds of activities which will help children to understand set, number, and numeration. But before we come to these, some further consideration must be given to the growth of thinking in pupils, especially as it relates to seriations and number.

In Chapter 1 there was a discussion of the growth of the child's ability to classify. It was indicated that by seven to eight years of age the pupil can carry out what may be termed additive composition of classes; that is, he can elaborate a set of nested classes where each one is included in the next larger one, which in turn is included in the next larger one, and so on. For example, he can subsume red and blue squares under the class of squares, red and blue circles under the class of circles, and circles and squares under the class of shapes (Figure 3).

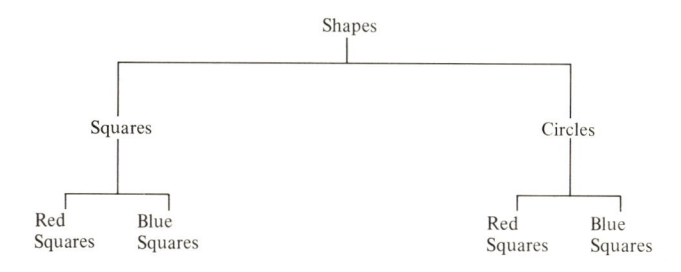

```
                    Shapes
              ┌────────┴────────┐
           Squares            Circles
          ┌───┴───┐          ┌───┴───┐
         Red    Blue        Red    Blue
       Squares Squares    Squares Squares
```

FIGURE 3

The child can also carry out what Piaget has called term-by-term ("bi-univocal") multiplication of classes. For example, he can appreciate that there are, say, boys and girls, who can be either swimmers or nonswimmers. Moreover, he can divide the total set into four subsets—namely, boy swimmers, boy nonswimmers, girl swimmers, girl nonswimmers. This skill will be needed when the concept of the product set (see Chapter 3) is used to illustrate the multiplication process.

## SERIATION

Another broad aspect of systematic ordering of thought is reflected in the child's ability to construct a series. This involves the grading and ordering of differences. All experience shows that children by three or four years of age have an intuitive grasp of grading and ordering. Indeed many well loved toys make use of this—for example, nesting cubes or rings graded in size to be placed on a stick. But there is no doubt about the child's behavior being intuitive rather than analytic. In the first place, the differences in size of the relevant objects are large, and the child's efforts are guided by his perceptual anticipation of the finished product: this is the figurative aspect of knowing. Second, these quite simple tasks are completed only after a considerable period of trial and error, so that although after a while the exercise may be done quickly, this is only because the behavior has developed into a specific habit.

Nevertheless, this kind of activity is helpful, for it gives rise to the growth of systematic concepts that involve asymmetrical transitive relations ($a > b$ and $b > c$ implies $a > c$). Then persons, objects, or classes can be arranged in order of length, weight, or other dimension (although not all at the same time), and they can be put into an asymmetric series in which the child recognizes that each element is in some respect greater than all the elements below it and less than those above it. When the thinking of the child reaches the stage of concrete operations, then transitivity "must be so," there is less need of perceptual support, and the concepts are the result of systematized thinking. It will be appreciated that this aspect of conceptual growth underpins the child's capacity for all physical scaling and a proper handling of spatial and temporal measurements and differences.

Thus it is found that if children up to about five years of age are given a set of rods graded in length, they are unable to put them into a series. In Piaget's view this is because the child is unable to realize that a particular rod is shorter than the one before it and longer than the one after it, since his thinking does not yet conform to a system or integrated structure and it is impossible for him, in thought, to pass through the series in both directions. Sometimes a subject who is asked to build a "staircase" with the rods will take no note of their bases but only of their tops, so that any rod can be made to fit into any position. However, at around six years of age the child will begin to make the series by trial and error, but if a few of the rods are held back at the start, then he has difficulty in inserting them into their correct positions in the series. But from the age of seven onward he can take the shortest rod, then the next in length, and so on, knowing in advance that he can build the series. Furthermore if with the graded series of rods he is also given a series of, say, cut-out figures of people graded in height, he will correctly assign the appropriate rod to each person. So the child reaches a stage in his thinking when he is able to carry out what Piaget calls the "addition of asymmetrical relations."

## NUMBER FROM THE PIAGETIAN VIEWPOINT

It has already been pointed out that by around seven years of age or soon after the child is able to look in on his thinking, monitor it, and distinguish between his experiences and the structure that he imposes on them. In this way he is able to attribute to a set the property of its numerousness. But the concept of number develops by stages. There is no doubt that much younger children have a simultaneous apprehension of the number of objects up to about four (as do some animals) and this number can be maintained when the objects are rearranged spatially. It is also true that they can assign the verbal labels one, two, three, and so on, to a small group of objects; that is, they can count. But counting, important as it is, does not necessarily imply that the child has a concept of number or that he can use it as an idea.

Piaget (1952) devised ingenious experiments which bring out some of the stages in the growth of the child's understanding of number. The following kinds of situation were used to test the development of his grasp of cardinals:

1. An equal number of beads was counted into each of two vessels of the same shape and size, so that the subjects could see that the two sets were equal quite apart from the counting. One set of beads was then transferred to a vessel of different shape and

size so that there would be marked perceptual differences. The child was then questioned as to whether the number of beads in the two vessels was the same.
2. Children were asked to match various sets of objects: for example, flowers and vases, by putting a flower in each vase. When this was successfully done, the experimenter took the flowers out and either put them in a bunch or laid each flower by each vase, and then spread out the vases. The child was again questioned as to whether there was the same number of flowers and vases.
3. The experimenter first matched, say, ten flowers with ten vases and then matched the vases with a second set of ten flowers. The child was questioned as to whether the first set of flowers had the same number as the second set. He was further asked how many flowers would be in each vase if the two, three, four matched sets of flowers were put into the vases.

All the experiments showed that it is not until around seven years of age that the number of objects is conserved regardless of their perceptual arrangement. Children then reply, "You've only changed the shape of the vessel, it makes no difference to the number of beads," or something equivalent. In the matching experiments it is not until seven or so that the child has a real notion of numerical equivalence and counting carries the day over appearance. Thus the child may reply, "You've only put the flowers in a bunch," or "You've only spread out the vases." Similarly in the experiment involving the equivalence of two or more groups, the seven-year-old recognizes the equivalence of the two or more sets of flowers originally matched with the vases. And in response to the last question he knows that there will be two, three, or four flowers in each vase as the case may be.

Other experiments by Piaget and Szeminska (1952) deal with ordinal numbers and series, and the relation between ordinals and cardinals. For example, children in the same age range as those taking part in the cardinal experiments might have to match a series of "walking sticks" which vary in length with a set of dolls which vary in height. The stages through which the child goes in solving this kind of problem have already been described, namely, total failure, partial success in easy cases, and finally a matter-of-fact solution which "must be so."

In Piaget's view (but see my later comments) the concept of number is not based on images, or on the mere ability to use symbols verbally, but on the fusion or synthesis in the mind of two logical entities, class and asymmetrical relation. A practical example may help to make this

## Set, Number, and Numeration

point clear (see Lovell, 1966, page 51). As the child picks out, say, all the red objects and puts them to one side, he comes to think of the red objects all together and eventually forms the concept of "class of all red objects." The concept of class, or the mental operation of classifying, is an internalized version of grouping together objects that are regarded as similar in some way.

Again, in his play activities the child puts, say, sticks in order of length, and from this type of activity he derives the concept of relation. The natural or counting numbers result from the union of classification and ordering; for the idea of the number 8, say, depends upon the child grouping in his mind eight objects to form a class, and upon placing 8 between 7 and 9; that is, in a relation. Put more formally, we can say that if a set of objects are counted and the cardinal-number value arrived at, say, 8, one treats the objects as if they were all alike and members of a common class. In other words, we disregard object differences in, say, size, color, texture, and so forth, and elaborate the homogenous unit 1, when assigning to a set its cardinal value. On the other hand, the objects put in the order in which they are counted form a series—a set of asymmetric relations—which are exactly analogous to a series of sticks of graded length. But the objects are not ordered in terms of their length but in terms of their ordinal position (for example, "second object counted," "third object counted," and so on). The child now has a concept of the natural or counting numbers, and he can think with it and use it. A unit is now looked upon as a unit, and a number is looked upon as made up of a number of units.

It can be seen that Piaget looks upon classes, relations, and numbers as developing in a closely linked, mutually dependent way. Whether there is as much structure in the child's thinking as Piaget suggests is doubtful. The correlations between one-to-one correspondence, conservation, and seriation are sometimes low. In practice, the cardinal-value property of the elements of a set may be present before the ordinal-value property. Indeed, it is certain that the synthesis of the ordinal and cardinal aspects of number is not achieved at once and for all numbers. Although the child may well realize that the next number is one more than the last one for small numbers (as in the case of 8 and 9), he may not understand this in respect of, say, 71 and 72, for which he has no physical experience. The smaller numbers can be conceived by him as forming part of real situations, since the property of numerousness is abstracted from the physical set. When the child is a little older, his uncertainty in respect of larger numbers disappears, and he can understand the relationship between $N$ and $N + 1$ for large as well as for small numbers.

Other examples are furnished by Piaget and his associates. Thus the child may know that the number which follows $N$ is $N + 1$, and the next one is $(N + 1) + 1$. But he still may not grasp that the third number is $N + (1 + 1)$. There is a gap in time, which varies for individual pupils, between the first and second instances, suggesting once more that the fusion of ordering and classification is not an "all or none" affair. To the normal child, long before he reaches the end of his elementary school career, it is patent that every other number is termed odd, and every other number is even. Yet a child may only realize this at first for small numbers, and it may be some time later before the synthesis of classification and ordering develops to the extent that he can use a recursive[1] argument. Only then can he explain, "Even, odd, even, add one more and it is odd," and so on. Experience suggests that frequent use of situations involving physical realizations of a one-to-one correspondence helps children to develop a recursive argument.

A final example which shows that it takes time before logical thought can be used with larger and larger physical sets has been supplied by Apostel, Mays, Morf, and Piaget (1957). In one experiment two rows of counters are placed in one-to-one correspondence. One of the sets is then divided into subsets. For example, when repeating this work, I started with two sets of twelve cubes, one set divided into subsets of 6, 4 and 2. A suitable screen is placed between the child and the cubes so that he can observe the set being divided into subsets without being able to count their members. He is then questioned as to whether the two sets (one of which is divided into three subsets) are still equal in respect to the number of their members. A number of stages can be found in the responses obtained. In the first, the subject denies conservation. During the second he asks to be allowed to count the members before he replies—this is an empirical test. Moreover, if the members are subject to a new subdivision—say, 4, 4, and 4—he wants to count them again. A little later this restriction is removed, and if the equality is maintained for one division of $n$ members, it is for all divisions. But in both these two instances, counting will only overcome perceptual differences, and so yield numerical equivalence of sets, when $n$ is small—say, 20 or so. In the final stage, which comes around age eight or soon after, counting up members of the subsets is no longer necessary. The numerical equivalence between the untouched set and the subsets is logically necessary—"it must be so"—so that an empirical test is unnecessary and, moreover, logical necessity now applies to sets of any size.

---

[1] A recursive argument is one that develops from mathematical induction. If $x_1 = x_0 + 1$ and $x_{n+1} = x_n + 1$, in essence the $(n + 1)$th term is defined in terms of the $n$th.

# Set, Number, and Numeration

## INTRODUCTION TO SETS

If one wishes to give pupils a deeper understanding of numbers, then the preparation for number must, as it were, be at a greater depth. Accordingly, a beginning is made with the notion of a set, for numerosity is a property of a set—a property attributed to the set by the mind. Thus number is a property of a set just as shape, size, and color are properties. In forming sets and subsets children are made aware of differences in properties, as in sorting, and of similarity of properties, as in grouping. This is equally true whether we are dealing with, say, objects, events, or ideas.

A useful beginning is to allow kindergarten children to suggest sets of things about which they are familiar; for example, train set (the collection of engine, cars, lines, signal box) or tea set (the collection of cups, saucers, plates, pot). In the discussion, different words conveying the same idea will arise, such as set, collection, group, and it can be pointed out that from that time onward it is better for everyone to use the word "set" so that teacher and child can understand each other.

At the same time, children need considerable free play with objects which give them much variety in shape, size, thickness, color, material, and texture, using, say, bricks, blocks, buttons, shells, nuts, leaves, and the like. It is helpful to have available both objects found in everyday life and commercially produced materials such as blocks which have been specially made to give variation in shape, size, color, and thickness. Moreover, it is suggested that the introduction to sets be made with objects rather than with pictures of objects. Pictures can be used after real objects. But there is some evidence that the use of real objects may be necessary for a longer period with disadvantaged children since they are less consistent in classifying pictures of objects compared with three-dimensional life-sized objects than are advantaged middle-class children. This is true even when the disadvantaged subjects can correctly label the objects in the pictures.

As already indicated in the preface, I hope that here, as throughout the book, teachers will vary the suggested activities to suit their own local situation, omit ones which they consider unnecessary for particular pupils, and make up new activities of their own to augment and reinforce the ones suggested here.

The kinds of activities in which children engage may form a progression along these lines:

1. The child makes his own free groupings in any way he wishes. It will be remembered from what was said in Chapter 1 that

children aged five or below may fail to keep to any kind of criterion.
2. Sets are made in terms of a property chosen by the child himself; for example, all the red things, all the shells. The property selected does not matter since any collection may be a set. In a sense all answers are correct.
3. Sets are made in terms of two properties; for example, all the small circles, all the green buttons. It is important to remember that the kindergarten child generally does this on the basis of the figurative aspects of knowing, for such children will be unable to "manipulate" two relationships in the mind.
4. Sets display a negative property; for example, all the toys without wheels, all the blocks which are not painted.
5. Sets are made by the child in terms of properties indicated by the teacher.

The criterion for defining a set is simple. The collection of objects (or events, qualities, ideas, and so forth) forms a set if the members are distinguished from one another and it is clear that a given object really does belong to the collection in the light of the criterion laid down. It will also be appreciated that in forming sets children naturally use relational terms such as "is smaller than," "as smooth as," "the same color as," and that the teacher or other adult must both use himself, and encourage children to use, precise language.

**SUBSETS**

Kindergarten pupils can also find out for themselves that a set can be divided into a number of subsets in terms of certain properties. The process of separating a set into subsets is, from the point of view of thinking skills, more important than the actual properties chosen as a basis for the division, provided of course that the properties are possible ones in a given instance. For example, the five- to six-year-old can grasp that all the children in a room form a set and that this set can be divided into the subset of boys and the subset of girls. Again, the subsets could consist of children with blue eyes and children who do not have blue eyes. If the number of children in the set is small, the division of the set into subsets could be recorded by the child as indicated in Figure 4.

Most of the work, will, of course, be done with actual objects and in terms of one property at first. The child first makes a set and then subdivides it into two or more subsets as he thinks fit. But pupils need to

# Set, Number, and Numeration

be questioned, individually, as to the basis on which the divisions are made, and the teacher must check that the properties specified by a child are being maintained throughout. At the same time, it must be

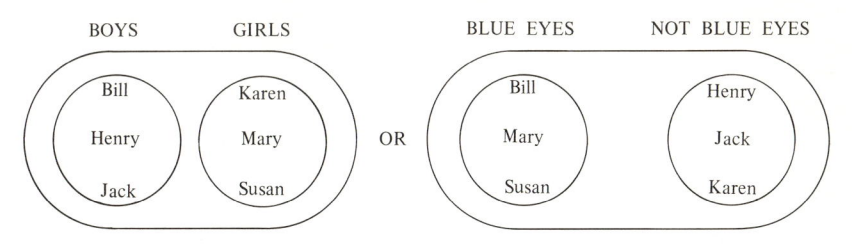

```
      BOYS         GIRLS                     BLUE EYES        NOT BLUE EYES
   ⎛  ⎛ Bill ⎞   ⎛ Karen ⎞ ⎞              ⎛  ⎛ Bill  ⎞   ⎛ Henry ⎞ ⎞
   ⎜  ⎜ Henry⎟   ⎜ Mary  ⎟ ⎟     OR       ⎜  ⎜ Mary  ⎟   ⎜ Jack  ⎟ ⎟
   ⎝  ⎝ Jack ⎠   ⎝ Susan ⎠ ⎠              ⎝  ⎝ Susan ⎠   ⎝ Karen ⎠ ⎠
```

FIGURE 4

realized that children may not always be able to verbalize how they sorted their objects into subsets. After work with objects that occur in everyday life, work with blocks is very helpful, for these have a number of properties as, for example, shape, size, color, thickness. Using these the pupil may select the set of round ones (circles) and he may divide these into subsets on the basis of the property of size or the property of color. These activities can be recorded in the form indicated in Figure 4; they make a useful lead-in to the use of the Venn diagram. Moreover if objects are sorted on the floor, chalk marks, rope, or hoops can be used to enclose the members of the set and subsets. Children themselves have sometimes to be divided into subsets for various purposes, and advantage should be taken of this to illustrate further the ideas we have been discussing.

If at this age objects are sorted on the basis of two properties, the subdivisions will often be made more on the basis of the figurative than on the operative aspects of knowing (see Chapter 1, in which the child had difficulty in classifying, and made collections rather than a true class because he had no overall anticipatory plan). For example, the members of the set may be all the blue circles; but these may also differ in size and thickness. The pupil must be asked to divide the circles into two subsets and to think about the ways in which he will do this. He may be quite correct in making subsets of large thin, small thin, large thick, and small thick circles, but he needs to be questioned as to how he performed the subdivision, for he is more likely to be representing to himself end states (figurative knowledge) than acting on and transforming reality (operative knowledge). Sorting by two properties is an exceedingly important exercise for children, but the teacher should be aware of the manner in which the sortings are made.

## CONSERVATION OF THE NUMBER
## OF MEMBERS OF A SET

It has already been indicated that for the five- to six-year-old the number of members of a set may alter if the members are rearranged spatially, and experience has to be given to pupils to help them toward conservation of number.

A useful approach is to start with a set of just three members, each member being of different shape, size, and color. For example, one could have, say, a small red cube, a tennis ball, and a nut. An equivalent[2] reference set is also formed using similar objects. If the members of the first set are moved around, the child knows through a simultaneous apprehension, and without counting, that the number of members has remained the same, while the members of the reference set are available for easy matching. Again, three children could be seated at a table or in the corners of a room; after they have changed seats, the child knows that the number of children remains the same. At least qualitative identity has been maintained even if there is not an intuitive grasp of number, for in both the above instances the five-year-old knows that the objects and the children "are the same." No change has been introduced by spatial rearrangement. Next, one might have, say, four blue counters matched against four yellow beads. If the yellow beads are now moved around, young children frequently realize that the number of beads remain the same. It is, of course, at best an intuitive knowledge based on the figurative aspect of knowing. On the other hand, if five (or more) blue counters are matched one-to-one with five (or more as the case may be) yellow beads and the latter spatially rearranged, then conservation of number may be lost.

Pupils thus need much experience of situations in which they have to establish one-to-one correspondences. By moving around the members of one set, the invariance of number may be established on an empirical basis at first. It is unnecessary for the child to do any counting of the members of each set at first: indeed, counting at first may be no more than mouthing appropriate words and pointing at the same time, and not performed with the awareness it will have later. Rather, the invariance of the numerousness of the sets may be established by laying pieces of string, or drawing lines using chalk, between each object and the "partner" with which it is matched. When the numbers of members

---

[2] Sets are equivalent if the members of one are exactly paired (matched one-to-one) with members of the other. The members of each set need be neither similar nor identical. Counters can be matched with counters, or drivers with elephants, to yield equivalent sets.

## Set, Number, and Numeration

in the two sets are unequal, pairing also enables the child to judge which set has more and which has fewer members, giving opportunities at the same time to use correctly terms such as "as many as," "fewer," "more." Thus one can have exercises of the following types:

1. Pair boys and girls to see if the number of children of both sexes is the same. The matching should be carried out physically at first, followed by the pairing of names which are recorded.
2. Pair cups and saucers; knives and forks; pens and pencils.
3. Pick balls from a bag and give one to each child; establish if there are more, fewer, or the same number of balls and pupils.
4. Lay out, say, seven circles and nine triangles in two rows, and let the child establish which set has the more members by linking the circles and triangles with string or chalk lines. Then spread out the seven circles so that they form a row longer than that of the triangles. Establish the child's views on the numerosity of the two sets, connecting the pairs again if necessary.

The exercises should be recorded pictorially by the child whenever possible. Sooner or later (except in slow children) the invariance of the number of members of the sets, regardless of the spatial arrangement of members, will become a logical necessity as the child's systematized thought develops. It is more than likely that the matching of flints to men, or the number of animals killed with the fingers of the hands, helped early man to establish his concept of the natural numbers. Indeed, one-to-one matching, or pairing, together with appropriate recording, seems to be an important type of activity for children today in the development of the concept of the natural numbers.

## THE EMPTY SET

If we give the members of a proposed set very complex or compound properties, it may be found that there are no members. For example, in a class of pupils there may be no girls with blue eyes who were born in the state of Montana. The properties remain, but there are no such pupils, so that the set corresponding to these attributes will have no members. It is the empty set. This is an important idea, mathematically, but a difficult one for children, and they need plenty of examples for discussion. It is, of course, the number of members in the empty set which later they must call zero, since the empty set has the property zero just as the set of six members has the property called six.

## PUTTING SETS IN ORDER IN TERMS OF THE NUMBER OF THEIR MEMBERS

Pupils now need to put sets in order according to the number of members in each set. To help them do this, it is useful to start with sets whose members consist of entirely different objects. For example, one set could have for its members triangular blocks, a second set could have shells as its members, while a third set could be of leaves. By pairing the members of each of two sets in turn the child can establish which set has the smallest number of members, which the next greatest number, and which has most. In similar fashion, he can order for himself four, five, or six sets in terms of the number of members which each contains. Many exercises of this general type are required.

At the same time, in order to help the idea of ordering more generally—for here we are ordering only in terms of the number of members of a set—exercises can be given which involve, say, the ordering of sticks in terms of their length, circles in terms of their size, and colors in terms of their shades. From what has been said earlier, it will be realized that before a child can know anything of ordering, except in a figurative sense, his thinking has to be approaching the stage where it is becoming systematized. However, the coordination of his actions as he attempts these activities is likely to aid the growth of such thought, which is essential for an understanding of asymmetrical relationships.

## COUNTING

Previously it was suggested that early man first matched, say, the animals he killed with the fingers of his hand. But with large numbers he had to resort to some kind of tallying. For example, he might have cut a notch in a stick for each object, or put a pebble aside for each animal. In essence there was a one-to-one correspondence between object and notch, or pebble and animal. Eventually there came to man, as there must to the child today, the realization that names (verbal labels) could also be used in one-to-one correspondence with the members of a set of objects, animals, events, and so forth. Words which were spoken, and later symbols which were written, took the place of notches and pebbles.

It is, of course, true that very young children can sometimes repeat the number names, but they fail to assign them correctly to the members of the set of objects in most instances. Or children may mouth the names correctly and move the finger correctly from object to ob-

## Set, Number, and Numeration

ject, but it is a learned procedure done without awareness. Instead of saying "one," "two," "three," "four," the child may as well say "fe," "fi," "fo," "fum," and point to each object in turn. It must be emphasized that it is futile to teach children to count by rote: in doing so they are not learning arithmetic. Real counting implies that the child is aware that he is pairing the term "one" with the first object, "two" with the second object, and so on.

In other words, a set of number names or numerals must be placed in one-to-one correspondence with the members of any set of objects. When this takes place, the child has the ability to compare the number of members in two sets directly. He has only to count the number of members in the first set, remember the number name paired with the last object, count the number of members in the second set, and finally compare the final number names. And with the use of spoken number names (the written symbols will come a little later) the child can easily deal with the number of objects even when the latter are not present. For example, he can go outdoors to the sandpit and count the number of spades, then go into the classroom, count the number of buckets, and compare the numbers. There is no longer any need to match spades with physical entities and then match the latter with buckets. Likewise he can compare the number of members in two sets whose formation is separated by time.

To the adult it is clear that a number and a number name, or numeral, are not the same thing. If a set contains eight members, the number is fixed; the corresponding numeral may be "eight," "8," or "VIII." While the teacher will obviously draw attention to the differing ways in which the number names may be written, there is little point in emphasizing the distinction between number and numeral with young children.

Earlier it was made clear that by about seven years of age the child monitors his own thinking and distinguishes between his experiences and the organization that he imposes on them. These intellectual skills seem to be brought about by the child coordinating his own actions as, for instance, in matching in one-to-one correspondence. This is logical-mathematical experience (Chapter 1). Slowly there evolves the ability to understand that the words "three," "seven," and so on, describe the property of a set containing a certain number of members—a property that the child's mind has imposed upon or imputed to the members of the set. The child is now at the second level of abstraction as far as his thinking skills are concerned: in the counting series he has constructed an abstract equivalent set in which number names are paired with objects, events, ideas, as the case may be. And developing roughly at the same time, since thought is becoming systematized, is the notion of order, so that each member of the counting series is known to be one more than the one before it and one less than the one that comes after it.

## SUMMARY OF WORK SO FAR INVOLVING PAIRING, COUNTING, AND NUMBERS

The following suggestions, put in summary form, concern the kinds of activities in which young children may engage as these seem to be potential learning situations for them:

1. Exercises to show that the numerousness (number of members) of a set is unchanged when the members are moved around.
2. Pairing of members of two sets when the number of members in each is (a) one to ten, and later (b) eleven to twenty. Establishing that there are the same number of members in each set introduces the child to the relational terms "as many as" and "the same as."
3. Pairing the members of two sets when the number of members is unequal. This gives opportunities for use of the relational terms "more than," "less than," "fewer than." In all the activities mentioned, children should work with sets whose members consist of a variety of different objects.
4. Worksheets may be given on which the child draws a set containing "as many as," "fewer than," "more than" members, compared with the number of members in the set shown in a diagram.
5. The pupil should have many opportunities to use as many relational terms as possible and to record these in written or pictorial forms. For example:

    is taller than       belongs to
 John $\rightarrow$ Tom $\rightarrow$ William   Red hat $\rightarrow$ Katherine

Other relational terms that will come to mind are "is the aunt of," "runs faster than," "has the same color as." And very important are the terms "is greater than," "is less than."

6. As has been shown, the child learns that number (natural) is a property which is attributed to a set. The number names are first learned for sets whose members range in number from one to ten, the extension from eleven to twenty being made as the child is ready. To help pupils establish the sequence of number names, rhymes, jingles, and finger plays are of help. Naturally teachers will use material which is familiar locally, but a typical rhyme is:

## Set, Number, and Numeration

One, two, three, four, five,
Once I caught a fish alive.
Why did you let it go?
Because it bit my finger so.

Six, seven, eight, nine, ten,
Shall we go to fish again?
Not today, some other time,
For I have broke my fishing line.

7. The symbol (1, 2, and so on) corresponding to each number name has now to be learned, but it is not my intention to say how this should be done. Further, the child has to be able to read the written form of the number name. It will, of course, be appreciated that unless some concept of number has been elaborated, the reading off of number words and symbols will convey little meaning. However, assuming that all is well, the child is now in the position where he can match spoken word, written word, and written symbols with a set which has the appropriate number of members. Thus for written words and symbols we have (Figure 5):

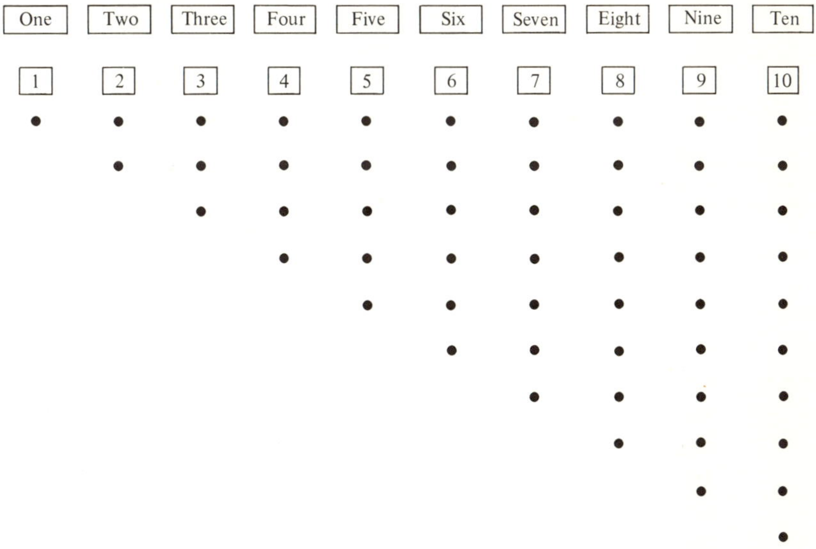

| One | Two | Three | Four | Five | Six | Seven | Eight | Nine | Ten |
|---|---|---|---|---|---|---|---|---|---|
| 1 | 2 | 3 | 4 | 5 | 6 | 7 | 8 | 9 | 10 |

FIGURE 5

Naturally the exercises provided for the child when matching word, symbol, and members of a set will vary greatly in content and spatial arrangement. For example, the symbol 4 can be associated with, say, sticks, shells, blocks, taps on the table, and children working in the sandpit.

8. The ability to write the number symbols must also be mastered. Exercise in writing numbers can be obtained through recording house numbers, telephone numbers, automobile numbers, bus numbers, and so forth.

9. Attention must be paid to the ordinal-value aspect of number. Experience must be given in laying objects on the table and the child saying "first-ball," "second-pencil," and so on. Or children can be put in a line and listed: "first-Tom," "second-Mary," "third-Kate," and so on. Later a record should be made in writing as the child makes the list.

10. The pupil is now ready for further experiences involving the ordering of sets in terms of the number of members that they contain, and for the use of ordering words and signs. After comparing pairs of numbers, such as 3 and 7, he can, for example, lay out sets containing three, seven, and nine members (Figure 6). Underneath the first (left-hand) set he places the

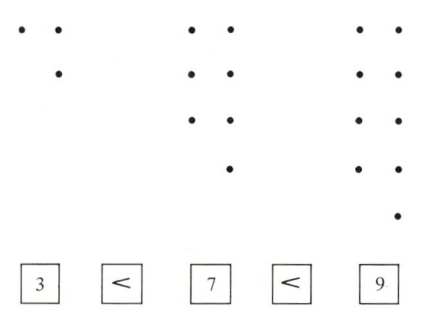

| 3 | < | 7 | < | 9 |

FIGURE 6

figure 3, underneath the middle set he places 7, and underneath the right-hand set the figure 9. Then in between the 3 and 7 he inserts a card bearing the sign meaning "is less than" ($<$), a similar sign being inserted between 7 and 9. Similarly appropriate sets can be made up and the "is greater than" sign introduced, as in $6 > 4 > 2$.

11. To give further experience in the use of ordering, exercises can be provided in the form of rows of numbers, in which the smallest is underlined by one line and the largest by two lines. But for some pupils a great deal of experience may be required

Set, Number, and Numeration 39

on the number ladder before they have the ability to carry out ordering in symbolic form with any facility. Thus a ladder (as large as is feasible) can be made from wooden slats and propped against the classroom wall (Figure 7). "Little men"

FIGURE 7

can be made from pipe-cleaning or other suitable materials so that they will attach to the rungs. Two pupils can play together using dice or drawing numbers written on cards from a box. It is better if they invent their own activities; if not, there must be teacher guidance. Eventually one looks for the following general type of activity. One child gets, say, a 7 and the other a 3. The little men are then placed on the appropriate rungs of the ladder and a recording made: "Tom drew 7," "Jack drew 3," "Tom's man is higher up," "7 > 3." It is unnecessary for all results to be recorded, but a good proportion of them should be. Naturally three children can play together, leading to recordings of the type "8 > 5 > 2."

Use can also be made of the number strip (Figure 8) made from wood or card. Counters, pebbles, or little men can be moved along the strip of necessary to accord with the throws of dice or the draws from a hat.[3] If the number line is drawn

[3] It is important that the numbers be exactly opposite the interval marks and not between them.

on the classroom floor or in the playground, children can actually make the appropriate number of jumps along the line. Eventually pupils must be able to order numbers in symbolic form and without the use of these concrete aids. They then move from the figurative to the operative aspects of knowing.

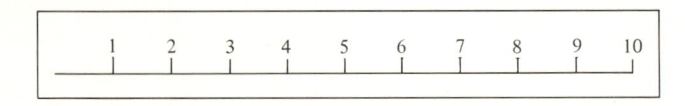

```
| 1   2   3   4   5   6   7   8   9   10 |
```

FIGURE 8

## ZERO

It was seen earlier that the empty set has the property zero. That is to say, the number of members in the empty set is called zero just as the number of members of other sets may be called three or five as appropriate. However, zero remains a somewhat difficult idea for the elementary school child, and his understanding of it will remain intuitive. Zero will remain contaminated, as it were, with nothing, as in "nothing in my pocket" or "nothing in the drawer." This does not greatly matter, though, for he has enough grasp of zero for his needs at the moment. The term *zero* will not be understood as the mathematician would wish it until the individual's thinking is at the level of formal operational thought, just as we shall see later that the pupil does not understand the term *point* as the mathematician does until adolescence. The pupil must, of course, be taught the symbol which represents zero.

## PLACE VALUE

The numerical notation we use involves concepts which can cause difficulty for many pupils. In everyday situations we use the Hindu-Arabic system of numeration, with 10 as the number base. Hence usually we use a decimal system, although on occasion this is not so. Indeed our system of numeration can be used with, say, base 2 or base 5 if it is so wished. The Hindu-Arabic system has three important properties which makes it superior to other systems of numeration. First, it is an additive system: the numeral 524 names the number $500 + 20 + 4$. Second, it is a place-value system. For example, in the numeral 555

## Set, Number, and Numeration

each 5 stands for a different number. The 5 on the right represents 5 ones; the middle 5 stands for 5 tens; and the left-hand 5 indicates 5 hundreds. Thus the position of a numeral, relative to other numerals, represents its value. This makes the numeration system a simple one from one point of view, yet it is a difficult idea for some pupils to grasp. It is simple in the sense that by using only ten numerals (0 to 9) it is possible to represent any number. A moment's thought will indicate how cumbersome a system would be, and what a memory store would be required, if each number was represented by a separate and distinct numeral. Third, the Hindu-Arabic system of notation has a zero symbol.

These properties make the system an efficient one. Teachers may wish to look at some of the other numeration systems and compare these with each other and with the Hindu-Arabic one. For example, a study of the Egyptian numeration system (developed by 1800 B.C. at the latest) was a decimal system and had an additive principle but made no use of place value. The Babylonian numeration system (developed by 1500 B.C.) on the other hand was a place-value system of a kind, but it had no zero symbol. Thus the Egyptian system was less efficient than the Babylonian. Examination of the Roman numeration system reveals that it used an additive principle but was a place-value system in special instances only, such as IX, where there is a significant relationship between adjacent numerals. If it is thought that a comparative study of the numeration systems would be helpful in the case of certain pupils, it is imperative that the children themselves construct the various counting aids, or symbols, using sand (for tracing), sticks, plasticine, paper, and pencil.

As was said earlier, in spite of the fact that the Hindu-Arabic system is simple in one sense, it is difficult for some pupils because of the incorporation of the principle of place value. In the work outlined so far in this chapter the child will write the numeral 13 to represent the number without considering numeration as such—13 is merely the symbol for that particular number. It does seem that often, although not always, the difficulty arises because pupils do not have enough opportunities to construct a practical situation using appropriate materials, where the position and consequent value of the number symbol can be readily seen.

The following suggestions are thus made for types of practical work using base 10; the question of introducing other number bases will be raised later.

Children need much experience in counting out pebbles, beads, sticks, or matchsticks to twenty or thirty to begin with, and later to, say, twenty-three or thirty-five. As each group of ten is counted it is put aside, and any objects left over are placed together. This gives the opportunity to emphasize the idea of putting objects into sets of ten members. If sticks are used, each set of ten members can be bundled, using a rubber band, with a certain number of individual sticks left unbundled at the end. In this type of activity a larger pebble can replace each set of ten pebbles, and a larger stick each set of ten sticks. The next stage in this general approach is to have a rather shallow box divided into two sections, one of which is clearly marked for Tens and the other for Units (Figure 9). The large pebbles or sticks, as the case

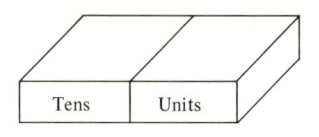

FIGURE 9

may be, are placed in the Tens section and the remaining small ones in the Units section. Through plenty of practice in this kind of activity, followed by the pupil writing T U in his book and writing the appropriate numerals underneath, as T U (with the box and its contents
2 4
still in front of him), he is given a realistic approach to the position and consequent value of the numeral.

Two further points may be made. It is preferable to start with numbers in the twenties or thirties rather than in the range 11 to 19. In this range the symbol, as pronounced, gives the unit symbol before the ten symbol. Second, after familiarizing himself with place-value notation in the twenties and thirties, the pupil needs to have much experience in counting out objects up to ninety-nine and in grouping these larger samples into sets having ten members each.

Activities involving various forms of the abacus are very helpful in aiding pupils to understand place value.

Various forms of structural apparatus may be used with much profit. These may vary from, say, Dienes' multibase arithmetic blocks using base 10, to the materials provided in the Stern apparatus, to the Cuisenaire rods.[4]

The child must make the necessary abstraction and recognize the "sameness" in these three types of activity. Abstraction must take place

[4] Dienes' multibase arithmetic blocks, obtained commercially, give bases of 3, 4, 5, 6, 10. The Cuisenaire rods, also obtained commercially, consist of colored rods representing the numbers 1 to 10.

*Set, Number, and Numeration*

so that the child does not think that place value is linked with particular materials. Only then will place value be understood. Later the concept of place value must be extended to hundreds, tens, and units with the same kind of activities being used. It will be readily appreciated from all that has been said of number itself that place value will not be understood until the child's thinking has become systematized in respect to number.

## NUMBER BASES OTHER THAN TEN

The properties of the Hindu-Arabic system of numeration are applicable not only to base 10 but to other number bases as well. But opinion is divided as to how much time children should spend on number bases other than 10. Dienes (1960), who devised the multibase arithmetic blocks, is naturally a keen advocate of using varied number bases. Using many number bases is likely to aid the generalization of the concept of place value and enable the child to see base 10 as just one instance of the place-value numeration system. Again the Binary Scale (base 2) is useful today since the only symbols used, 0 and 1, can be represented by *on* and *off* and hence it provides the basis by means of which the digital electronic computer can handle the operations it is instructed to perform.

If it is decided to introduce other number bases, then adequate exercises must be given to the child in representing a given number by one numeral in one number base and by a different numeral in another base. For instance, he must find for himself that the number represented by 11 in base 2 is represented by 3 in base 10, while the numeral 24 in base 10 represents the same number as 44 in base 5. Moreover the same number should be expressed in symbol form using different bases. Thus the pupil should discover that the number written as 53 in base 10 is written as 65 in base 8, as 203 in base 5, as 311 in base 4, and as 1222 in base 3. Some teachers who have used other number bases claim greater understanding of the concept of place value on the part of the pupils and greater facility in handling place value in exercises which demand its use. There is no doubt that many elementary school children aged seven and up will work in different number bases with much enjoyment and interest. Nevertheless, to be able to see place value as a general structure which holds across different number bases will require the thinking skills of formal operational thought. But early work in different bases could aid the recognition of the general structure later.

On the other hand, there are those who argue that working in number bases other than 10 is unnecessary for the majority of elementary school pupils. Thus Fehr (1966)—a distinguished American worker in the field of mathematics education—says that it has never been proved that work in number bases other than 10 helps to develop the understanding of the decimal system and that base 10 remains sufficient for the needs of the great mass of future citizens. Thus the argument on this side is not that children are confused by working in different bases (as the teachers may be, because their thinking may have become somewhat crystalized) but that it does little positive good for the majority of children who will need to work only in base 10.

Unfortunately it is impossible to decide between these viewpoints on the basis of experimental evidence. Teachers must make their own decisions, taking into account, among many other factors, the ability level of their pupils.

# 3
# Operations and Mathematical Sentences

Readers will recognize that parts of this chapter are concerned with work which is suitable for the older children in the age range considered in this book. Such work must be included because of pupils in grades 2 and 3. However, actions upon objects of the types described in the text are entirely suitable in some cases for the five- to seven-year-olds with the use of symbols and recording coming later.

It was pointed out earlier that the term *operation* has a different meaning in mathematics than it has in Piaget's developmental system, and it is important for the reader to keep the distinction in mind. In mathematics a binary operation is performed on a set when any two members are combined according to some stated rule and produce a third member of the set as the only result. While this chapter does consider—although lightly—mathematical operations in terms of sets, it must be stressed that with young children the emphasis must be on the numerical rather than on the logical relationships. We begin then with some simple sorting and recording activities of the type that should be undertaken by pupils.

## WAYS OF RECORDING LEADING TO THE USE OF THE VENN[1] DIAGRAM

Consider a ball, toy airplane, rag animal, teddy bear, plate, saucer, and blue block. The kindergarten child, given these objects, can sort them into a set of objects whose members are hard and into a set whose

---

[1] Venn (1834–1923) was a British logician. Euler (1707–1783) had earlier used such diagrams; hence they are often called Venn-Euler diagrams.

members are soft, as we saw in the previous chapter. Moreover if the objects are now put together again, he can, if the objects are, say, either yellow or blue, sort them into a set whose members are yellow and a set whose members are blue. But the child at the stage of concrete operational thought can build up the following table in which the objects are sorted in terms of hard, soft, yellow, and blue, for he is now capable of working out a term-by-term multiplication of classes.

|  | Hard | Soft | Yellow | Blue |
|---|---|---|---|---|
| Ball |  | Yes |  | Yes |
| Toy Airplane | Yes |  |  | Yes |
| Rag Animal |  | Yes | Yes |  |
| Teddy Bear |  | Yes | Yes |  |
| Plate | Yes |  | Yes |  |
| Saucer | Yes |  | Yes |  |
| Block | Yes |  |  | Yes |

The construction of such a table by a child whose thinking is at the concrete operational level leads naturally to the drawing by him of the diagrams shown in Figure 10. In Figure 10a, one simple closed curve

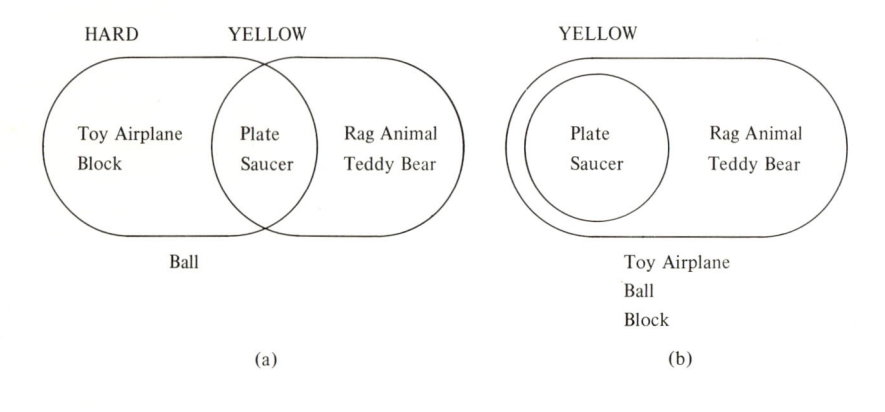

FIGURE 10

surrounds the hard objects, and another the yellow objects. But the two curves intersect, for some objects are both hard and yellow. Note that the ball is not included in either set. In Figure 10b the outer closed curve gathers within itself all the yellow objects. But inside this closed curve is another closed curve which includes all the hard yellow objects. Again, note that the toy airplane, ball, and block remain outside

## Operations and Mathematical Sentences

the set of yellow objects. In early activities of this nature, objects comprising such sets (and subsets) can be enclosed by rope or hoops; later the results of the activities can be committed to paper and pencil directly. Thus in sorting, say, large beads and red beads the child will find that some beads are both large and red, and he may illustrate his results directly, as in Figure 11. Many activities of this general kind are needed,

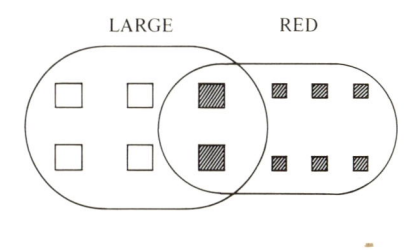

FIGURE 11

employing beads, blocks, sticks, leaves, and so forth, yielding differences in hardness, color, size, and texture.

Different diagrams are obviously obtained according to the attribute used. One attribute—say, hard—implies separation of a set into two classes, hard and not hard, or yellow and not yellow. It is important for the teacher to appreciate that the two chosen attributes must be compatible; thus hard and soft could not be the chosen attributes, for they give the same classifications, one being the negative of the other. Again, pupils must learn that the area and shape of the Venn diagrams are not important, as the diagrams merely illustrate the relations between two or more sets.

It might be objected that some children will complete a Venn diagram in a situation where simple and familiar materials are sorted at five or six years of age and before the onset of concrete operational thought. Indeed, some children do, but in this case their action is directed by the figurative, and not the operative, aspects of knowing. The teacher needs to know, for each child, the basis on which such diagrams are constructed. He obtains such knowledge by questioning the child and by discussion with him.

## INTERSECTION OF SETS

The activities just described are the obvious lead into the intersection of sets. This refers, when objects are being classified, to a subset of objects having two or more of the stated qualities or attributes. In other words, the intersection of two sets $A$ and $B$ is the set of all objects that are members of both set $A$ and set $B$. Another type of practical illustration for children is the road intersection (Figure 12). The dotted area

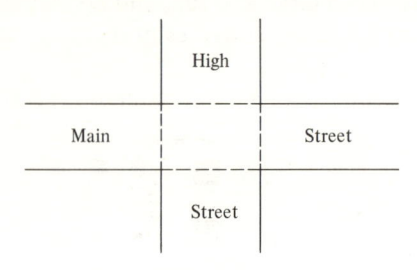

```
                    |  High  |
                    |        |
        _____+--------+_____
                    |        |
            Main    |        |    Street
        _____+--------+_____
                    |        |
                    | Street |
                    |        |
```

FIGURE 12

is seen by the child to be part of both High Street and Main Street. Chalk marks can be drawn on the classroom floor or in the playground, and children can stand within the dotted area to emphasize, to them, that the area is common to both streets. Activities which involve the child in the construction of set intersections helps the child to exercise and strengthen his new found thinking skills of term-by-term multiplication of classes. It is also hoped that they will help him to appreciate, later on, that the arithmetic operation of addition may be looked upon as the union of two sets in which the set intersection is empty—that is, the two sets do not have any common area in the Venn diagram.

## UNION OF SETS

Partitioning by two properties also leads to the union of sets. Stated in more formal terms, the union of two sets results in the set of objects that have the first property, or the second property, or both properties. In the example given earlier of the child sorting large beads and red beads, the union of the set of large beads and the set of red beads will result in the set of beads which is either large or red or both (Figure 13). The union of sets is a more difficult idea for the child than is intersection, because *or* is involved, whereas in the latter instance it is *and* which is the key word. Nevertheless the union of two sets which have no members in common (they are disjoint sets or the intersection is empty) is the precursor of the arithmetic operation of addition. While the importance of the notion of the union or putting together of two

*Operations and Mathematical Sentences* 49

sets cannot be overstressed, in the age group with which we are concerned the emphasis must be on the numerical rather than on the logical relationships.

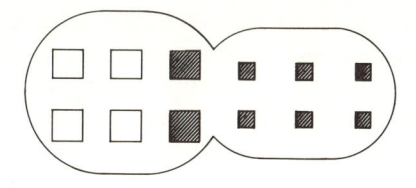

FIGURE 13

## COMMUTATIVE AND ASSOCIATIVE PROPERTIES APPLIED TO SETS

As we shall see in Chapter 7, it is hoped that many of the eight- and nine-year-olds will begin to discover, with the aid of the teacher, the defining properties of the number system. Indeed many children aged seven to eight years and up can be helped to find that the counting numbers have the property of being commutative and associative as far as the operation of addition is concerned, although these terms for the properties will not be used. Children within the age range considered here will not, however, attempt to discover that the operations of union and intersection of sets, *per se*, have commutative and associative properties. But from later activities involving the union of sets, it is hoped that they as high school pupils will realize that in the case of the natural numbers we have a special case of commutative and associative laws operating for addition.

## SYMBOLS

In the age range considered in this book there is no need for the introduction of written symbols associated with sets. At most, the written symbols for intersection and union may be introduced to selected nine-year-olds. Written symbols are, of course, a form of language. In the Piagetian view, symbols, like other forms of language, act as a symbolic vehicle for thought, aiding in the storage and retrieval of information but not greatly helping in the coordination of the input information. In other words, the symbol plays a facilitating role but not a central role in the growth of mathematical thinking. While both teachers and child must use precisely terms such as sets, empty sets, number of members, and so forth, there is no need for the use of symbols associated with sets in the elementary school. The only written symbols necessary in such a school are numerals, those to indicate the relations of greater than, less than, equality, and equivalence, those to indicate the operations of addition, subtraction, multiplication, and division, and the occasional grouping symbol. This general point of view on the use of symbols in the elementary school is supported by Fehr (1966).

## INTRODUCTION TO ADDITION

An introduction to the addition of the natural numbers can be made by putting together the members of two disjoint sets. This has great appeal to children. On the table the child lays out, say, two red counters and five blue counters (Figure 14). Underneath the sets he lays out the

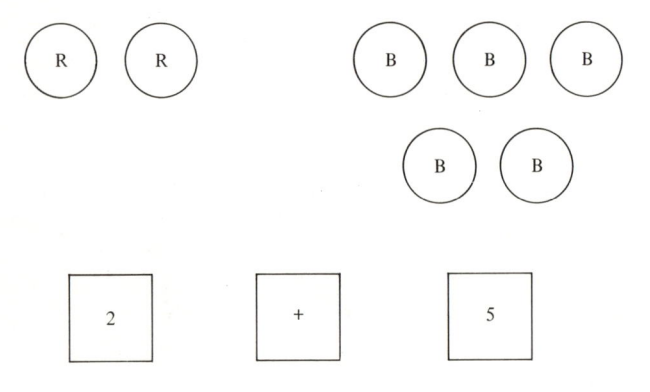

FIGURE 14

numerals 2 and 5 (written on cards) and places the "putting together" or the sign for addition (written on a card) appropriately, as in Figure 14 If the child now puts the two sets of counters together (combination of disjoint sets) to form a new set and counts the number of members in the latter, he finds he has a set of seven members. So he is introduced to a number of ideas: a new whole is formed from two given wholes with the latter now forming part of the former; putting together the members of the two sets is called addition; the number of members in the new set can be written as 2 + 5 or as 7; 7 represents or stands for the same number as 2 + 5; and 2 + 5 or 7 are said to be the sum of 2 and 5.

## Operations and Mathematical Sentences

Pupils need many activities of this general type in which they use, as members of the sets, very varied objects. At the same time they must record what they are doing in the form 2 + 5 is 7, or 2 + 5 altogether 7. Practice will have to be given in writing the sign for addition as earlier practice was needed in the writing of numerals. Pupils then often move on to the use of worksheets on which are pictures of sets of objects, and they have to complete the expression, say, 1 + 7 is ____. The move to worksheets should not be hurried. Putting together physical objects and counting the total number is a more useful activity in the early stages, from the point of view of the child understanding what he is doing in addition, than is the mere counting up of the number of objects depicted on the worksheet. As was pointed out in Chapter 1, logical-mathematical experience is abstracted from one's actions and not from the materials themselves. In the third stage the child will work without objects or pictures of objects and will complete exercises of the type 5 + 3 is ____, and 3 + 5 is ____.

So far the problem of recording has not raised any difficulties, but from this point opinions differ as to the way in which a child should record for a while. Some mathematicians are happy that the words "is" and "altogether" should be replaced by the equal sign so that the child writes 1 + 3 = 4 or 5 + 4 = 9, and so on. On the other hand, the view of the British Nuffield Mathematics Teaching Project is that in the early stages recording should be in words and that the sign for mathematical equality should be avoided. It is argued that while the child needs concrete materials, he may well understand the statement "I had three marbles and John gave me six so that I have nine marbles altogether." But he will not appreciate 3 + 6 = 9 as the mathematician does, because equality defined as "represents the same number as" is a special case of the more general equivalence relation that we shall discuss later.

Instead the Nuffield Project recommends the introduction of an elementary form of mapping (the topic of mapping will be discussed more fully in Chapter 6) so that children record their earliest activities involving addition as shown in Figure 15. The use of the arrow is explained by saying to the child, "It tells you where to go." This form of recording can be made perfectly understandable to the child. On the other hand, it must be remembered that it is a form of recording and its use in no sense guarantees understanding. I have seen children using the notation $5 \xrightarrow{\text{add } 3} 8$ in rote fashion as well as children writing 5 + 3 = 8 without understanding.

```
            Add 3
1 ——————————→ 4
4 ——————————→ 7


            Add 5
2 ——————————→ 7
5 ——————————→ 10
```

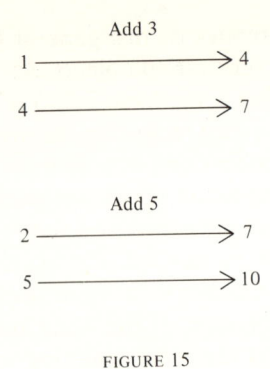

FIGURE 15

When the Nuffield Mathematics Project introduces the equal sign, it is taken to mean "represents the same number as," just as it was used in the opening paragraph of this section. Readers should ponder carefully over the question of the sense in which the equality sign should be introduced to pupils. The seven- to eight-year-old will not, however, be able to appreciate "having the same image under addition mapping." Moreover, as we shall see later, while the elementary school child must have an intuitive grasp of the Reflexive, Symmetric, and Transitive properties that relations may have, he will not possess the ability to structure these and have a well developed concept of Equivalence relation or Equivalence class until the advent of formal operational thought.

From this point on, children need experience in the following kinds of activities, among others, to help develop both their understanding of number relationships involved with addition and their skill in carrying out the operation.

1. Writing out the combinations of numbers which yield a total of 5, 10, and so on, using objects as aids if necessary at the outset. In the case of 5 we have:

$$5 + 0 = 5$$
$$4 + 1 = 5$$
$$3 + 2 = 5$$
$$2 + 3 = 5$$
$$1 + 4 = 5$$
$$0 + 5 = 5$$

Using a mapping notation, the child can map pairs of numbers to 5, 10, and so on. In the case of 5, the mappings are illustrated in Figure 16a. Either method of recording brings out the commutative property of addition.

## Operations and Mathematical Sentences

2. Construction of the addition table as in, say, Figure 16b. This helps to systematize the basic number bonds under the operation of addition. The table should be used by the pupil in working examples.

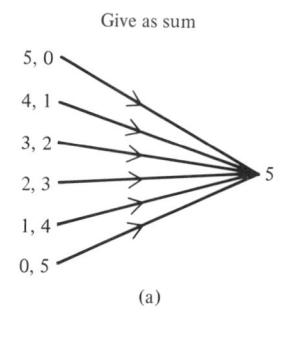

Give as sum

5, 0
4, 1
3, 2
2, 3
1, 4
0, 5

5

(a)

| + | 0 | 1 | 2 | 3 | 4 | 5 |
|---|---|---|---|---|---|---|
| 0 | 0 | 1 | 2 | 3 | 4 | 5 |
| 1 | 1 | 2 | 3 | 4 | 5 | 6 |
| 2 | 2 | 3 | 4 | 5 | 6 | 7 |
| 3 | 3 | 4 | 5 | 6 | 7 | 8 |
| 4 | 4 | 5 | 6 | 7 | 8 | 9 |
| 5 | 5 | 6 | 7 | 8 | 9 | 10 |

In high school the pupil will see the diagonal in terms of $x + y = 5$

(b)

FIGURE 16

3. Working examples which involve "collecting" all the tens in one column and carrying that number of tens to the next column to the left. An understanding of place value (Chapter 2) is essential for this, as is the slow discovery of the commutative and associative properties of the addition of natural numbers if the addition of two- and three digit numbers is to be meaningful (the words "commutative" and "associative" will not, of course, be used at this stage). So exercises of the following type must be provided:
$$53 + 29 = 50 + 3 + 20 + 9 = (50 + 20) + (3 + 9)$$
$$= (70) + (12) = (70) + (10 + 2)$$
$$= (70) + (10) + (2) = (80) + (2) = 82.$$
But if the child chooses to work the examples as $53 + 7 + 2 + 20 = 60 + 2 + 20 = 60 + 20 + 2 = 80 + 2 = 82$, he should be encouraged to do so. It is for the child to develop a number of strategies, as it were.

4. Counting in twos, as in 2, 4, 6, 8 or 1, 3, 5, 7; also in threes and fours. There should also be experiences in counting backwards and starting from different numbers, as, for example, 12, 14, 16, ... or 27, 23, 19, ....

5. Working exercises which involve totals of 10, 20, 30, and so on, up to 99. Later there will be a further progression using totals in the hundreds. By the end of the third grade, pupils can be expected to work examples involving addition with totals up to 9999.
6. Structural apparatus of all kinds can play a most useful role in the understanding of the operation of addition. Such apparatus shows ordinal and cardinal relations between numbers in a concrete form. It is a model of the counting numbers, and actions on it are analogous to various operations used in arithmetic.
7. If examples of the type $6 + 9 =$ , $16 + 9 =$ , $26 + 9 =$ are given, they direct the child's attention to the problem of place value.

In a later chapter we shall deal with the approach to addition through the number line.

## INTRODUCTION TO SUBTRACTION

If a set consisting of, say, six counters is counted out by a child, and he removes from it a set consisting of four members, he finds by counting that the number of remaining members is two. Thus when a set has removed from it a subset containing the same or fewer members, the number of members in the set which is left is equal to the difference in the number of members in the earlier sets. This approach to subtraction would be all right if the operation was confined solely to situations in which physical sets were involved. But later on pupils have to deal with the set of integers, and subtraction has to be unambiguously defined as the additive inverse of addition.

A more satisfactory way of looking at subtraction is to consider the difference between two numbers as the number which has to be added to the second number to obtain the first. In general terms, the difference of $x - y$ (read as $x$ minus $y$) may be thought of as what has to be added to $y$ to obtain $x$. In a numerical example, $6 - 4$ is the number that must be added to four to obtain 6. Stated rather differently, the child must learn that $6 - 4$ is another name for 2 and vice versa; also the expression $6 - 4$ says that 4 is subtracted from 6.

The "add on" process is perfectly understandable to pupils whose thinking has reached the stage of flexible concrete operations in regard to number. In everyday life, problems arise involving "How many

## Operations and Mathematical Sentences

more?", "How many less?", while the shopkeeper regularly calculates the amount of change to be given by the method of complementary addition, that is, through adding on. To help the child to understand that subtraction is the additive inverse of addition, he can put out a set of, say, four counters, and two more counters, and then subtract two from the sum. The operation can be recorded as $(4 + 2) - 2$, and he finds that he finishes with four counters. Put in language that he can comprehend, we can say that subtraction undoes addition and vice versa.

This approach gets over a major difficulty encountered when the operation of subtraction is illustrated in principle by the removal of a physical set; namely, that such removal is only sometimes a model of mathematical subtraction. One can argue a strong case against ever saying to the child, "one minus three you cannot," as in the example $31 - 13$. When he is older he will have to handle the set of integers, as distinct from the natural numbers, and he finds that he will be able to subtract 3 from 1.

Thus it is suggested that an intelligent trial and error approach to subtraction, which is perfectly feasible for a child with flexible concrete operational thought, is likely to be the best lead into subtraction. He will quickly see that if $7 + 3 = 10$ then $10 - 7 = 3$. In other words, $10 - 7 = 3$ is another way of expressing $7 + 3 = 10$. Using physical objects at first, then pictures of objects on worksheets, the child works exercises of the type indicated:

$$7 + \square = 10; \quad \square + 7 = 10; \quad \square + 9 = 10$$

If physical apparatus such as beads is required, he lays out the appropriate number of beads underneath the 7 and underneath the sum 10 (in the first two examples), and then finds the number of beads required to match the sum of 10. He must learn that one name for the difference set is $10 - 7$ and another name is 3, so that $10 - 7$ is 3 or $10 - 7 = 3$. Using a mapping notation, we should have:

$$\text{Subtract 7}$$
$$10 \longrightarrow 3$$

The inverse relationship between addition and subtraction needs to be supported by a number of examples of the type indicated earlier in which the child added two counters to four counters, giving $(4 + 2)$, subtracted two counters, giving $(4 + 2) - 2$, and found that four counters remained. He works this as:

$$(4 + 2) - 2 = 4$$
$$6 - 2 = 4$$

From this point pupils need to acquire greater facility in an intelligent trial and error approach to subtraction. To foster this facility they need to work through exercises of the following types:

$$8 - 5 = 3$$
$$14 - 6 = (14 + 4) - (6 + 4) = 18 - 10 = 8$$
$$\text{or } 14 - 6 = 10 + 4 - 6 = (10 - 6) + 4 = 4 + 4 = 8$$
$$25 - 7 = (25 + 3) - (7 + 3) = 28 - 10 = 18$$
$$16 - 9 = 16 - (6 + 3) = (16 - 6) - 3 = 10 - 3 = 7$$

At the same time as working an example of the type $25 - 7$ by adding 3 to each number, the child should be faced with the example $25 + 7$ in order to discover that here the answer is given by $(25 + 3) + (7 - 3) = 28 + 4 = 32$.

With good experience of physical materials and some flexibility in concrete operational thinking in respect of number, most pupils will understand what they are doing and not look upon subtraction as a set of tricks that work in some situations but not in others. As for working examples when they are set down in a vertical layout, it is suggested that say, $55 - 28$ be worked as

$$\begin{array}{r} 4\ 15 \\ \cancel{5}\cancel{5} \\ -28 \\ \hline \end{array}$$

for the pupil will appreciate that 55 can be replaced by 4 tens + 15. Such an example could obviously be worked as $(55 + 2) - (28 + 2) = 57 - 30 = 27$ and the child's previous experience of an intelligent trial and error approach will help him to understand what takes place when working subtraction in the vertical layout.

One word of warning is necessary at this point. While the thinking of most children at eight years of age is sufficiently flexible and systematized for them to be able to see the relation between $7 + 3 = 10$ and $10 - 7 = 3$, there is a proportion of school educable retarded pupils who will have difficulty in seeing this even when much older (see Chapter 1). It is perfectly true that they will use an "add on" approach to subtraction as they do when giving change. But it is a rote procedure for them, and they do not grasp that subtraction undoes addition and vice versa.

In Chapter 7 we shall look at subtraction again, using clock arithmetic.

## INTRODUCTION TO MULTIPLICATION

The mathematician knows that the operation of multiplication carried out by the elementary school child is a many-to-one mapping whereby

## Operations and Mathematical Sentences

every ordered pair of natural numbers is mapped on to a natural number defined as their product. We do not, of course, begin by defining the operation of multiplication, or product, in this way. Rather, to start with we look upon multiplication as the simultaneous joining together of sets that have the same number of members, making use of sets of objects at first.

It will be realized that in the expression $3 \times 4$ the numbers 3 and 4 have different roles. Some persons maintain that it indicates a set of 3 four times; others that it indicates three times a set of 4. There is no agreement on this issue, and the writer does not intend to enter the debate, as counting numbers possess the commutative property with respect to multiplication.

A child then needs many activities of the following types:

1. The arranging of, say, three rows each of four objects; also four rows each of three objects, as in Figure 17. Such arrays may

    • • • •      • • •
    • • • •      • • •
    • • • •      • • •
                 • • •

    FIGURE 17

    be constructed using counters, or pegboard and pegs. Each time the child has to establish that there is the same number of objects in each row, how many objects there are in each row, how many rows there are, and what the total or product is.
2. Given a number—say, twelve, sixteen, or twenty-four—of suitable objects, he must find, for each number, how many rows can be made with the same number of objects in each row. Thus, in the case of twelve, he establishes that he can have two rows of six, three rows of four, four rows of three, and six rows of two. Moreover, he must be given odd numbers of objects so that some odd numbers will yield rows which contain an equal number of objects (for example, twenty-one), and some which will not give more than one such row (as twenty-three). He will learn later that there is something rather special about the latter kind of number—the prime number.
3. Counting out objects in sets of two, three, four, and so on, and recording the number of members in each set and the total as, say,

$2 + 2 = 4; \quad 2 + 2 + 2 = 6; \quad 2 + 2 + 2 + 2 = 8$
$3 + 3 = 6; \quad 3 + 3 + 3 = 9; \quad 3 + 3 + 3 + 3 = 12$

4. The appropriate use of the various forms of structural apparatus available.

In all the above activities (except in the case of the prime numbers) equivalent sets are being joined, and children soon learn to associate the operation of multiplication with the joining of such sets; they also learn to associate the term *product* and the symbol $x$ with the results of such action. From laying out objects in front of him, a child finds for himself and then records that, say,

$$3 \times 4 = 4 + 4 + 4 = 2 + 2 + 2 + 2 + 2 + 2$$
$$= 1 + 1 + \ldots + 1 = 6 + 6 = 3 + 3 + 3 + 3$$

These activities are perfectly understandable to an average eight-year-old, although he may need much experience with objects. Eventually he will be able to systematize the results of his actions and begin to record his findings in table form. For example:

$1 \times 2 = 2 \qquad 1 \times 3 = 3$
$2 \times 2 = 4 \qquad 2 \times 3 = 6$
$3 \times 2 = 6 \qquad 3 \times 3 = 9$

where the equals sign ( = ) is again to read "represents the same number as." Furthermore, he will record his findings in the form of the multiplication table square. Four rows of such a square are shown in Figure 18. Such a square should be used by the child in working examples. Its use will help him to commit the facts to memory and should be used in preference to printed tables.

| × | 1 | 2 | 3 | 4 | 5 | 6 | 7 | 8 | 9 | 10 |
|---|---|---|---|---|---|---|---|---|---|----|
| 1 | 1 | 2 | 3 | 4 | 5 | 6 | 7 | 8 | 9 | 10 |
| 2 | 2 | 4 | 6 | 8 | 10 | 12 | 14 | 16 | 18 | 20 |
| 3 | 3 | 6 | 9 | 12 | 15 | 18 | 21 | 24 | 27 | 30 |
| 4 | 4 | 8 | 12 | 16 | 20 | 24 | 28 | 32 | 36 | 40 |

FIGURE 18

Recording can be made so that a table gives four sixes lying on a curve (Figure 19a). In high school the pupil will think of this curve in terms of $xy = 6$. Recording can also be made using a mapping nota-

*Operations and Mathematical Sentences* 59

tion (to be developed later) if that is preferred. This is illustrated in Figure 19b. But it is essentially through his activities that the child discovers that for every pair of natural numbers there corresponds another which is called the product.

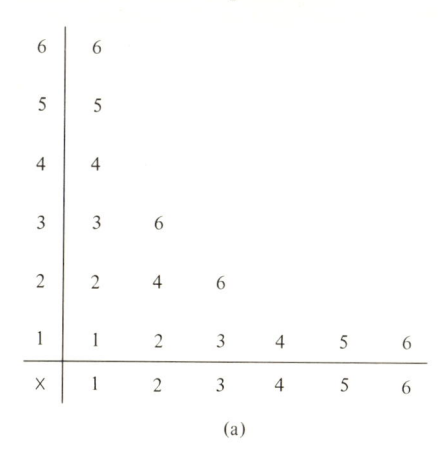

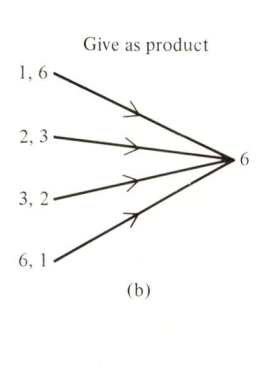

```
6 | 6
5 | 5
4 | 4                        Give as product
3 | 3   6                    1, 6 ──┐
2 | 2   4   6                2, 3 ──┤
1 | 1   2   3   4   5   6    3, 2 ──┼── 6
X | 1   2   3   4   5   6    6, 1 ──┘
        (a)                      (b)
```

FIGURE 19

Later, the relationship between the operation of multiplication and the formation of the product set can be shown if desired. To start with a nonmathematical example may be of help. Consider, for example, the dishes that are served at lunchtime (Figure 20). Let members of the

|  |  | Second Course | | |
|---|---|---|---|---|
|  |  | Cherry Pie | Ice Cream | Fresh Fruit |
| First Course | Steak | Steak/Cherry Pie | Steak/Ice Cream | Steak/Fresh Fruit |
|  | Chicken | Chicken/Cherry Pie | Chicken/Ice Cream | Chicken/Fresh Fruit |

FIGURE 20

first set be the dishes served on the first course, and the members of the second set the dishes served on the second course. Now the child at the stage of flexible concrete operational thought can carry out a term-by-term multiplication of classes as we have seen, and he can work out the six possible meals that he can have. He can establish the product set by pairing off each member of the first set with each member of the second

60               *The Growth of Understanding in Mathematics*

set, and he can grasp that the product set consists of six ordered pairs, since he well understands that he always takes his steak before his cherry pie, and so on. Finally he notes that the cardinal value of the product set is six. If we allow a dot to take the place of each ordered pair (Figure 21), then the operation of multiplication is reduced to counting, and once again the pupil can establish that $2 \times 3 = 1 + \ldots + 1 = 2 + 2 + 2 = 3 + 3$.

|  |  | Second Course |  |  |
|---|---|---|---|---|
|  |  | Cherry Pie | Ice Cream | Fresh Fruit |
| First Course | Steak | ● | ● | ● |
|  | Chicken | ● | ● | ● |

FIGURE 21

The introduction of the idea of product set is helpful when treating the multiplication of fractions (rational numbers will be dealt with more fully in Chapter 7) and in understanding multiplication by 0. For example, consider $2/3 \times 2/5$. Let the members of the first set be thirds and the members of the second set be fifths. Then the product set indicates that the product will be 4/15 (Figure 22).

|  | 1/5 | 2/5 | 3/5 | 4/5 | 5/5 |
|---|---|---|---|---|---|
| 1/3 | ● | ● |  |  |  |
| 2/3 | ● | ● |  |  |  |
| 3/3 |  |  |  |  |  |

FIGURE 22

However, the justification for the introduction of the child to the product set is the opening of his mind to wider issues, namely the ordered pair; the product set of two sets when one is the empty set; as well as practicing the skill of term by term multiplication of classes. He will understand, for example, that if there are four members in each of sets $X$ and $Y$, the cardinal value of the product set will be 16 (Figure 23a), for each member of $X$ may be paired off with each member of $Y$ yielding sixteen ordered pairs. On the other hand, if there are no members in set $Y$—that is, it is the empty set—the child can see that no ordered pairs can be constructed so that the product $4 \times 0 = 0$ (Figure 23b).

## Operations and Mathematical Sentences

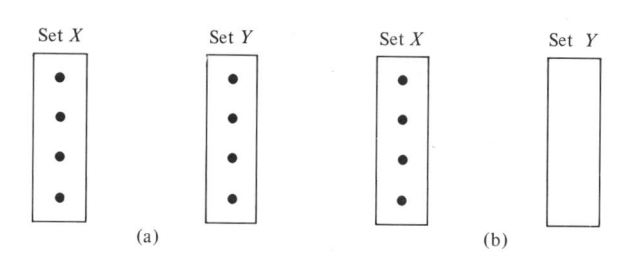

```
      Set X        Set Y        Set X        Set Y
       •            •            •
       •            •            •
       •            •            •
       •            •            •
        (a)                       (b)
```

FIGURE 23

A word must be said about the multiplication tables. While it is of the utmost importance that children learn that the operation of multiplication involves the joining of equivalent sets, and learn how to build up the multiplication tables, it is also necessary for them to commit the results (the products) to memory. They need to be able to compute quickly and accurately. While many pupils will need considerable time and a variety of experiences before they are able to memorize the results of the tables, most pupils do obtain a grasp of them. But some do not, even when in high school, and they need the aid of a reference table. Figure 24 shows the first four rows of a multiplication square which pupils

| × | 0 | 1 | 2 | 3 | 4 | 5 | 6 | 7 | 8 | 9 | 10 | 11 | 12 |
|---|---|---|---|---|---|---|---|---|---|---|----|----|----|
| 0 | 0 | 0 | 0 | 0 | 0 | 0 | 0 | 0 | 0 | 0 | 0  | 0  | 0  |
| 1 | 0 | 1 | 2 | 3 | 4 | 5 | 6 | 7 | 8 | 9 | 10 | 11 | 12 |
| 2 | 0 | 2 | 4 | 6 | 8 | 10| 12| 14| 16| 18| 20 | 22 | 24 |
| 3 | 0 | 3 | 6 | 9 | 12| 15| 18| 21| 24| 27| 30 | 33 | 36 |

FIGURE 24

should construct for themselves. Note that in Figure 24, but not in Figure 18, the results of multiplying by zero are included.

It is not intended here to outline methods which are likely to help pupils to commit to memory the results of these tables, as this book is concerned essentially with understanding mathematics. But it should be said that there is no one best method for all children, although all pupils do seem to need much preliminary experience of counting on in ones, twos, threes, and so on, always starting with zero, and counting as, say:

0, 3, 6, 9, . . .
0, 5, 10, 15, . . .

Counting backwards is also important:
30, 27, 24, 21 . . .

## INTRODUCTION TO DIVISION

In everyday situations children frequently share, say, their sweets or their toys, as when they give the same number to each of their playmates. They may also be familiar with the school situation where a number of pupils are divided equally into, say, four teams. This notion of sharing is a very real one for children, and when we help them to carry out the process of sharing we are, of course, introducing them to division.

The suggestion made here is that the best way to introduce the operation of division is to consider it as undoing multiplication, just as earlier we considered subtraction as undoing addition. The link between the operation of division and multiplication is so strong that children whose thinking is characterized as being concrete operational will discover the strength of the link for themselves. We may begin then by giving a pupil, say, twelve counters and asking him to put them into three piles so that there is the same number in each. If he has understood the operation of multiplication, there is a strong possibility that he will understand the mathematical statement $\square \times 3 = 12$, and through the actual manipulation of the counters, he should be able to insert the correct number in the box. In practice there is a need for considerable experience of sharing physical objects—a finding out of how many sets, each containing the same given number of members, are needed to contain a given number of objects; or a finding out of how many members will be in each of a specified number of sets necessary to contain a given number of objects when the numerousness of the set is the same in all instances. The former instance is illustrated by the problem "How many teams can be made from twenty children if each team has five pupils in it?" The latter is indicated by the problem "How many oranges will each child get if twenty are shared equally among five pupils?"

In essence then, the child works with physical apparatus and writes down the appropriate mathematical statement, such as $5 \times \square = 20$. He finds the number, or more strictly the numeral, corresponding to the set of counting numbers which makes the statement true and inserts the appropriate symbol in the box. Eventually he is introduced to the symbolism $20 \div 5 = 4$.

# Operations and Mathematical Sentences

Apart from sharing problems, the building up and use of conversion tables regarding, say, length or other measures is a useful type of exercise. The child has to find, for example, how many feet measure the same distance as two yards, and how many yards measure the same distance as fifteen feet. Again the number strip may be used for problems such as "How many times must I step off seven to reach twenty-one?" But having introduced the child to the operation of division as the opposite operation to that of multiplication, and having given him the opportunity to engage in plenty of activities of the type indicated, it may be best to refrain from a great deal more work in division until pupils have an understanding of other kinds of numbers such as $1\frac{3}{4}$ or 3.5.

But the child can at this stage be introduced to the term *quotient* (the quotient of 16 and 8 is 2) as he was to the term *product* (the product of 8 and 2 is 16), and he should be introduced to a way of recording when there is a remainder. In the case of the mathematical statement $4 \times \square = 17$ it is helpful to get the child to think through the statement and rewrite it as $4 \times \square + \square = 17$. An intelligent trial and error approach using apparatus and small numbers will aid the child in putting the correct symbols in the boxes. This book is not primarily concerned with methods of recording, vital though these be, but it is important to stress here that the rephrasing of the mathematical statement by an intelligent trial and error approach does lead the child to the point where he can record $17 \div 4$ as 4 Rem 1. It is for the teacher to decide at this point, as indeed it is when any of the four operations are introduced, how much drill and practice is required by a particular pupil.

It has been stressed that concrete operational thought is necessary for the strong bond between addition and subtraction, and between multiplication and division, to be grasped. Many school educable retarded children, and some other pupils, will throughout the elementary school years find it difficult if not impossible to appreciate the relationship between addition and subtraction, and between multiplication and division. They may well learn some of the addition, subtraction, multiplication, and division "facts," but they will not see their interconnectedness.

## MATHEMATICAL SENTENCES

In this section we discuss the introduction of mathematical sentences to children. As the reader will be aware, the child has already met such sentences, but here we are to look at them more closely. We begin by listing the different kinds of symbols used in mathematics with pupils within the age range covered by this book.

First, there are the number symbols or numerals like 0, 3, 91, 675; second, the symbols indicating the four operations, $+, -, \times, \div$; third, symbols expressing relationship but limited to the use of $=, >, <$; fourth, one grouping symbol or bracket generally indicated by ( ); fifth, what is known as a placeholder, confined at our age level to symbols like □. In later grades of the elementary and high school, placeholders will also contain symbols such as *a, b, x, y*. By the time the child is ready to look at mathematical sentences—these are confined to number sentences in this book—he will obviously have experienced the symbols indicated above, and used them correctly.

In order to write a mathematical sentence we write a relational symbol in conjunction with one or more of the above types of symbol. The sentence is not, of course, defined in this terse way to the child. Rather examples are given, such as:

$$14 - 5 > 2 + 4$$
$$1 \times 3 < 10 \div 2$$
$$11 + 6 = 17 - 0 \text{ or } 11 + 6 = 17$$
$$4 \times 0 = 5 - 5 \text{ or } 0 = 5 - 5$$

By examining such instances and through discussion with teacher and peers, the child can learn the defining characteristics of the number sentence. The pupil needs much experience in making up such sentences, which the teacher must check.

Now a mathematical sentence which does not contain a placeholder is either true or false but not both. So the next task for the pupil is to examine such sentences and determine if they are true or false. He thus makes up such sentences, designating each as true or false; or he works through examples, provided on worksheets, of the following and related types:

$$\text{T or F: } 8 + 2 = 10$$
$$24 \div 6 > 4$$
$$4 \times 5 < 23 - 7$$
$$3 + 5 = 12 - 4$$

To this point the pupil has looked at certain kinds of sentences and decided upon their truth or falsity. He must now be led to look upon sentences more closely in order to learn more about when they are true or false, or when it is not possible to determine which they are.

As a beginning, consider the following three sentences, which are suitable for adults and not for children:

*Operations and Mathematical Sentences* 65

1. U Thant was elected Secretary General of the United Nations.
2. The first President of the United States was elected Secretary General to the United Nations.
3. The man was elected Secretary General to the United Nations.

Sentence 1 is true and sentence 2 obviously false, but we cannot determine the truth or falsity of the third sentence until the words "The man" are replaced by his precise name.

We can now take an example that is suitable for use with children. Let us suppose that the teacher's name is Miss Macaulay and get the child to examine these sentences:

1. Miss Macaulay is my teacher.
2. Buffalo Bill's wife is my teacher.
3. The lady is my teacher.

Sentence 1 is obviously true for the child, sentence 2 is easily seen by him to be false, while he cannot decide on the truth or falsity of sentence 3 until the lady's name is inserted.

With this illustration the child can be taken back to the mathematical sentence and led to consider, through discussion with the teacher, the truth or falsity of the following kinds of sentences, or whether it is impossible to determine this as they stand—that is, their truth is conditional.

1. $4 + 3 = 7$;   $18 \div 3 > 2 + 1$
2. $5 \div 1 = 8$;   $20 - 5 < 4 \times 2$
3. $10 - \square = 6$;   $17 + 7 = \square \times 6$

Those sentences in the first group are true, those in the second group false, while it is not possible to say anything about those in the third group until the placeholder is replaced by a numeral. The last category of sentences, which are neither true nor false until a numeral has been put into the placeholder, are called *open* sentences.

Through his experience of the four operations, the child will have met many open sentences. Now he needs further experience, using worksheets, of classifying mathematical sentences as true, false, or open, and in the case of the last named of replacing the placeholder with a numeral. The child should have his attention directed to the fact that more than one numeral can often be put into the placeholder: $2 + \square > 8$.

It will be readily recognized that the pupil must have flexible and systematic thinking before he can handle mathematical sentences in a satisfactory manner. But the ideas outlined here are important, for they serve as a basis for later work. In the higher grades of the elementary school, and in high school, he will need to elaborate the concept of solution set—that is, the set of replacements for the variable (placeholder) in the open sentence that makes the resultant sentence true.

Teachers hope that their pupils will be able to solve problems. Alas, many pupils find difficulty in problem solving, although they may be able to apply learned rules to operations in rote fashion. Essentially when they are unable to solve problems, either the problems are too complex, or they are couched in language the pupils do not comprehend, or the pupils' grasp of the mathematical ideas involved is too tenuous, or their thinking shows little capacity for transfer from situation to situation. There is no one set of rules that can be given to children to help them solve problems, nor is there any one way in which mathematics can be applied to solve real life problems. But we can attempt to help children to think about and organize the data given in the problems.

Basically in problem solving the child is presented with a "number story," and the English sentences have to be translated in some way or other into mathematical sentences. Of course, not all English sentences can be so translated. For example, there can be no mathematical translation of the sentence "The boy is honest." But we can translate into a mathematical sentence the English sentence "If John has eight marbles and I have three more, how many have I?" What the child must do is to think out the implications of the sentence and form an open mathematical sentence which corresponds. Thus the child should be encouraged to write:

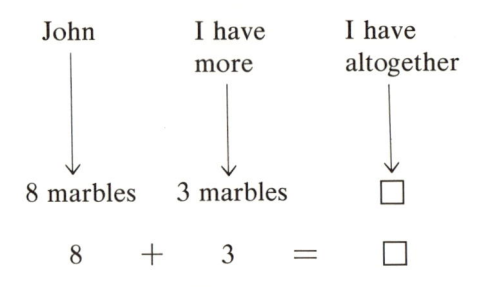

$$\begin{array}{ccc} \text{John} & \text{I have more} & \text{I have altogether} \\ \downarrow & \downarrow & \downarrow \\ \text{8 marbles} & \text{3 marbles} & \square \\ 8 & + \quad 3 \quad = & \square \end{array}$$

Again we can translate the English sentences "Tom is two years younger than Mary, and she is now ten years old. How old is Tom?" The child is now encouraged to lay out his data as:

## Operations and Mathematical Sentences

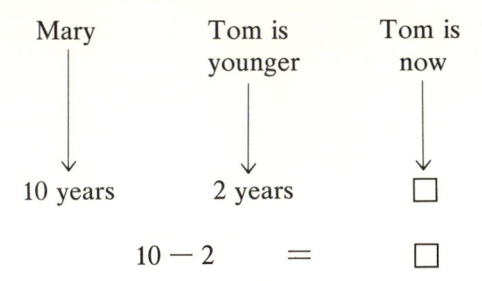

```
    Mary         Tom is        Tom is
     |          younger         now
     |             |             |
     ↓             ↓             ↓
  10 years      2 years         □

              10 − 2    =       □
```

A third example may be helpful in that it may emphasize to the reader the great importance of this help to children. We can translate the English sentences "Five boys each have three pets. How many pets do they have altogether?"

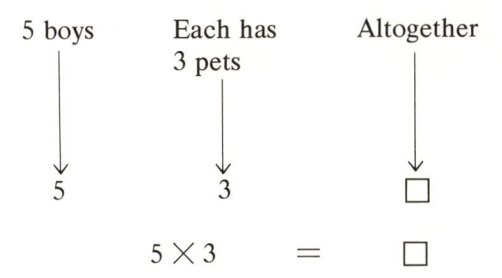

```
    5 boys       Each has     Altogether
                  3 pets
      |             |             |
      ↓             ↓             ↓
      5             3             □

              5 × 3     =         □
```

If the problem deals with situations familiar to the child and is couched in suitable language, he can be helped through many examples to reflect on his data, lay it out in diagrammatic form, establish the operations involved, form the open sentence, and solve the problem. Eventually the diagrammatic layout of the material will be unnecessary. But there is no royal road to problem solving. Each child needs much experience in formulating the mathematical sentence, along with encouragement from, and discussion with, his teacher.

# 4
# Space

**IMPORTANCE OF SPATIAL WORK**

There is little doubt that spatial work has, in the past, been neglected in the education of young children. Accordingly this chapter opens with three reasons for dealing with concepts of space, including those of measurement and metrical geometry, in the kindergarten and elementary school.

The first and fundamental reason for studying spatial relationships is to develop the individual's intuitions about space. Both as a child and later as an adult—whether it be as architect, engineer, bus driver, or housewife—one needs an intuitive grasp of the properties of space and of objects in it. Second, mathematical relations are often presentable in the form that the mind can grasp using diagrams and geometrical language. Simple graphical representations can be used with a six-year-old, as they can with backward adults; while the average and above average high school pupil, judged in respect of his attainment, finds that a vivid way of illustrating the solution set to a pair of simultaneous equations is via the intersection of their graphs. Third, mathematicians are interested in structure in a very general sense. Children, however, are unable to grasp abstract structures, so if we want to stress them we must find concrete realizations of such structures in the real world. Spatial relationships are often rich in such structures at varying levels of difficulty. For example, the rotations of an ordinary envelope or of a piece of cardboard in space can be made to illustrate the structure of the mathematical group.

## PERCEPTUAL AND REPRESENTATIONAL SPACE

The term *perception* is sometimes defined as the process of becoming immediately aware of something. Others have used the term in a wider sense to include the actual identification of an object or situation. In the latter usage, perception is sensory awareness as affected by the person's knowledge, mental set, attitudes, expectations, motivation, and general ways of thinking. Piaget (1954–55) takes an intermediate view: "We will call perception the most direct or immediate possible knowledge of a present object in the sensorial field (without affirming, however, that there exists a knowledge which is completely direct or immediate)." This discussion of perception is necessary, for Piaget and Inhelder (1956) are claer that the growth of spatial relationships takes place at two levels—the perceptual level and the level of thinking or representation.

The growth of perceptual space starts at birth and cannot be dealt with in this book except to say that the actions and experiences of the sensori-motor period seem to be of great consequence. From the point of view of the school, the position is this: Long before a child can deal with, say, perspective in thought, or measure the length of an object using operational thinking (see Chapter 5) he can perceive things projectively and understand certain metric relationships by perception alone. The ability to recognize, say, circles, squares, and triangles is greatly in advance of his capacity to represent these to himself at the level of mental images or representational thought. Indeed the infant and many animals can distinguish these figures when presented visually. Thus thinking has to achieve at its level—of representation as distinct from direct perception—all that perception achieved within the limited field of direct contact with the object. Indeed, in Piaget's view, some years separate the two constructions, for it is not until seven to eight years of age that measurement, the coordination of perspectives, the construction of axes of references, and so forth, result in the elaboration of a conceptual space.

Nevertheless both constructions have, in Piaget's view, a common factor; namely, both are dependent upon the motor activity of the child. The case for motor activity underlying elementary perceptions cannot be argued here. In brief, it is Piaget's view that perceptual space results both from direct perception and from sensori-motor activity applied to the control and direction of various movements which in turn determine what the perception in centered on. On the other hand, spatial concepts are internalized actions; they are not just images of external events or things—or even images of one's actions. It is true that at times one thinks of a static pattern, as when the image of a square is conjured up (the figurative aspect of knowing), but at other times one thinks of the rotation of a square about a side (the operative aspect of knowing). Indeed, using his knowledge of spatial concepts to predict the effect of such a rotation, a child can operate on objects mentally and not merely evoke images of them. Put in another way, we can say that to arrange a series of objects in the mind is not just to arrange a series of objects set in order, or even to imagine the act of arranging them, but to carry out actions, internally, on symbolic objects. In other words, the series must be arranged operationally—by logical thought.

The role of the spatial image decreases as the active component of thought becomes better organized, although this is not to deny that the spatial image is of help from time to time in child and adolescent thinking. Indeed spatial images may serve as a support for spatial reasoning at times, and there is certainly a greater awareness and feeling for isomorphism, or similarity of structure, between image and operation in the area of space than of logic. Summing up in a rather different way, we can say that spatial ideas do not derive from a "reading" or direct apprehension of the physical properties of objects, but from an action performed on them.

It is because of the internalization of actions that the mind can eventually go beyond the physical limitations of objects, for such actions permit the creation of operational thinking. At the level of concrete operational thought the mental actions may be sufficiently logical and precise for the image to be no longer indispensable, although, as said earlier, the image may still have its uses. But at the level of formal operational thought, action on space is a purely abstract deductive affair; indeed such images of, say, point or continuous line as can be conjured up are quite inadequate for operational thinking, as will be seen later.

In the remainder of this chapter, there is a discussion of the growth of some very basic spatial concepts, namely, point, projective concepts, and axes of reference. Later, consideration is given to the kinds of activities which children might engage in to assist the development of these spatial ideas together with those of symmetry and simple transformations.

## POINT

We begin with a discussion of the growth of the child's concept of point. On the surface this is an apparently simple idea and one beloved by mathematicians, yet in fact it is an extremely difficult one for pupils in the elementary school. This fact is often forgotten. For example, in a well-known and currently used text on elementary school arithmetic it is stated: "It is important for children to learn that although dots . . . are of different sizes, the points represented by these dots do not differ in size. Thus . . . a point is not a physical object and can thus be thought of as being without size in the physical sense." Unfortunately children cannot think of an abstract point as adolescents and adults can, for it is not intuitable. Indeed the teacher must be extremely careful when using the term in the elementary school. To illustrate these difficulties for the child, an outline is given of some of Piaget and Inhelder's relevant experiments and findings (Piaget and Inhelder, 1956).

Basically four problems face the child. First, he is given a sheet of paper, and, in suitable language, he is asked to draw the smallest possible square on it. Then on a second sheet he is asked to draw the largest possible square. Second, he is asked to continue subdividing, say, a straight line, or a circle, square, or triangle. If he is shown a line, he is requested to draw another half its length, then half of a half, and so on, and to continue doing this "in his mind," and then asked what he is left with or what remains at the end. Third, the child is questioned regarding the actual shape of the end product of the subdivision. If he uses the term "point," he must be asked what shape the point will be, while if he says "nothing at all," he must be questioned as to what is left just before nothing at all. Fourth, the pupil is asked about the recreation of a figure or line out of its ultimate elements.

This is an important issue in Piaget's view. Indeed, the teacher wants to know at what age the child can conceive of a line or surface as a set of points. The verbal questioning must be supplemented by getting the child to draw a series of dots and then insert as many dots in between the former as possible, or to draw two limiting dots and then insert as many dots as possible in between, all with the intention of finding out if he believes that the dots will eventually form a line.

In the writer's experience these tasks make clear the growth of the child's understanding of point, although the various age levels appear to be more variable than Piaget suggests. The latter maintains that up to seven to eight years of age the pupil, being unable to form a series, finds difficulty in drawing the largest and smallest squares. Only a limited number of subdivisions of a figure or line can be made ("half of a half" is beyond the grasp of many pupils), while what the subject maintains is that the final or ultimate element has recognizable size and is of the same shape as the original; so that if we start with a square, the final element is also a square.

With the onset of more systematized thought, around seven or so,

# Space

the nature of the responses begins to change. The largest and smallest squares can be drawn; many more subdivisions of a figure or line can be admitted, but the child does not regard them as being infinite in number, nor are they generalized beyond the tangible—that is to say, at the level of concrete operational thinking the pupil can handle only intuitable data. The shape of the ultimate elements is dependent upon the manner in which the original was subdivided; if a line is constantly subdivided, the end shape will be "long," or a triangle may end as "a little bit pointed." However, the end shape is not isomorphic with the original shape as earlier. On the other hand, the end shape is never regarded as without surface area and consisting of an infinite set of points.

The responses to the fourth task are interesting. While the pupil can increasingly consider making a whole out of constituent elements as the reverse counterpart to subdivision, his understanding is no more than an intuitive grasp of continuity. Indeed he remains in a quandary, for he cannot reconcile the continuity of, say, the line which results from the reunion of dots with the discontinuous nature of the dots themselves out of which the line is to be formed.

Finally, with the onset of formal operational thought at around eleven to twelve years of age in the brightest pupils, and around fourteen to fifteen years of age in ordinary adolescents, further changes begin. Subdivision can increasingly be thought of as limitless, points become homogeneous regardless of the original shape from which they were derived and are, of course, without shape or surface area. Unlimited subdivision and synthesis of the whole are regarded as reverse processes, although for a further period there may still be some contradiction between a continuous whole and the discontinuous nature of the points out of which the whole is formed.

This short account will give readers some idea of the growth of children's understanding in regard to point and line, or surface area, considered as a set of points. For further details Piaget and Inhelder's original work should be studied. It will be realized that pupils whose ages are covered by this book will have, at best, the understanding provided by a flexible concrete operational thought. Readers who are particularly interested in the growth of the concept of limit point in elementary school pupils, admittedly able and privileged ones, should also consult Taback (1969).

## PROJECTIVE CONCEPTS

In the view of Piaget and Inhelder (1956) both projective and Euclidean concepts begin to emerge around the age of six or soon afterward as the child's thinking begins to move towards systematization. Projective space begins psychologically, in their view, when an object is no longer thought of in isolation but begins to be considered in relation to a "point of view." Thus projective relationships, like Euclidean relationships, seem to demand the intercoordination of objects which are separated in space. In other words, the growth of logical thought permits the simultaneous development of both projective and Euclidean concepts, because such thinking permits the coordination of objects within a more general system of organization.

## The Projective Straight Line

We begin our study of projective concepts by considering projective straight lines—straight lines constructed through taking aim—since they illustrate very clearly that children who have for a long while recognized straight lines still have difficulty in constructing one. Such lines also suggest how simple perspectives come to be constructed. In order to study the growth of the child's ability to construct the projective straight line, Piaget and Inhelder (1956) devised the following experiment.

Two matchsticks, each stuck into a small amount of plasticine, are set up about eighteen inches apart and one inch from the edge of a rectangular table ($A$ and $B$ in Figure 25a). The child has to place his

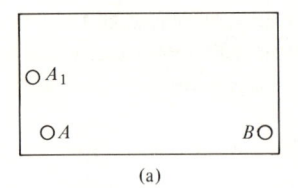

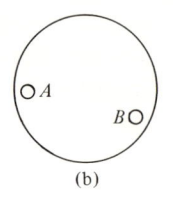

FIGURE 25

matchsticks (stuck in plasticine) in a straight line between the two end matchsticks. In the next part of the experiment, $A$ is moved to $A_1$ and the subject has again to make a straight line $A_1B$ with his matchsticks. The third part of the experiment consists of putting a hoop on the table, placing two matchsticks at the end of a cord about two feet long (Figure 25b), and asking the child again to construct a straight line $AB$ with his matchsticks.

A number of stages in the growth of the child's ability to construct the line are claimed by Piaget and Inhelder. Between about four and

Space

six years of age the child is able to construct the straight line $AB$ (Figure 25a) by placing his matchsticks more or less parallel to the edge of the table. But he is unable to break away from the perceptual influence of the edge of the table when the line $A_1B$ has to be constructed (Figure 26a), a line which is essentially at an angle to the edge of the table.

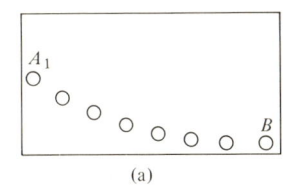

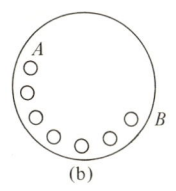

FIGURE 26

Similarly in Figure 26b he constructs his "straight" line around the circumference of the hoop. But starting around six, and extending to seven years of age, the child is said by Piaget and Inhelder to overcome his errors in constructing the straight line by a process of trial and error, while from around seven years of age onward he makes the line correctly no matter where it is situated. He does this by putting himself in line with the first and last matchsticks and sights along, or "takes aim" along the trajectory.

I have found that children do pass through these stages but at rather earlier ages than indicated by the Geneva school. Moreover, children use methods not indicated by Piaget and Inhelder, such as laying hands along the table to see if the line is straight and drawing imaginary lines with their fingers which the matchsticks must follow. And a few children as young as four and a half to five have been found who will "take aim" from behind one of the posts.

However, apart from these findings, children seem to pass through the stages suggested by Piaget and Inhelder. Young children have no clear idea as to what constitutes a straight line in spite of the fact that they can recognize one and distinguish it from one that is not straight or one that is broken. The Geneva school indicates that the child begins to construct the straight line when he discovers that some points of view are better than others for correcting imperfect alignments. In other words, he begins to distinguish between points of view and grasps that the two points $AB$ (or $A_1B$) can be related to himself through the agency of the line of sight $AB$. The conceptual straight line differs from the perceptual straight line because in the case of the former the child has become aware of the part played by different points of view.

## Perspectives

The straight line is the only shape that remains unaltered by perspective changes. Thus an essential requirement for forming perspective is the ability to imagine, compared with merely perceive, straight lines facing in any direction. For example, a child must be able to imagine the foreshortening that would take place if one end of a stick is placed on the table in front of him and the other end points away from him.

In Piaget and Inhelder's (1956) experiments, changes are made in the displacement of objects relative to the child, and a study is made of how the latter sets about representing these objects in perspective. Thus the subject is presented with, say, a disc or stick and is asked to imagine what apparent shape each object would have when placed in a number of different positions. It is, of course, imperative to get the child to understand that we are interested in the apparent shape ("how it looks") and not the real shape. To make sure that this is the case, the child is asked to draw, say, a stick. But he must draw it not as it appears to him at $A$ (Figure 27) when it is rotated through 90° with its base fixed, but

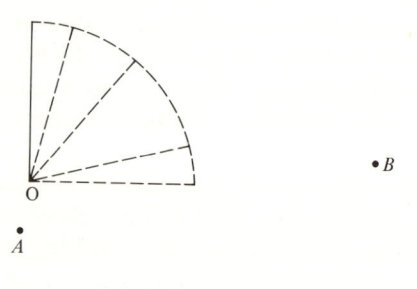

FIGURE 27

as it would appear to a doll representing another child at $B$ (Figure 27). The plane in which the stick is lowered is perpendicular to the plane of the table and also to $AO$. If the child draws the doll at $B$ as ultimately seeing a dot or small circle, we may be sure that the child at $A$ understands that he has to draw the apparent and not the real shape. Again, in order to get over the difficulty that lack of drawing skill will be a handicap, subjects are also shown a number of drawings, some incorrect, some correct, and they are asked to pick out the one which corresponds to a given position of the stick (or disc).

In this type of experiment, objects are necessarily near the child, but studies can also be made in which distance is involved. For example, children notice the common perspective distortion of parallel lines converging to a point in the distance, as in the case of railway lines or the edges of a road. Thus subjects are also asked to draw a picture

# Space

of straight railway lines going far away into the distance and then to add the drawing of the ties. Finally they are asked to pick out a correct drawing of such lines from a set of prepared drawings.

A number of stages are identified and described by Piaget and Inhelder. As we shall see in a moment, these stages are not, in the writer's experience, as clear cut as the Geneva work suggests. However, for Piaget, children between about four and six years of age either indicate the same viewpoint—and thus the same shape and size—regardless of how the observer is related to the object, or at best they make some slight change in orientation. But toward the end of this period there is some awareness of the inadequacy of their drawings, while for end-on views of the stick the paper may be turned to a similar position. In the next stage, which lasts from about six to seven years of age, children begin to choose between different viewpoints mainly through the selection of drawings, although in their own drawings there is less obvious progress. That is to say, it is easier to select a drawing than to elaborate the representation for themselves. Likewise they may choose a picture showing converging railway lines but draw the lines as parallel. Even during the next stage, which lasts from about seven to eight and a half years of age, changes in apparent shape may be indicated in only a general way; the foreshortening of the stick will not always be correctly indicated, while some pupils find it hard to accept a disc as a straight line, although the changes in the apparent shape of the disc are grasped in a general way. Finally, from eight and a half years of age onwards, perspective is systematically applied to all drawings. The child now draws things as he sees them and not as he knows them.

These stages can be observed in the growth of the child's ability to handle perspective, with the more advanced stages coming somewhat later. Moreover, there is a great deal more specificity in the stage reached according to whether the child is concerned with stick, disc, or railway line than Piaget would allow. The child's experience with specific objects may advance the grasp of some aspects of perspective relations in respect of those objects. Moreover, in my experience it is only the occasional child at nine years of age who has mastered perspective in all situations. Again, there is some variation in the child's performance in the use of a single piece of apparatus; for example, in the case of many children, the end-on view of the stick is easier to imagine than the foreshortened view.

**Coordination of Perspectives**

The growth of the child's ability to master perspective relationships is slow. Indeed he can do so only when he can coordinate a number of viewpoints, including his own, with others. Piaget and Inhelder point out that being aware of one's own viewpoint involves separating it from that of others and thus coordinating it with them. To study the growth of the coordination of perspectives they devised an experiment which involved the perspectives of a group of objects as seen by an imaginary observer from different positions. This enabled them to study the construction, by the child, of a global system linking a number of viewpoints, and to examine the relationships which he builds or establishes between his own viewpoint and those of others.

In essence the experiment consists of providing a model on a base 1 meter square; the model has three mountains ranging in height from 12 cms to 30 cms—a grey one (the largest), a brown one (medium size), and a green one (the smallest). The child is placed in position *A* (Figure 28) and given pieces of card colored the same as the mountains. He is

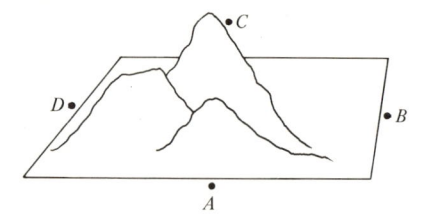

FIGURE 28

asked to arrange these and make a picture of the mountains as seen by an "observer" (a doll) placed at *B, C,* and *D*. The child, of course, stays at *A* while he constructs the view as seen by the observer from *B, C,* and *D*. In addition he is shown a set of pictures of the mountains and asked to pick out the one most suited to the view seen by the doll from each of the positions.

A number of stages are, according to Piaget, found in children's performances, although it must be said that the level of performance varies somewhat according to the method used; for example, whether the child arranges the cards or selects pictures. Up to about six years of age the child can produce only his own viewpoints. Between six and seven and a half years of age one sees the attempt of the child to break away from his own viewpoint, and sometimes he approaches the doll's. There is a dawning awareness that things look different according to where the observer is, but there is no real grasp of the fundamental relativity of perspectives. In the next stage, which lasts from about seven and a half to nine years of age, there is increasing evidence that the child discovers that left-right, before-behind relations between the mountains vary according to the position of the observer. But there is still no comprehensive coordination of viewpoints. Finally, by around nine to ten years of age the ability to master perspective is complete. Once again, however, my own experience is that children do go through the stages broadly outlined by the Geneva school but that there is a considerable spread in the ages of children reaching any one stage.

Piaget and Inhelder argue that the various perspectives can only be grouped through an act of intelligence which links together all possible perspectives by means of operations—using the term in the Piagetian sense. Moreover the stages that have been identified are conceptual, not perceptual, in character.

**Geometrical Sections**

The mental operations involved in making a geometrical section are applicable to both Euclidean and projective geometry. For example, one could imagine cutting a cone with a knife (Euclidean section) or putting a screen in the way of a cone of light (projective section). In the view of Piaget and Inhelder, sectioning is as applicable to the "geometry of viewpoints" as it is to the "geometry of objects." In the form in which they devised their experiments the investigators concerned themselves with the latter type of geometry, but it has the closest bearing on the overall development of projection and perspectives.

Sectioning involves a process of interaction between the perspective and projective operations of the geometry of viewpoints, with the operations of displacement and positioning which belong to object geometry. For example, a child must be able to imagine the line of intersection of the knife and the periphery of the solid. But he has to be able to do this not just for the side facing him, but for the solid as a whole, and to be able to do this means that the child must be able to imagine the solid in projection. That is to say, he must be able to imagine it from a number of viewpoints.

In the Geneva experiments the child had to look at a series of increasingly complex solids made of plasticine, such as cylinder, prism, sphere, cone, followed by irregular shapes like twists, snail's shells, and the like. After looking at them he had to predict the shape of the section produced when the solid is cut along various planes. Thus a cone cut parallel to its base will give a circle.

In work carried out under my own direction, beechwood models have been used and sectioned; the investigator presenting each solid to the child in such a way that he sees only that part of the cut that he would normally see if he began the sectioning process with a preliminary knife-scratch. By this means a uniform model is presented to each child, in contrast to plasticine models, which change shape while sectioning is in progress. For each model the child is asked (a) to draw the predicted section, and (b) to pick out the predicted section illustrated in a series of drawings. He is also asked for his reasons. Sectioning is then carried out if desired so that he can compare his predictions with the actual results of sectioning.

The stages in the growth of the child's ability to forecast sectioning is, according to Piaget and Inhelder, as follows. From almost four to six years of age he cannot distinguish any of the internal viewpoints which represent the section of the objects. This is true even in the case of the transverse section of the cylinder where the section, a circle, is identical with the exterior of the cylinder. In the six to eight year age range, the section shape is slowly distinguished from the intact shape in the case of some models, so that there is an increase in ability to imagine the projection of the solid if it were cut along some imaginary plane. But it must be stressed that the sectioning of some solids is easier than that of others. For example, the sectioning of a rectangular block is easier than that of a twist. A third stage begins around eight years of age when there is an immediate prediction of various sections of some solids. Thus in the case of the cone, the child can predict the circles or ellipses which would result from cutting the cone. But in the case of more complex solids, this prediction comes a few years later.

In the writer's experience the child does pass through the broad stages that have been indicated, but there are even greater discrepancies between the stages reached by a child using the various solids than the Geneva school admits. Moreover, the more advanced stages come rather later.

It seems clear that both experience with solids and the growth of thinking underpins the pupil's ability to predict geometrical sections. To be able to imagine a sectioned surface a child has to be able to abstract or dissociate a particular shape in relation to the general shape of the object.

## EUCLIDEAN CONCEPTS—
## AXES OF REFERENCE

Over the last few pages we have been discussing the growth of projective concepts. Developing alongside such concepts we find the growth of Euclidean concepts, and it is to the concept of systems of

# Space

reference—a Euclidean concept—that we now turn. Other Euclidean ideas will be discussed in the next chapter.

Children do not have an innate knowledge of a frame of reference. They do not from the earliest years fit objects automatically within a grid of horizontal and vertical coordinates. This frame of reference, which adults take for granted, is slowly built up, in spite of the fact that walls, floors, street crossings, tall buildings, and the like are in front of the child virtually all day long, and in spite of the fact that he himself has ample experience of standing up, walking around, and lying on a bed at night. In the view of Piaget and Inhelder (1956) the construction of this frame of reference is possible only to the extent that his thinking conforms to a system. Some of the types of experiments devised at Geneva to illustrate this growth include the following:

1. Children are shown two narrow-necked bottles, one with straight parallel sides and the other with rounded sides. Each is about one quarter filled with colored water. They are then asked to indicate by finger and gesture the level of the water on similar empty bottles under various degrees of tilt. The bottles containing the water are then tilted varying degrees, and subjects are asked to draw what they see. Moreover, they have always to sketch in the edge of the table on their drawings so that this horizontal, directly perceived, may help them in judging the position of the liquid level. Each child is, of course, individually tested.
2. A plumb line is suspended inside an empty jar, the plumb bob being shaped to represent a fish. The child has to predict the line of the string when the jar is tilted at various angles. After the jar is tilted he is asked for drawings of what he sees.
3. The child is given a model of a mountain and is asked to put in posts on the mountain side "nice and straight." He is also asked to draw in such posts, as well as houses, on a prepared outline sketch of the mountain.

A number of stages in the growth of the child's understanding of horizontal and vertical axes can be observed:

1. The child has no grasp of planes at all. He represents the water level as a ball or scribble, and the trees and houses as lying flat on the mountainside.
2. In the next stage the liquid is imagined as simply contracting

or expanding, with the water level remaining parallel to the base of the jar when the latter is tilted. But sometimes the liquid is thought to move towards the mouth of the jar, leaving the lower part of the jar empty. Posts are placed at right angles to the mountain side and without reference to the base of the mountain (table top) while the subject is unable to predict the direction of the plumb line.

3. The child is unable to draw the surface of the water in the tilted bottle as level, but he does show that the level is no longer parallel to the base of the vessel. He fails to coordinate his predictions with any reference system—the table—but connects the water line with, say, the corners of the jar (Figure 29). Posts are now placed upright on the mountainside but remain drawn perpendicular to the hillside. They fail to predict the correct inclination of the plumb line.

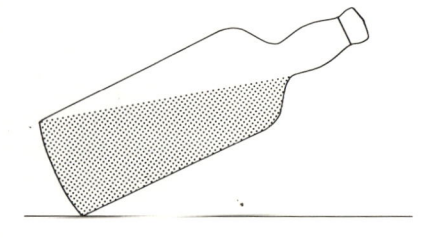

FIGURE 29

4. Beginning around eight years of age, the final stage is in evidence. At first the principle of horizontal and vertical axes comes to be applied gradually to all cases, although at the beginning the level is still made oblique at times. Later the child begins with immediate prediction of horizontal and vertical so that both water level and plumb line are drawn correctly from the outset.

My own experience has shown that there is considerable variation in the ages at which children reach stage 4. In general the ages that Piaget suggests for this stage are on the old side. Moreover this experiment brings out one of the gaps in Piaget's developmental system in that horizontal differentials are often experienced. For example, a child may be at a different stage in the tasks involving bottles compared with those involving the mountains, or in drawing posts as compared with putting posts on the mountainside. Nevertheless the overall progression is clearly visible.

It must also be pointed out that Smedslund (1963) has shown that mere observation of the horizontal level of a water surface when the container is tilted brings about no learning concerning horizontality in five- to seven-year-olds who have no concept of the horizontal to begin with, and brings about only limited improvement in those who have only initial traces of the notion. Again Beilin and others (1966) studied the ability of 180 pupils of average age seven years, six months to represent the water levels in jars tilted at various angles. Unsuccessful subjects were then trained either by showing them the water level after their forecast (perceptual training) or by using verbal methods. While training resulted in improved performance using jars of the same shape as used in the experiment, there was no transfer to jars of a different shape.

Piaget and Inhelder point out that children's experience of, say, water play allows a child to discover that water levels remain horizontal. But this knowledge comes to the child empirically; it is not deduced *a priori* and is thus not a case of "it must be so." Why then, ask Piaget and Inhelder, is some stage in the intellectual growth of the child necessary before this is possible? Why do the older pupils rapidly conclude that water levels will always be horizontal? They themselves answer their questions.

It is the indispensable role of the frame of reference which makes these things possible. Younger children are usually aware of the need for some kind of anchorage for horizontals and verticals, for they will either draw in the table top or say that they looked at it, but there is as yet for them no comprehensive system which links together objects in two- and three-dimensional space. The ability to organize global space into a two- or three-dimensional system of rectangular coordinates is not innate. Rather the growth of a system of reference depends upon the growth of concrete operational thought and the operational coordination of all fields with one another.

## SOME CLASSROOM ACTIVITIES

The following are some suggestions for activities within the classroom and home likely to aid the growth of some of the basic ideas which have been discussed, together with others.

Opportunities in everyday situations, including play, must be available in order to help the child recognize spatial relationships and the appropriate vocabulary to indicate them. For example, the following relationships are vital: left, right, under, over, above, below, before, behind, on top, underneath, thick, thin, large, small, far, near.

Experience indicates that the last two terms are more difficult than the others for many children. But readers will appreciate that these words may be handled correctly when used singly long before two or more of the relationships can be coordinated. For example, it is much easier to use the word "small," as in "That is a small doll," than to be able to coordinate two or more terms, as in the situation indicated by "The doll is to the left of the doll's house and behind the sofa." The first instance can easily be described by the child in kindergarten; the second requires concrete operational thought before the appropriate coordinations can be effected. Moreover, the kindergarten pupil may well understand the word "left" in relation to himself, but he finds it very difficult, if not impossible, to indicate the left hand of the child facing him. In Physical Education and in Movement many opportunities are provided for the child to become aware of himself and his movements in space. He will learn of situations in which terms like *line, bending, leaning,* and *straight* are applicable. Further, he will be standing upright (vertical) and lying flat (horizontal); however, we must not necessarily expect the child to be able to coordinate these into a frame of reference all at once, as we have seen earlier.

Provision for familiarization with, and labeling of, the commoner 3D and 2D shapes[1] must be made. Such shapes as cube, sphere, cylinder, square, circle, and triangle will have been recognized by the child for some years (that is, he will have perceptual knowledge of them), but now there must be a closer examination and discussion of such objects. Moreover, associated terms such as *surface, corner,* and *edge* must be introduced. Both 3D and 2D materials should be sorted by shape, size, or other relevant attribute, and once again it is hoped that objects will be classified before pictures of objects. In addition there is a need for a partitioning of objects by folding, cutting, taking apart, and so on, as appropriate, and then reassembling the parts.

The use of bricks and blocks, erector kits, paper-folding, tearing and fitting, jigsaw puzzles, nesting toys, and the laying of mosaics provide for either free imaginative constructions and pattern-making or such construction and pattern-making to some kind of specification.

Pegboards and geo-boards provide an easy means whereby 2D shapes

---

[1] Shape is a property of an object; it is one by which objects are often classified.

can be altered. In Chapter 5 it will be seen that this kind of activity may help the older elementary school child to understand that under some changes, perimeter but not area is conserved, under other changes area but not perimeter is conserved, while under yet other changes neither is conserved. At the same time experience is required in changing the shape of 3D materials, as in playing with plasticine and clay, and pouring water from one container to another of an entirely different shape.

Exercises are required which are relevant to the conceptualization of a straight line. Suitable tasks are: paper-folding, stretching a piece of elastic, "taking aim" as along a ruler's edge or along two or more objects, as in the situation described earlier in the chapter.

Opportunities can be provided which involve a frame of reference. For example, in Movement and Physical Education attention should be drawn to the child's own body positions—horizontal, vertical, leaning over, at an angle to. Likewise there can be a discussion of such everyday situations as streets intersecting at right angles, floor of a room and its walls, and mast of a ship. Facilities can be provided so that the pupil can experiment with, say, wood floating on water, a plumb line, spirit level, toy cars moving up and down a slope, paper folding to make a right angle, compass in an outdoor situation. In the case of the older children in the age range with which this book is concerned, terms such as *flat* and *curved surface, convex,* and *concave* must also be introduced.

Experiences are needed which enable the child to engage in the construction of the commoner 2D figures such as rectangle and square. This can be achieved through the use of paper printed out in squares and drawing around a given number of squares, and using geo-boards, wire, straws, strips of card, and paper-folding and cutting. Triangles can be made by cutting along the diagonal of a square or rectangle, and shapes can be made through combinations of squares, rectangles, and triangles. The use of templates in drawing shapes is also helpful. A circle can be drawn by tracing around the edge of a saucer, tin lid, or disc. It can also be drawn by means of a pin and piece of string and later with the aid of compasses, although pin and string perhaps draws the child's attention more directly to the fact that all points on the circumference are the same distance from the center, as does reference to the spokes of a wheel.

Objects need to be seen from different angles and positions. Related activities in the general field of projective concepts involve drawing objects, as from position $X$ while viewing it from $Y$ (the distance $XY$

being gradually increased). Likewise pupils need experience in sectioning the simpler 3D objects such as a cylinder in order to expose various sections.

Opportunities should be provided for the folding and unfolding of surfaces (for example, a cardboard box or carton). A useful task is to make a cube or cuboid from the corresponding developments. The latter is first drawn on paper to given measurements, then cut from the paper, bent as appropriate, and glued.

With the older of the children we are considering, there should be familiarization and labeling of some of the less common 3D and 2D shapes, such as pyramid, cone, quadrilateral, parallelogram, and polygons more generally.

Further examples of types of activities involving spatial relationships are given in the next chapter.

## SYMMETRY

Euclidean geometry, or the geometry that deals with metric and measurement, deals with properties of figures that remain constant when the figures are subjected to a particular class of transformation, namely, rigid motions. For example, if a triangle is rotated or moved in any way, either in or out of its own plane, we obtain another triangle congruent with the first. Under this type of transformation, length of sides and size of angles remain unchanged. There are other kinds of transformations too: for example, projective and topological transformations. In the former, lengths and angles are distorted depending upon the relative position of the objects drawn, but a point always projects as a point and a line as a line; in topological transformations all metric and projective properties are lost. Consider, for example, a circle with two diameters at right angles, drawn on a sheet of rubber. If the sheet is stretched in one direction, the circle will become an ellipse, the diameters will no longer be at right angles nor will they be the same length. But the centre of the original circle is still the midpoint of the ellipse, and it still stands at the midpoint of both diameters.

This discussion concerning a rigid motion transformation and the comparison with a projective transformation was necessary before a look is taken at symmetry. In everyday life the term suggests that a pattern is well balanced in its spatial characteristics, that it is well proportioned, and that in short it looks "perfect." The two wings of a butterfly are an example of symmetry which readily comes to mind and which displays this beauty. But in mathematics the term *symmetry* has a more

Space

precise meaning. A symmetrical pattern is one which remains unchanged under a certain kind of rigid motion. Essentially then, in symmetry, one is dealing with congruences—that is, with objects which have the same shape and size both before and after certain kinds of rigid motion transformations. These transformations are those of rotation, translation, and reflection. For example, if equilateral triangle $ABC$ is rotated $120°$ or $240°$ about an axis through its center and perpendicular to the plane of the triangle, then the shape is identical in orientation with the original.

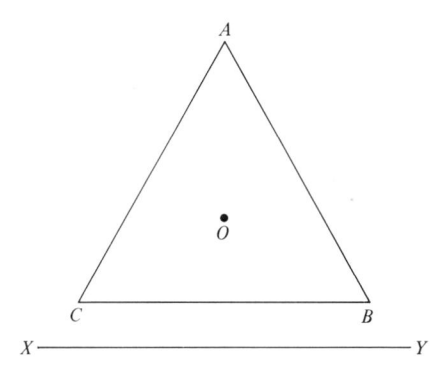

FIGURE 30

Again the shape and size of the triangle, and also its orientation, remain identical with the original if the latter is translated or moved along a line without rotation. Finally the mirror image remains congruent with the original if the latter is reflected in a line which lies in the plane of the triangle, as in the case of line $XY$ in Figure 30.

There are many opportunities for children to learn of the different kinds of symmetry. A five-year-old may spill some paint on a sheet of paper. Frustrated, he may fold the paper before throwing it into the wastebasket. But before actually dropping it in, he may by chance open the paper and discover to his surprise that the pattern has been duplicated. He has hit upon the simplest kind of symmetry, namely, symmetry about a line or axis. The butterfly's wings, already mentioned, are an excellent example of this.

Two tests can be made to establish the presence of this kind of symmetry. In some instances a pattern can be folded about a central axis, and it can be seen whether or not the two halves are coincident. In other cases folding is impractical. But if a mirror is placed vertically

88                    *The Growth of Understanding in Mathematics*

along what is thought to be the axis of symmetry, then half of the shape seen directly, together with its image seen in the mirror, coincide precisely with the whole of the original shape.

An examination of leaves, flowers, shells, and animals furnish opportunities for the child to discover whether line symmetry is present or not. Paper-folding and the cutting out of shapes also provide many examples. If a sheet of paper is folded along the axis $AB$ and a triangle cut from the edge formed by $AB$, then when the paper is opened out again the diamond shows symmetry about the axis $AB$ (Figure 31a). Further, if a

(a)

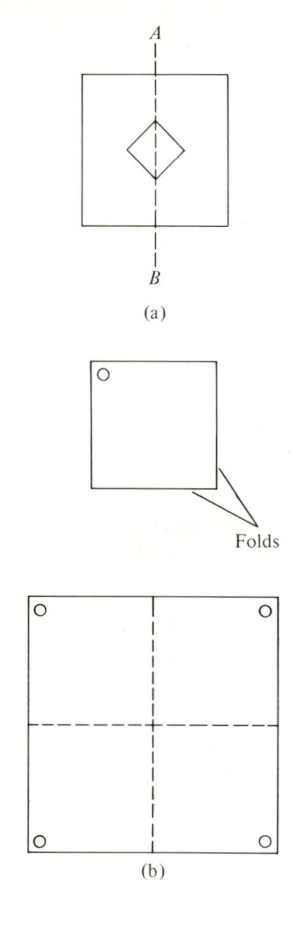

Folds

(b)

FIGURE 31

sheet of paper is quartered by folding and a pattern cut through the four folded pieces, then there will be symmetry about two axes (Figure 31b). Some naturally occurring objects can only be cut in one way to obtain a mirror image (for example, the backs of some beetles) whereas many flowers can be cut in two or more ways and mirror images obtained. The letters A, M, V, and W are also examples of symmetry about a line. In the case of the letter V it is very easy for the child to see that for every point (the pupil in the age range covered by this book will think of the point as a dot, as we have seen) on one side of the axis of symmetry there is a corresponding point on the other side and at the same distance from the axis, with the line joining the point to its image being perpendicular to the axis. It must, of course, be made clear that this holds in all instances of line symmetry—the letter V making a simple, easy-to-see example to start with.

A second kind of symmetry is known as translational symmetry. A child will be familiar with railings or fences in which the posts are repeated at regular intervals. Likewise he will have seen a number of wallpapers in which the pattern repeats itself around the room. Moreover when he stick prints, threads beads on a string in which a square bead and a round one succeed one another in turn, or makes a "chain" with his bricks, putting a long and short one alternately, he is making patterns which repeat themselves. Such examples will serve as a basis for discussion with pupils.

Put more formally, we can say that if some parts of a pattern can be moved a definite distance along a line to cover an identical part of the pattern, and if by a succession of such moves the whole of the pattern can be covered, then the pattern is said to be a repeating one, and it is further said to be characterized by translational symmetry. Strictly this term should be linked only with a pattern that extends infinitely in both directions, but in practice it is used to cover patterns which are finite but which in imagination can be extended to infinity. However, as we know, children with whom we are concerned in this book will not be able to consider what is beyond the tangible or intuitable. Finally it might be said that from the mathematician's point of view, translation carries a pattern into itself.

There are many opportunities for children to discover, under teacher guidance, examples of nonrepeating and repeating patterns in nature and in natural situations. Moreover in the classroom, children can provide their own instances of translational symmetry with brush and paint, bricks, beads, or whatever materials are at hand. Further, and very important, pupils should be helped to recognize the repeated patterns of rhythms that occur in music and poetry.

A third type of symmetry is rotational symmetry. In this case we are dealing with a symmetry resulting from the rotation of a shape about an axis through the center of the shape and perpendicular to its plane. A very simple example is that of a cross made of two wires equal in length, which intersect at their centers and which are at right angles to one another (Figure 32). Coincidence with the original pattern is main-

FIGURE 32

tained if the latter is rotated thrgugh 90°, 180°, and 270°. This is also true of rotations of 0° and 360°, but these are said to be trivial in the sense that any object rotated through 0° and 360° is coincident with the original whether it possesses rotational symmetry or not. Pupils should be encouraged to look for examples of such symmetry in nature as in, say, flowers or the starfish; in everyday situations as when they encounter the spokes of a wheel, a circle, square, or stars; and in more specific instances as in the design on, say, a saucer, plate, or bowl, or in the points of the compass. The test of rotational symmetry is to find which rotation less than 360° (and excluding 0°) gives coincidence with the original positions.

Many of the brighter eight- and nine-year-olds may discover that some shapes possess both line symmetry and rotational symmetry. Both a square and a star show rotational symmetry, as do the letters *S* and *N;* they also show symmetry about certain lines drawn through the center of the figure and in its plane. It should also be noted that while there is no discussion of symmetry applied to 3D objects, teachers may wish to develop such ideas with some pupils. And there are other more complex symmetries which may be described mathematically but which do not concern us at all in this book.

In his work in art, the pupil will have many opportunities to create examples of all the kinds of symmetry we have discussed. Again, as was suggested earlier, he should be helped to find examples of symmetry in music and poetry, for they will both heighten his enjoyment of these arts and help him to appreciate that symmetry is a principle of wide applicability. From the point of view of mathematics the hope is that through engaging in these various activities, children will make abstractions and recognize that different patterns may possess the same type of symmetry. The ideas that have been discussed here will be made use of in mathematics later on.

Space

## SOME SIMPLE TRANSFORMATIONS

It is possible to introduce some simple transformations to the oldest and ablest pupils in the age range that we are considering, for such pupils will already be familiar with symmetry about a line and also with rotational and translational symmetry. Furthermore, they will be aware of the idea of reflecting a shape in a mirror, and from this point we can introduce the idea of reflecting a shape in a line. Thus, using Figure 33a, we can discuss with pupils what the reflections of the flag shape would

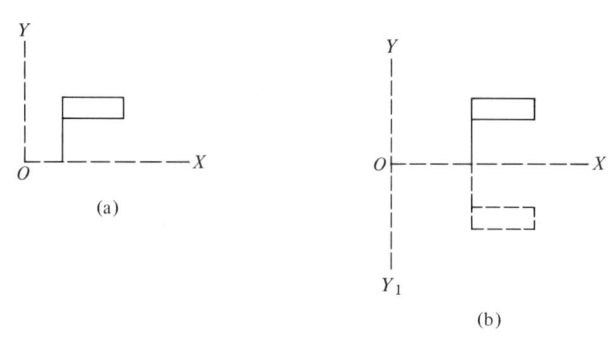

FIGURE 33

be in lines $OX$ and $OY$, introducing a mirror whenever necessary to make the position clear. In the next stage one might consider what happens when the flag shape is first rotated 180° about $OX$ into the dotted position shown in Figure 33b and then reflected in the line $YY_1$.

By means of such a graded approach it is possible to lead the child to the following type of exercise in which he has to carry out a number of tasks of increasing difficulty (Figure 34). A few typical such tasks are listed.

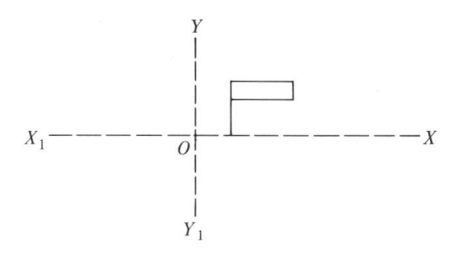

FIGURE 34

Draw the position of the pattern after
1. Translation along $OX$

2. Rotation through 180° about *OX*
3. Reflection in $YY_1$ followed by translation along *OX*
4. Reflection in *OX*, followed by rotation of 180° about *OX*, followed by reflection in $YY_1$
5. Translation along *OX*, followed by reflection in $YY_1$, followed by reflection in *OX*

How can we get the pattern in its final position in (5) back into its original position?

Teachers will wish to make the grading of the questions less steep than that shown here. Also, children can make up such questions for each other to work.

At the same time, and as a supporting type of activity, the oldest and ablest pupils can build up the table involved in an exercise of the kind indicated below, actually making the turns on the ground themselves if necessary. Suppose, for example, a boy faces north. The exercise is for the child to make up a table showing if he is facing south or north after performing the given actions (Figure 35). The instructions at the

|  | | First Operation | | |
|---|---|---|---|---|
|  | | Stand still | Do one about turn | Do two about turns |
| Second Operation | Stand still |  |  |  |
|  | Do one about turn |  |  |  |
|  | Do two about turns |  |  |  |

FIGURE 35

top of the table indicate the actions (first operation) which are then followed by the actions indicated by the instructions given on the left-hand side (second operation).

## SOME RELATED ACTIVITIES IN THE NUMERICAL FIELD

So far we have dealt with operations within the spatial field. But a main role of mathematics is to show links and common structure be-

# Space

tween what are apparently unrelated topics. Thus after having completed an exercise of the kind illustrated in Figure 35, the child can construct a table to show, say, what kind of numbers (odd or even) result when an odd or even number is added to an odd or even number (Figure 36).

| + | Even | Odd |
|---|---|---|
| Even | | |
| Odd | | |

FIGURE 36

Similarly by discussing, say, the movements of the large hand of a clock in terms of the number of halves of a whole revolution which it makes, the pupil can complete the table given in Figure 37. The num-

| + | 0 | 1 |
|---|---|---|
| 0 | | |
| 1 | | |

FIGURE 37

bers across the top indicate the nature of the first operation in terms of half-turns, and those at the left side give the nature of the second operation, again in terms of half-turns. By means of such a table the pupil is led to clock arithmetic (miniature systems of finite numbers). But he is also given experience with operations yielding transformations in varied situations.

It will be much later in their school career that pupils will be able to see the nature of the links, but at this early age the oldest and ablest of the pupils we are considering can be given understandable concrete realization of mathematical structures which are embodied in very varied situations. Even young children enjoy carrying out the kinds of activity indicated here, for they find pattern in the results. At the same time, however, readers will appreciate that a pupil's thinking must be systematized and flexible before he can appreciate the operations he is carrying out in these concrete situations.

Throughout the work described in this chapter, it is possible for a child to arrive at some correct solutions to problems posed through the figurative rather than the operative aspects of knowing. Once again it is important that teachers discuss with their pupils the reasons for the solutions suggested and attempt to establish how the pupils arrived at their answers.

# 5

# Geometry

The previous chapter dealt with some basic spatial concepts. This chapter continues the process, but it includes some concepts which involve metric and measurements. The ideas presented in Chapter 4 do not necessarily precede those of this chapter. Indeed, the ideas covered in the first part of this chapter should be considered along with those outlined earlier, although area and loci will be introduced at the upper end of the age range which is the concern of this book.

**CURVES**

The child will have a perceptual recognition of curve (including line) years before he enters kindergarten, but, as we have seen, a conceptualization of a straight line comes much later. To aid the child in regard to the straight line, exercises involving paper-folding, stretching an elastic band, and "taking aim" were suggested. At the same time an attempt must be made to get the child to obtain some concept of a curve and to realize that a straight line is a special instance of a curve. The teacher knows that a curve may be thought of as any path traced out by a moving point, but children cannot be given this definition. Instead, examples must be explored which occur in everyday situations with the hope that the child will make the necessary abstraction, or "taking from," in order to derive the concept of a curve. Thus the following kinds of activities might be found very useful:

1. In discussion it can be pointed out that every time the child writes, or draws any kind of line or lines, with pen, pencil, crayon, paintbrush, and so on, he is making a curve.
2. Children can join hands to form various arrangements from, say, straight lines through open curves to closed ones.
3. A rope can be placed, or chalk mark made, on the floor, and pupils can stand at intervals on the curve so formed. The curve can be reformed into any desired curve. In this exercise and in the previous one listed, it is important that the child does not confuse the children that represent the curve with the curve itself.
4. Pupils can trace around the edges of varied objects.
5. With the aid of finger or stick, children can draw curves freely in sand or construct them using plasticine.
6. A discussion can be held of sets of objects in curves or lines; for example, parked automobiles in a row, automobiles moving on a bend, trees lining a curving road, lines of soldiers, ticker tape used in a ticker-tape welcome.

Whereas in the case of the straight line the child comes to realize that it is always going in the same direction, in the case of the curve this is not necessarily true. As a child once put it, "A straight line is a curve that always goes the same way." This is an important distinction for the child to make, and he must hold this in his mind as he is introduced to other subsets of curves.

As the pupil draws around some objects like, say, the rim of a saucer, it becomes apparent to him that the starting and stopping points are the same. Likewise if he draws a *V*, the curve does not touch or cross itself. On the other hand, when he writes the letter *f*, or draws an *X* or a picture of a ball resting on a table (Figure 38), the curve does cross or

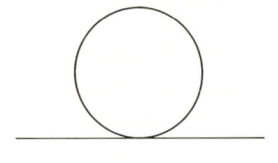

FIGURE 38

touch itself. The former types are called simple curves and have to be explored much further; the latter are termed nonsimple curves and will occasion us no further interest in this book. It will be appreciated that sufficient examples must be provided to bring out clearly the differences

*Geometry* 97

between the two types, such examples being offered by both teacher and child.

Simple curves can be further subdivided into those that are open and those that are closed. Thus $V$ is an example of a simple open curve, because it has end points, and so is the curve drawn to represent a horseshoe. But the curve obtained from drawing around the rim of a saucer is a simple closed curve, as is the curve drawn to represent a star; such curves have no end points. The child can be helped to make this distinction by referring to his own drawings; by standing with other pupils on rope or on chalk lines and forming open or closed curves; by making curves in plasticine; through studying shapes in advertisements in magazines; and by discussion of curves drawn by teacher and pupils on the blackboard.

It is thus possible to summarize the discussion of curves so far by Figure 39. But the diagram also indicates that simple open and closed

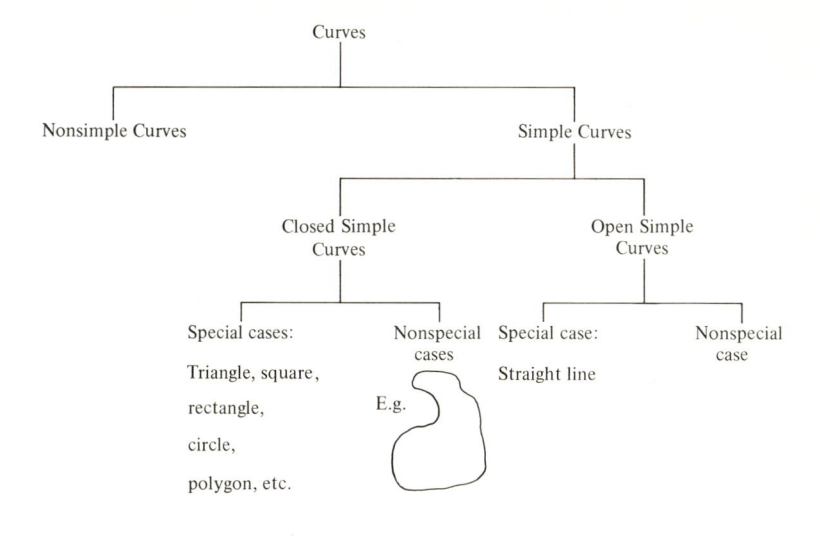

FIGURE 39

curves can be further subdivided. The former can be divided into the special case—the straight line—and the nonspecial cases including, say, the letter *S*, the horseshoe, or any irregular open curve. Simple closed curves can be divided into the special cases such as triangle, circle, square, rectangle, and polygon more generally, whereas the nonspecial cases include any irregular closed curve. The special cases of the closed curves must be drawn, made, and discussed. Such discussion would bring out, for example, that the square is a special instance of a rhombus as the square is also a special instance of a rectangle. The term *perimeter* must also be introduced and discussed, as should terms such as *corner, edge, inside, outside, on, off.*

With suitable experiences the kindergarten child can distinguish simple open from simple closed curves, recognize special instances, and learn something of the vocabulary. But it will require much experience in drawing and making, considerable discussion about their names and properties, and flexible concrete operational thought before the various curves can be conceptualized and regarded in a hierarchical classification as indicated in Figure 39. Moreover, even the nine-year-old will still have only an intuitable grasp of curve. He will not think of it as a set of points or as a path traced out by a moving point, although the older abler ones may well consider it as a path traced out by a moving object of tangible size—for example, a dot, fingertip, or ball. Indeed, the case of the ball traveling along a curve—this means a straight line at times—is a useful concrete exemplar. Moreover when the activities suggested at the beginning of the chapter were undertaken, some consideration should be given to properties of curves intimated here.

There are other ideas associated with curves which must be introduced. The simple closed curve which is in one plane may be thought of as a *boundary* in the sense that it separates the *region* inside the curve from that outside. It is easy to introduce these new terms using the situations already discussed. Again the seven- to eight-year-old can discover and understand, using plasticine, wire, rope, or human chains, that both simple open and closed curves can, respectively, have their shapes changed, but they cannot be changed one into another. Further, by drawing simple open or closed curves on a sheet of rubber and stretching or compressing it, or by drawing them on the surface of a balloon and inflating and twisting it, he can learn that one can bend, pull, stretch, and so forth, such curves into a variety of shapes, but they always remain simple open or closed curves as they began.

One may wish to introduce to some of the older pupils the terms *half line, ray,* and *segment.* Defined formally:

1. A given point divides a given line into two subsets called half lines, the point being the boundary for each half line.
2. The union of the set containing the boundary and one of the half lines is called a ray.
3. The segment is a subset of a line that includes two points in the line and all the points between the two given ones, which are called the endpoints of the segment.

Geometry

No such formal definitions will, of course, be attempted with the pupils this book is concerned with. Rather, these concepts will be discussed informally and examples given. By seeing instances where these terms are and are not applicable, the child will come to grasp the ideas. Further, it is important to remember that the nine-year-olds, and indeed all elementary school pupils except the oldest and brightest, will have only an intuitable understanding of half line, ray, and segment. Again, the eight- and nine-year-old well understands that in the case of a closed curve he can start at some point in the curve, trace around it with his finger, and end up at the point at which he started without lifting his finger and without passing through the same point twice. By the same token he will have only an intuitive, and not a formal analytic, understanding that one property of a closed curve is that a segment determined by a point in its interior and a point in its exterior must contain an odd number of points on the curve.

## ANGLES

Pupils can be helped to obtain an intuitive notion of angle by getting them to think of it in terms of a change of direction. Suppose the child is walking along the straight road *ABC*, but at *B* he turns down road *BD* (Figure 40). He has changed direction, or "the way he's going," by

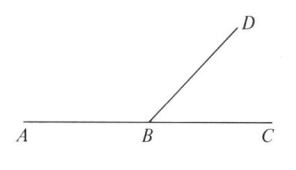

FIGURE 40

amount *CBD*. Examples of angles are all about him; for example, the angles between the blades of open scissors, the covers of a partially open book, the hands of a clock, and between two intersecting straight lines which he draws on paper. Likewise when out of doors he can be helped to appreciate that the wind changes direction so that whereas it was, say, blowing from one corner of a field—perhaps the west—it is now blowing from a different point—perhaps northwest.

The special case of the right angle is of particular importance. As soon as the child has elaborated a rectangular framework (Chapter 4) he can have a conceptual and not merely a perceptual grasp of a right angle. Pupils meet this angle in innumerable activities; in paper-folding and cutting, fitting square and rectangular tiles, playing with bricks and blocks, and in using a set square. In addition they encounter the angle in many everyday situations; in the corners of many tables, doors, floors, walls, ceilings, and so forth. Such activities and situations provide the opportunities for discussion regarding this special angle, and pupils must be helped to recognize a right angle regardless of the orientation, in space, of its arms. Questions should be asked, and discussed, concerning the number of corners that a square and a brick have, and the number of right angles on the faces of a brick.

By cutting or folding a paper square from one corner to its opposite, the child can be introduced to another special angle, namely the half right angle. Then, using folded paper to give right angles and half right angles, pupils can use these to check if other angles are of the same size. This in turn leads the way to the use of the simplified protractor to check the size of an angle and not, at first, to measure its magnitude in degrees. Such a protractor can be constructed from a card by cutting a circle, dividing it into four quadrants, and further dividing the circumference of, say, the top right-hand quadrant. This protractor is placed appropriately against the arms of, say, a half right angle and the points on the protractor marked corresponding to the arms. It can similarly be used to check the size of any other angle. Moreover, this use of a simplified protractor is a natural lead to the more elaborate protractor, later on, to measure an angle in degrees.

So the pupil is helped to acquire an intuitive grasp of a right angle, and to be able to recognize it however it is oriented in space. This is the opportunity to introduce the term *perpendicular* and for the child to find which shapes that he uses, and which everyday objects, have one side perpendicular to another, or two faces at right angles.

This is also a suitable point to introduce the notion of *parallel;* not by defining the term in any formal way at this early stage, but by considering examples and counterexamples until the idea is made clear to the child. Thus he can find edges which are perpendicular to one another, as in the case of the adjacent sides of squares, rectangles, and some tables. He can also find examples of lines which cross or meet, as in the case of the capital letters $X$ and $V$ respectively. Finally he can find examples of lines which are parallel; for example, the lines of the exercise book, railway lines, and the opposite edges of squares, rectangles, and many tables. Having obtained some idea of what is meant by parallel, the child needs to be questioned if parallel lines drawn on paper remain parallel if the paper is rotated. It is also necessary to encourage him to think what happens if the lines get longer and

Geometry

longer and whether or not they would then meet. Children in the age group cannot, of course, consider infinity, for, as we have often stressed, in the period of concrete operational thought they can consider only intuitable data.

## DISTANCE, LENGTH, AND MEASUREMENT

Piaget, Inhelder, and Szeminska (1960) have described a number of experiments which show the stages through which a child passes in elaborating the concepts of distance, length, and measurement.

Young children make a distinction between distance and length, the former term referring to the linear separation of objects or "empty space." On the other hand, length refers to the "filled in" space as in the case of, say, the length of a row of bricks or sticks. To demonstrate this one can place, say, two dolls of the same height on a table and about twenty inches apart. The child is then asked if the dolls are "far apart" or "near one another," all direct reference to length or measurement being avoided. After the child has given his answer, a screen which is taller than the dolls is placed between them. He is asked if the dolls are still as "far apart" or "as near one another" as before, and asked for his reasons. Up to five years of age or so, children tend to say that the distance is less when the screen is interposed, for they consider only one of the two parts into which the distance is divided. It will be realized from what has been said earlier that children at this age find difficulty in the whole to part relationship, although they cannot, of course, verbalize this difficulty. Between about five and seven years of age the overall distance is still said to be less, but the reason advanced is that part of the distance has been taken away since the screen is "filled space." Finally from seven to eight years onward distance is, in the view of the Geneva school, conserved in spite of any objects in between.

In studies I myself have done, much the same kinds of responses were found as those reported by Piaget, Inhelder, and Szeminska. For example, one five-year-old conserved distance ("as far as before") between the dolls ($X$ and $Y$) when the screen was interposed, but he did not maintain that the distance $XY$ was the same as $YX$. Another five-year-old could not conserve the distance when the screen was interposed but recognized the symmetrical character of the interval $XY = YX$. While some eight-year-olds gave good reasons for conserving distance ("the dolls haven't moved") other eight- and nine-year-olds were not conserving distance in this situation.

The Geneva school maintains that it is the conservation of distance which brings about both the notion of a homogeneous and stable environment, and conservation of length ("filled in space"). In its judgment, conservation of length is possible only when the child understands that the size of a site previously empty remains the same when filled by an object, and that the site occupied by an object remains the same length when the object is removed.

Having seen then that the young child has difficulties with distance and length, we now turn to the problem of measurement of length. Measurement, using the term more generally, is the process whereby a number is assigned to a physical object such as a piece of wood or lumps of iron; to a mathematical construct like a line segment; or to, say, a period of time. The number then answers questions such as "How heavy?", "How long?", or "What length of time?" In this chapter we are, of course, concerned only with measurement of length and area. However, for Piaget, the concept of measurement used in a general sense depends essentially upon the growth of logical thinking. The child must first grasp that the whole is comprised of a number of parts added together. Second, he must understand the principles of substitution and iteration—that is, the transport of the applied measure to another entity (such as length or area) and its repeated application to this other. In this view, measurement is the synthesis of division into parts and of iteration, just as in the view of the Geneva school, number is the synthesis of classes and serial ordering.

**The Measurement of Length**

One prerequisite for measurement of length is that the child understand that the length of an object remains the same whatever changes occur in its position. Yet such conservation is not a sufficient condition for measurement, for the latter involves subdivision and the construction of a unit. Piaget, Inhelder, and Szeminska neatly illustrate the development of conservation of length by the following experiment. The child is presented with two identical straight rods each about two inches long; they lie parallel to one another, and their ends are in alignment. He is asked, in essence, if the rods are of the same length or if one is shorter than the other. If he agrees that the rods are the same length, the experiment proceeds. One of the rods is then moved about 1/5 of an inch, being kept close to, and parallel to, the other rod; or the two rods are placed to form a $T$ shape; or they are inclined at an acute angle to, but touching, one another. Whatever the rearrangement, the child is again questioned about their lengths—whether the rods

Geometry

are equal or different in length. Once again it is shown that length is not conserved until around seven to eight years of age. Just prior to that, children may conserve length when the rods are in one arrangement but not in another. But at seven to eight years of age the average child knows that the rods must be the same length (logical necessity), and he will argue that "you've only moved them" or similar replies, whatever the rearrangement.

Once the child conserves length, he may be ready for the next step, the measurement of length. To illustrate the stages through which a child goes in mastering this, use is made of an experiment of the type provided by Piaget, Inhelder, and Szeminska. In work carried out under my own direction, the child is presented with strips of cards arranged in various shapes and pasted onto hardboard, the strips being presented in pairs (Figure 41). Three pairs of such strips have been used; their dimensions are given in Figure 41.

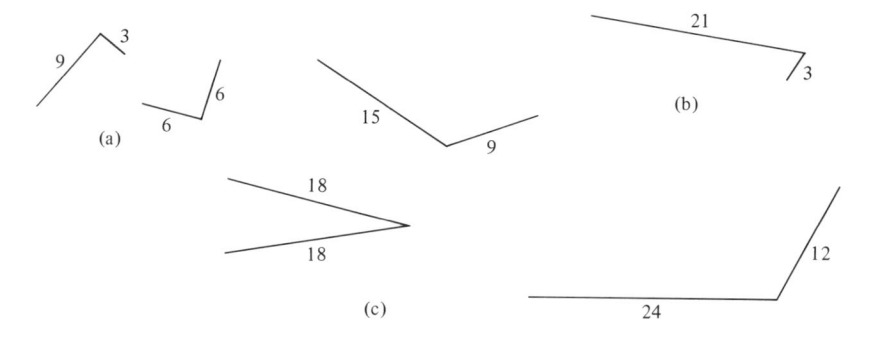

FIGURE 41

The child is asked to compare the "lines" and say if, in the case of each pair, they are equal or if one is longer than the other. When he has made a response, he is provided with short strips of card three and six units long, and asked to measure the lengths to verify his initial estimates. If he is unable to make use of the cards, the experimenter shows him how to apply the three-unit card by marking off two or three intervals on one of the first pair of lines. The intervals are regarded as "steps" which a man makes as he walks along "the road." The subject is asked to find how many steps the man takes if he walks from one end of the road to the other, for each of the two lines in the three pairs presented for comparison. Thus the child is helped to check the accuracy of his original estimates concerning the lengths of the lines in each pair.

A number of stages are found in the child's ability to measure and understand measurement. In the first stage there are a variety of behaviors. A child may run his fingers along the lines and make a comparison. Another may transfer the width of two or three fingers from one line to the other. This, although rough, is the beginning of the idea of subdivision. Some children at this stage slide the cards along in arbitrary fashion, making pencil marks as they go. Others may begin with subdivision and ignore iteration. For example, a three-unit card may be laid along one part of the line but not along the whole length of the line, it being thought, seemingly, that this is enough to judge the lengths of the two lines. In short, pupils at this stage do not see the need for unit measures or for placing the unit card accurately. At least, if they do see the need, the concept of unit is vague, for they may count the subdivisions they have made and not care whether they are equal or not. Again readers will appreciate that measurement involves a unit (for example, a finger or a three-unit card) which, in this experiment, is first applied to one length and then to another, and the movement between the lines may involve a change in length in the measuring unit for these pupils.

At the second stage, children begin to understand subdivision and respond to prompting by the experimenter. They can move a reference card in definite order, place reference marks fairly accurately, and thus break up a line into successive segments. It is, however, a kind of "learned" understanding, for it does not immediately lead to subdivision in terms of homogeneous units. Subjects will still count the number of steps used but ignore whether or not they are all the same length (whether they are of three or six units).

By eight to eight and a half years of age pupils can, in the Geneva view, make an operational fusion of subdivision and change of position. There is now systematic measurement, a comparison of three- and six-unit cards, and an ability to realize that the length of a line can be expressed as a multiple of, say, either three or six units. It is clear to the child that the different numbers of units so obtained indicate the same length of line.

These results do not, of course, imply that all work on measurement of length should be postponed until the child fully understands what he is doing. Rather the experiences derived from activities involving measurement, which the child carries out at the teacher's suggestion, provide the basis out of which understanding arises with the growth of thinking skills. The important point for the teacher is to realize to what extent a child is carrying out measurement operationally—that is, with full understanding—or to what extent it is being carried out in rote

## Subdividing a Straight Line

In the previous task children were presented with lines already segmented and the choice of unit imposed on them. In the task described in this section the technique is reversed (see Piaget, Inhelder, and Szeminska, 1960). Children are asked to locate a segment on a straight line equal in length to a segment on another straight line. Two wires $X_1Z_1$, $X_2Z_2$ of the same length (about twenty inches long in our experiments) are placed parallel to one another with their ends in alignment (Figure 42).

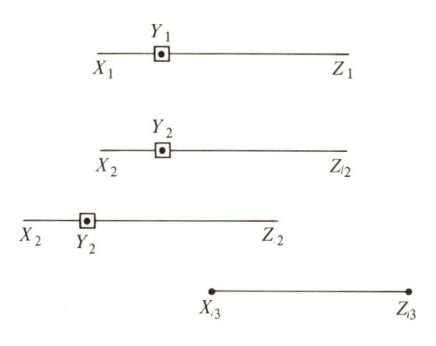

FIGURE 42

The child is told that a bead on the wire is a train traveling along a railway line, or a car along a road. The experimenter moves his bead from $X_1$ to $Y_1$, and the subject is asked to "do a journey" of the same length. He is provided with a ruler, string, and strips of card of varying length which he is invited, but not shown how, to use. The child watches the experimenter move his bead from $X_1$ to $Y_1$ and is asked, in essence, to move his bead from $X_2$ so that the segment $X_2Y_2$ equals the segment $X_1Y_1$. The experiment is then repeated with the child having to move his bead from the other end ($Z_2$) so that $Z_2Y_2 = X_1Y_1$.

In the next experiment the wire $X_2Z_2$ is moved a few inches (four in our experiments) to the left of wire $X_1Z_1$, with the wires still remaining parallel to one another. The child is again asked to move his bead from $Z_2$ and make $Z_2Y_2 = X_1Y_1$. Then, keeping $X_2Z_2$ in the same position relative to $X_1Z_1$, the experimenter moves his bead fifteen inches (in our case) from $X_1$—a distance greater than the length of any of the measuring instruments provided. The child is again asked to locate $Y_2$ so that $Z_2Y_2 = X_1Y_1$. Finally the wire $X_2Y_2$ is replaced by the wire $X_3Z_3$, which is shorter than $X_1Y_1$. The wires are still parallel, but $X_3Z_3$ is displaced (four inches in our experiment) to the right of $X_1Z_1$. After the experimenter moves his bead about six inches from $X_1$, the child is asked to move his bead the same distance from $Z_3$.

In children's progress toward solving these tasks, four stages can be observed:

1. The child moves his bead until it is opposite that of the experimenter, so the problem is solved only when the points of departure are in alignment. At this stage he is quite unable to think of lengths as coherent systems of nesting intervals or parts.
2. Some tasks are solved intuitively, that is, by visual inspection. But there is still failure when the wires of the child and the experimenter are of different length, and when the child is asked to move his bead from the opposite end of the wire. He may try to measure, but he does not realize the need for accurate subdivision or for taking into account both the point of departure and the point of arrival. Moreover, when he does measure, it is merely to verify a judgment that has been already reached by visual estimate.
3. Measurement of the length which the experimenter's bead has moved is possible in some instances, namely, in those cases in which the ruler, piece of string, or other measuring instrument is equal to or longer than the distance to be measured. If the distance to be measured is longer than any of the instruments provided, the child will improvise a suitable line of objects; for example, he may place a pencil at the end of a ruler. These are then transferred to the subject's wire and the bead moved accordingly. A qualitative transitivity is achieved, for he knows that if $A = B$ and $B = C$ then $A = C$.
4. The child now applies a short ruler using iterative stepwise movements, thus reducing the total distance to multiples of unit length. In Piaget's view this stage begins around eight years of age; I have found it begins at an earlier age in some pupils.

It is certain that readers will have observed these kinds of behavior in young children. One can even see much older but backward pupils responding in the way indicated in stage 3. For true measurement of distances and lengths, the child must be able to recognize that any length may be decomposed into a series of intervals which are known

# Geometry

to be equal, and that one of them may be applied to each of the others in turn. Moreover it is instructive to note, once again, that for Piaget the arithmetic unit or number is a similar element in a synthesis of a class and of an asymmetric relation. But, he argues, unlike the unit of number, that of length occurs not at the beginning stage but at the final stage of the achievement of operational thinking. This, in Piaget's view, is because the metric unit involves an arbitrary disintegration of a continuous whole. Thus although the operations involved in measurement exactly parallel those in the child's construction of number, the elaboration of the former is slower. Unit iteration is the fundamental element in the construction of the concept of measurement; and at seven years of age, when the concept of number is elaborated, measurement is still only qualitative (the child merely knows that if $A > B$ and $B > C$ then $A > C$). The views of Piaget on this particular point have been given without comment.

Later in the chapter suggestions will be made for appropriate activities to give children experience in measuring and recording length.

## AREA AND ITS MEASUREMENT

The term *area* may be defined as the amount of surface within a closed curve. It can more precisely be developed for the child as the size of a region on a surface bounded by a closed curve (usually a simple closed curve). The child in his everyday experiences encounters, say, coins and plates of different sizes, large and small tables, bricks and tiles of different shapes and sizes, together with a hundred and one other objects that display a surface. Furthermore, in his play, he often places one object over another. Slowly he builds up the notion that some surfaces are larger than others or there is more room on some surfaces than on others; for example, he can stretch his arms and cover some tables but not others. So he slowly discovers that shapes are of different sizes or areas, although he does not use the latter word at first. But before the concept of area is well defined for him, he may center on an aspect of an area, such as length, and maintain that a particular surface which is longer is also bigger. Even when area is conserved, the child, like adults, takes a "short cut" and says that one table is bigger than another when he means that the surface area of one is larger than that of the other.

Piaget, Inhelder, and Szeminska (1960) devised a number of experiments which illustrate that area, like length, is not conserved with change of position in the case of young children. In one such experiment, children are shown two rectangles, *a* and *b* in Figure 43, which are recognized as congruent. This can be seen by placing one over the

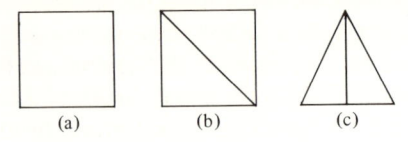

FIGURE 43

other. One of these—say, *b*—is cut into two halves along its diagonal and the pieces are placed together to form a triangle as in *c*. The child is then questioned as to whether the rectangle *a* and triangle *c* have the same area or are the same size. To five or six years of age, area is not conserved; while around six to seven years of age, the judgments made are often correct but are made intuitively. From seven onward, however, area is conserved and sound reasons are given.

But the fact that area is conserved in no sense ensures that the child can measure area. We adults know that in the same way as we use linear length to find the number which is the length of a segment, we use a square measure (square centimeter, square inch) to find the number that is the area of a region bounded by a simple closed curve; for example, rectangle, square, triangle, circle. It is not, of course, necessary to use a square as a unit of measure of area; one could use, say, half a square, or we could find the area of a closed curve in terms of the area of a unit triangle. But, as stated earlier, it is usual to employ a square of side one linear unit as the measuring unit. However, the child finds difficulty at first in measuring area, and it is to a consideration of these difficulties that we now turn. Piaget, Inhelder, and Szeminska used two techniques—namely, measurement by superposition and measurement by unit iteration.

**Measurement by Superposition**

The pupil is given a right-angled triangle and a rather larger but irregular shape (Figure 44). Measuring cards are provided in the form of a number of smaller unit squares, rectangles composed of two squares, and triangles made of the squares cut diagonally. All the cards (rectangles, squares, and triangles) together just cover the irregular shape. The task of the child is to compare the areas of the two shapes. Responses obtained from children can be classified into a number of stages.

# Geometry

In the first stage, pupils have to be prompted to cover the shapes with cards, and their judgments are based on perception, not on logic.

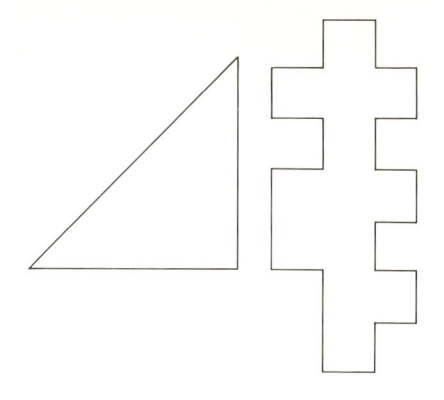

FIGURE 44

Even when they find that the irregular shape needs all the cards to completely cover it but the large triangle does not, they are still capable of saying that the triangle is larger. During the next stage, children slowly discover that the irregular shape is larger because more pieces are needed to cover it. But they still need prodding to use the cards as a common measure rather than as a mere covering.

Then, in the third stage, two developments are seen. At first, pupils certainly use the cards as a common measure to compare the areas of the two shapes, but they count all the cards used regardless of their size. In other words, they treat all the cards as equal units and ignore their inequality. Finally, they grasp the notion of a unit of area so that the size of the measuring card or element is taken into account. Thus an area requiring, say, two rectangles, three squares, and one triangle to cover it is seen to need fifteen triangles as an alternative, and so it has an area of fifteen unit triangles.

## Measurement by Unit Iteration

Using this technique, the child is first given shapes made up of squares, together with a separate unit square as a measuring instrument (Figure 45a). He is also given shapes made of squares, or of squares and adjoining triangles (made from cutting a unit square along a diagonal (Figure 45b), together with a unit square, a rectangle of two squares, and a triangle again formed by cutting a unit square along a diagonal.

In the second instance, there is the additional problem of converting a rectangle into unit squares, and the number of unit squares into unit

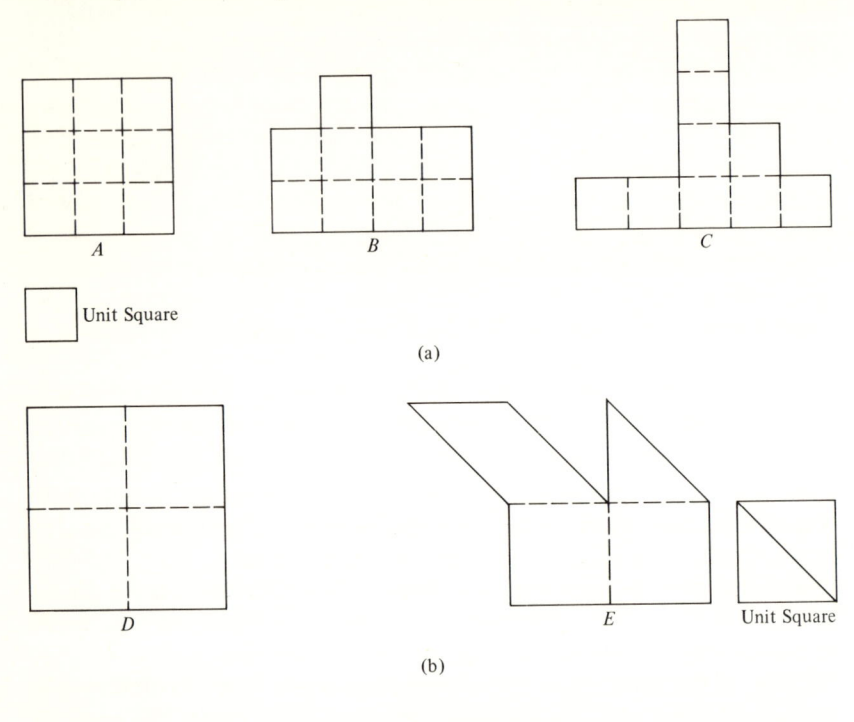

FIGURE 45

triangles, because the area of complete shapes can at times (as in $E$ in Figure 45) be expressed as whole numbers only in terms of unit triangles. The overall task for the child is to compare the areas of the shapes within Figure 45a and within Figure 45b.

Once again a number of stages are found in the child's progress. In the first, the size of the shapes $A$, $B$, $C$ in Figure 45a is judged in terms of perceptual appearance, so that they may be said to be of different sizes. This is so even after the pupil has been shown how to mark off unit squares (dotted lines) within the shapes and he has satisfied himself that the same number of squares can be drawn inside each of the three figures. The subdivision into unit squares has no operational significance at this stage. The value of a unit square may change with change of position for the child (nonconservation), while he does not yet comprehend that the whole is equal to the sum of the parts. Moreover, there is no idea of a unit of measurement; thus the transport of an applied measure and its repeated application is beyond him.

Geometry

In the second stage, the shapes in Figure 45a are now judged to be equal in area, because each is composed of the same number of squares. But in the case of the shape in Figure 45b, the same child will still treat squares and triangles as equal in area, so that in comparing the areas of $D$ and $E$ he will be in error. However, taken as a whole, there is an improvement in the child's performance, for there is increased understanding of a whole having been subdivided into units, also that the value of a unit does not change with change of position. But the two ideas are not well coordinated, and there is still no idea of a measuring unit.

We find in stage three a better coordination of the two operations—substitution and iteration—leading to the construction of a unit of measurement. At first the child still counts squares and triangles as equivalent units until his error is pointed out. Later the pupil measures area by the repeated application of a *unit* measure inside a larger area. In my experience, children vary greatly in the age at which they reach this final substage. This age can range from seven and a half to nine years for ordinary pupils. Readers particularly interested in the child's conception of area measure should also consult Wagman (1968).

We now discuss a matter of considerable importance as far as the pupil's understanding of the calculation of area is concerned. Somewhere between seven and a half and nine years of age the pupil can measure, say, square $A$ of Figure 45a and know that it is composed of nine unit squares. It will have an area of nine square units. But, it might be argued, that result could have been derived directly from the linear measurements of the square and without any thought of the application of a unit area inside a larger area. If we think of the area of the larger unit in terms of the application of a unit area inside it, then no more is required than the logical multiplication of lengths in two dimensions (Figure 46). But as Piaget, Inhelder, and Szeminska (1960) point out on the basis of experimental evidence, it requires formal operational thought before a child can make a *direct* transition from length to area—with understanding—by a process of arithmetic calculation.

One can teach the child that the area of a square or rectangle is given by the product of the length of its sides. Indeed teachers do this on the basis of the successive application of a unit area within a larger area. But, given two lengths, say four inches each, perpendicular to one another and starting from the same point or origin, the calculation of an area sixteen square inches amounts to reducing the area to two infinite sets of lines with each member of one set being perpendicular to each member of the other set, and within each set members are all parallel. In short, we have a grid with the lines infinitesimally close. This is analogous to the situation where, at the stage of formal opera-

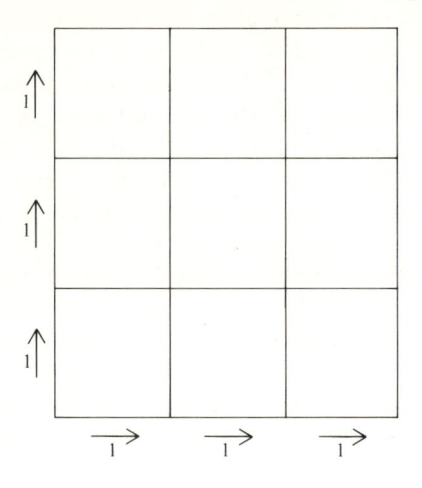

FIGURE 46

tional thought, a line becomes an infinite set of points, as we saw earlier. While we know that the area of a rectangle is given by the product of the length of its sides, this situation is intelligible only if it is understood that the area itself is reducible to infinite sets of perpendicular lines; for, as Piaget and the others point out, a two-dimensional continuum amounts to an uninterrupted matrix of one-dimensional continua.

It is thus seen that constructing a coordinated system within an area and using successive applications of a unit area (as in Figure 45) is a very different matter from generating an area by multiplying lengths. In the former instance we have a limited number of elements, in the latter a continuous structure with an infinite set of elements. Naturally one commences in the classroom with unit iteration within a larger area. Then pupils are taught to multiply together the lengths of the sides of a rectangle in order to calculate the area, illustrating the process with a finite number of lines. But a direct transition from length to area through a full understanding that area is reducible to an infinite number of lines is possible only at the stage of formal operational thought.

Lunzer (1968) has provided a neat experiment which shows the difficulties which pupils have with the conservation of area and perimeter under certain changes. The tasks involved have been given to children at each age level from five to fifteen years, both in Switzerland and in England. The results are substantially the same. The first task employs

# Geometry

a board with sets of nails which form the corners of a series of rectangular figures (Figure 47). A square is marked out with a heavy black

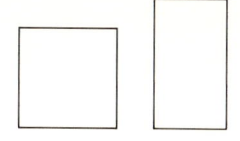

FIGURE 47

line, and the child is first shown the figure with a fixed length of string around the square. The string is then moved from the square to a series of rectangles in turn, with each rectangle getting taller but narrower and with the string always exactly fitting around the rectangle. With younger pupils appropriate stories are told about farmers walking around their fields, and amounts of grass, in order to clarify the terms *area* and *perimeter*. Each child is questioned about the conservation of both the area and perimeter of the rectangle under these changes.

Another piece of apparatus consists of a piece of green card in the shape of a square and five further squares cut as in Figure 48 but with

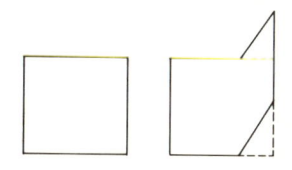

FIGURE 48

the triangular section progressively increasing in height. Once again the child is questioned about the conservation of area and perimeter.

In the first task there is, at nine years of age, correct conservation of perimeter, but in addition the area is falsely conserved. The child maintains both conservations in spite of the perceptual evidence that the area varies. In the second task, area is correctly conserved but so is perimeter (incorrectly) although occasionally a nine-year-old recognizes that there is an increase in perimeter. The results show that even among the oldest of the pupils considered in this book, area and perimeter are not clearly dissociated. Indeed the experiment shows that it is not until fourteen years of age that pupils can unambiguously conserve perimeter in the first task with loss of conservation of area, and in the second case conserve area but recognize loss of conservation of perimeter. Thus it is only at the level of formal operational thought that area and perimeter can be clearly dissociated, although it must be admitted that such understanding comes a little earlier when perimeter rather than area is deformed.

## GEOMETRICAL LOCI

The study of geometrical loci[1] is particularly interesting, for the child is unable to construct the relevant figures unless he can make a generalization, which in turn is based upon an action or an operation that is repeated indefinitely. In essence the pupil has to recognize the principle of recurrence, which is as fundamental in geometrical as it is in arithmetical reasoning. Thus in studying geometrical loci we have, once again, to be concerned with the problem of the growth of general reasoning.

Piaget, Inhelder, and Szeminska (1960) have provided a number of interesting experiments which enable us to study this topic. Two will be discussed here: one relates to the locus of points equidistant from two points in a straight line, the second to the locus of all points equidistant from a fixed point. In respect to the first experiment, work carried out under my direction involved the experimenter and child sitting on opposite sides of a rectangular table. The child is given a number of small beads or other suitable objects, and told that the game is to place a bead so that "it is as far from you as from me," or something equivalent. Then he is asked to place another bead similarly, then a third bead, and so on.

In another experiment the child is asked to place the beads so that they are equidistant from two coins or two toy trees. Whatever the exact apparatus used, the subject is frequently asked, in suitable language, if there are points other than those indicated which satisfy the conditions. This is necessary, for the child may place all the beads on one side of the line joining himself to the experimenter (or the two coins or trees) and forget about positions on the other sides. In the second task the child is asked where children should stand, or where marbles should be placed, so that each is the same distance from ("as far as") a marble used as a "jack" when playing marbles. It is stressed that the children or marbles must be the same—exactly the same—distance from the target. Once again the child is frequently asked if there are points other than those indicated which satisfy the conditions.

---

[1] The word "location" is sometimes used instead of the word "locus." The former term is obviously linked to the word locate and means place. "Location" is met more often in everyday life than is "locus."

*Geometry* 115

A number of stages are found in the development of the child's notion of loci:

1. Objects are placed at random, for there is a lack of an intellectual grasp of distance.
2. In the case of the straight line, the subject finds the particular case of the midpoint of the line joining himself to the experimenter. This is done by perceptual estimate and is fairly accurately performed. The locus is either confined to this point or to a few points nearby. In the case of the circle, the children or marbles are arranged in a row or in an irregular ring around the center, without making any attempt to measure the distance between any of the children (or marbles) and the center.
3. There is a beginning of generalization, although it is manifested as a single repetition of behavior rather than as a genuine iteration of actions. The understanding of locus is rudimentary; it is achieved by extending the method used in placing the first central marble and then placing one marble behind another in a continuous line following the same direction. Nevertheless some children at this stage do show the beginnings of generalization in relation to symmetry, for they place some beads on both sides of the midpoint; in relation to continuity, for they interpolate beads in the intervals between beads; and in relation to infinity, for they will progressively iterate on both sides of the line joining experimenter and subject. In the case of the task involving a circle, the child shows evidence of mastering continuity while the "ring" becomes more regular.
4. From seven and a half years of age onward (much later in some pupils) there is no doubt on the part of the child as to what he seeks—namely a series of points characterized by equidistance from the center. There is now reasoning by recurrence, for after a small amount of experimentation to find out what form a particular locus will take, he concludes that all points on the straight line or circle must have the required common property.
5. There is a later stage when formal operational thought becomes available to the pupil. Then the responses are the same, but there is a far more refined notion of point, continuity, and infinity.

In Piaget's view the study of loci as indicated in these experiments is the finest example of the direct transition from induction based on empiricism and intuition (indicated here in stage 3) to operational generalization which is deductive (indicated here by stage 4). The end is reasoning by recurrence. Unfortunately reasoning by recurrence does not always occur in number and in loci at the same time. Here is another example of a horizontal differential (see Chapter 1).

## SOME SUGGESTED CLASSROOM ACTIVITIES

Earlier in the chapter we suggested some classroom activities in connection with curves and angles. Further activities are now suggested which relate to length, area, and loci. It is assumed that the teacher will, at the same time, give the child adequate experience in using, say, ruler, compasses, set square, and trundle wheel,[2] so the pupil will become physically adept in working with them.

1. *Comparison of rods or strips of cardboard of differing lengths, or children of different heights.* Thus rod 1 (longest) is compared with rod 2 (middle value), and rod 2 compared with rod 3 (shortest). Such activities give the child experience in comparing lengths, using the correct relational terms like "longer than," "as long as," and so on, and ordering elements in terms of a dimension, while at the same time the elements demonstrate the principle of transitivity.

2. *Tasks which might help to promote the conservation of length.* The pupil may be given two equal rods or sticks which lie side by side (Figure 49a). Each has a number of equally spaced notches cut on it.

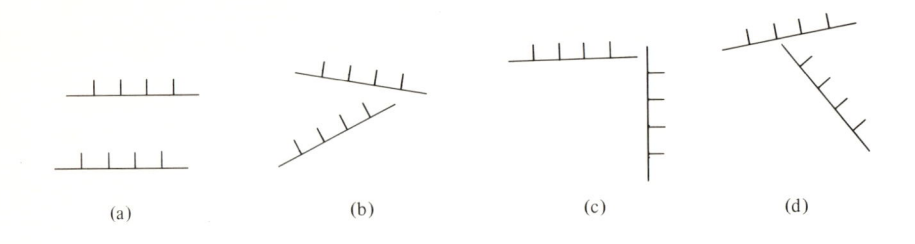

(a)　　　　　(b)　　　　　(c)　　　　　(d)

FIGURE 49

One or both of the rods is moved so that they assume positions as in Figures 49b, c, d, and the child is questioned as to the equality or otherwise of the lengths of the rods now. If length is not conserved, he is asked to count the number of parts on each rod in each position or to

---

[2] A circular wooden disc (diameter 1 yard) attached to a long handle. The child pushes the wheel and an attachment "clicks" after each rotation. By counting the number of "clicks," he can measure the length he has traversed.

# Geometry

measure the rods each time against some reference unit.[3] It is also useful to construct a framework of four rods (Figure 50a) and to allow the

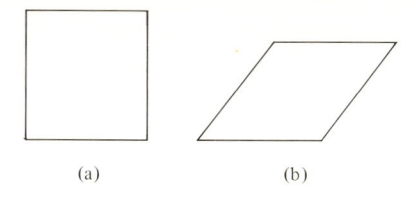

FIGURE 50

child to examine it when it is in the form of a square. Each side is compared with a reference unit. The square is then pushed out of shape into that of a parallelogram and the subject again questioned as to the equality of the sides. Each side can be compared once more with the reference unit.

3. *Measurement of length using informal methods.* A chalk line can be drawn on the floor, and a child can traverse the whole line by carefully putting one foot immediately in front of the other. Another child with a different size foot does the same. The length of the line is obtained by finding the number of foot units. Such an exercise brings home markedly to the child that measurement involves subdivision and iteration, and that we get different numbers to indicate the number of units of length according to the size of the child's foot which does the measurement. Alternately a line can be completely covered by pieces of wood first, say, six inches in length and later nine inches in length. Or a shorter line can be measured by the iteration of one child's hand span and then by another child's hand span. This type of activity brings out both the nature of measurement and the need for some standard unit of reference before we can measure the length of a line and be in a position to compare its length with that of another line.

4. *Introduction of the yardstick and measurement of a line drawn on the classroom floor or playground by laying down a line of yardsticks (not more than about six).* This is followed by the introduction of the foot rule and the measurement of lines by the number of foot rules required to be laid down. So far the lines have been drawn to accommodate an exact number of yardsticks or foot rules, but lines must then be introduced which have "pieces left over." This is the time

---

[3] It is well realized that there is a logical flaw here which cannot be circumvented. The child could think that the distance between notches changed as the rod changed its orientation, or that the rod changed its length as it was reorientated with respect to a reference unit. In practice this general approach is the only one.

to mark the yardstick in inches and measure the line in terms of the number of yardsticks and the number of inches "left over." Similarly a shorter line could be measured using the yardstick as, say, sixteen inches and converted into one foot, four inches. So far we have spoken of the prolongation of the yardstick by laying down a number of such units until the line is covered, but readers will appreciate that pupils must be weaned away from this to the iteration of the yardstick (or foot rule) as soon as possible. If desired, the meter stick can first be introduced instead of the yardstick, and then marked in centimeters.

5. *Early in their school careers, pupils need to be encouraged to estimate the length of lines before they measure their lengths.* This early estimation of length is important. Without such experience the high school pupil and adult are often wildly inaccurate in their judgment of length.

6. *The drawing of lines first freehand and then to a given number of inches is a necessary activity.* Drawing a line to a given length is more difficult for the child than measuring it, and considerable teacher guidance is often required.

7. Further practical activities involving measurement include measuring the lengths of perimeters and diagonals of rectangular figures; the circumference of a wheel by rolling it along a straight line; the length of a curve by means of the trundle wheel; and the dimensions of, say, paths, walls, and flowerbeds using a tape measure or surveyor's chain.

8. *Pupils should have the opportunity to discover empirically that the perpendicular to a line passing through a point is the shortest distance from that point to the line.* Let the pupil draw any line $BC$ and mark a point $A$ some six inches from the line. Let him draw the line $AD$ perpendicular to $BC$ (Figure 51), using a set square. He must discover that

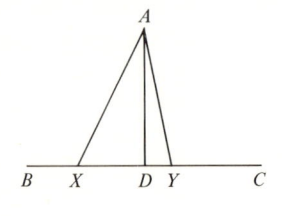

FIGURE 51

$AD$ is shorter than $AX$ or $AY$, however close he can make $X$ and $Y$ approach $D$. This knowledge will be needed later in dealing with loci.

9. *There should be a comparison of the areas of squares and rectangles as there was for length of rods.* In regard to the conservation

*Geometry* 119

and measurement of area, it is suggested that a pupil should practice the drawing of one-inch squares on paper (one-foot and one-yard squares are best drawn on the blackboard or floor). He also needs to be provided with a number of squares of stiff cardboard or hardboard each one inch by one inch or, say, one centimeter by one centimeter. A square can be made out of, say, thirty-six squares, and the latter can be rearranged to form rectangles of varying dimensions—eighteen by two or twelve by three, and so on. This kind of exercise is likely to "precipitate" the child's understanding of conservation of area when his thinking skills are nearly ready for this, for the number of unit squares remains constant. It also provides an opportunity to appreciate that the area of a shape that is not a square is, nevertheless, composed of a number of square units.

10. *Plenty of activities must be given in which the child has the opportunity to count the number of units required to cover a flat surface.* Thus a child is set the task of drawing a series of squares and rectangles —say, six by three, four by four, and so on—and dividing each into unit squares. He has then to cover the whole area with unit squares, or apply a unit square successively (that is, iteration of a unit square), until the whole area is covered. It is by these means that the pupil is helped to find that instead of counting up the number of squares to cover each square or rectangle, or instead of counting the number of times the unit square has to be applied, he can multiply the number of units of length by the number of the same units of breadth to obtain the area of the figure.

Pupils also need experience in measuring larger areas marked out, say, on the floor or playground. Such can be measured in square feet or square yards. A variety of objects ranging from doors and windows to parts of the school garden can have their areas measured in appropriate units. But it is also essential for children to grasp that areas can be measured in nonsquare units. Thus the area of a triangle can be measured as counts of a unit triangle, the area of a rectangle as counts of a unit rectangle, and so on. Irregular polygons—made of rectangles and triangles—can also be measured in terms of unit triangles.

11. *It is often necessary to help a child to appreciate that the area of the surface within a closed irregular curve (more formally, the area of a region on a surface bounded by an irregular closed curve) can be expressed as a number of square units.* He can sometimes be helped by getting him to draw on a grid, or on paper ruled into squares, an irregular closed curve, and then shade in, and count, the total number of *whole* squares enclosed. In discussion it can be explained that the *parts* of squares remaining within the boundary could themselves be re-

arranged to form a rectangle or square and this in turn would have an area which can be expressed in terms of unit squares. If the flexibility of his concrete operational thought is insufficient for him to make this rearrangement, it is best to leave this task for the present and give it to him again, say, three to six months later.

12. *Certain problems in loci can profitably be discussed.* For example, the locus of the point which moves so that it is equidistant from a fixed point is admirably illustrated by the points on the circumference of a bicycle wheel, and the locus of the point which moves so that it is equidistant from two parallel lines, by the movement of a man walking midway between two railway lines.

13. *There is a need for precision in the use of language.* Thus a child should be encouraged to say that twelve inches measures the same distance as one foot, or a measure of one hundred centimeters is the same as a measure of one meter, rather than "twelve inches equals one foot."

# 6
# Relationships and Mappings

As we saw earlier, mathematics is the study of structures or of systematic patterns of relationships. Consequently it is of great importance that children be led to discover relationships and record them in different ways. In everyday situations pupils have innumerable opportunities to find relationships which can be understood by them at their level of intellectual development.

Thus the four- or five-year-old can well understand the utterance "That's my red hat," which expresses a relationship between him and a certain hat. If the teacher writes the names of pupils on the blackboard together with the color of their hats (indicating in colored chalk the appropriate color), then a particular child can well indicate with a chalk mark the relationship between himself and a hat. Thus in Figure 52 each child indicates by an arrow the relationship "wears." As the

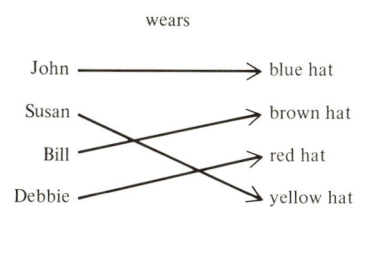

```
              wears
  John ─────────────────→ blue hat
  Susan ╲             ╱→ brown hat
         ╲           ╱
  Bill ───╲─────────╱──→ red hat
           ╲       ╱
  Debbie ───────────→ yellow hat
```

FIGURE 52

child gets older and his experience of life increases, his ability to understand rather more difficult relationships also grows, and he is able to express and record these in different ways as his vocabulary gets larger and his power of symbolism develops. Many relationships can be expressed by means of an arrow, which has to be given a specific meaning on each occasion. Thus once heights and speeds can be put in a series, the relationship between the heights of Jack, Mary, and Susan may be expressed as:

$$\text{Jack} \xrightarrow{\text{is taller than}} \text{Mary} \longrightarrow \text{Susan}$$

and the relationship between the speeds of jet plane, automobile, and bicycle as:

$$\text{jet plane} \xrightarrow{\text{is faster than}} \text{automobile} \longrightarrow \text{bicycle}$$

The child should, in his activities, be encouraged to be on the lookout for, and record, relationships. In the tasks that he will encounter in the field of number, length, area, capacity, buying and selling, arithmetic operations, social situations, and so forth, he will meet these, and many other, relationships:

| | |
|---|---|
| is taller than | can be exchanged for |
| is lighter than | has the same price as |
| is longer than | represents the same number as |
| weighs more than | have as product |
| holds less than | lives on the same street as |
| is the brother of | went earlier than |

These and other relationships can be expressed by a simple arrow notation or in a mapping notation (to be discussed later).

But other relationships are more complex, for an object or child may be involved in two relationships at the same time. Consider the set of objects indicated in Figure 53. Airplane, coin, and balloon are silver in

The relations involved are:
is as hard as
is as silver in color as

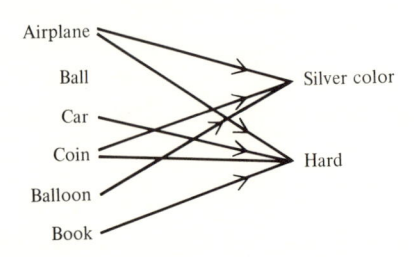

Airplane
Ball
Car          Silver color
Coin         Hard
Balloon
Book

FIGURE 53

color, while airplane, car, book, and coin are hard. The child is seven to eight years of age before he clearly understands and can explain

*Relationships and Mappings* 123

why more than one arrow leaves a member of the first set. A younger child may, of course, put the arrows in correctly, but we have again to distinguish between the figurative aspects of knowing displayed by the younger child and the operative aspects displayed by the child entering the stage of concrete operational thought.

## PROPERTIES OF RELATIONSHIPS

Certain properties of relationships are of particular interest to mathematicians. The latter are enthusiastic to know if a relationship possesses reflexive, symmetric, and transitive properties. Here the treatment of this matter will be from the point of view of the child, and the discussion will involve the kinds of relationships that the teacher can use in making clear to him that a particular relationship may possess one, two, or all of these properties.

First, a relationship among males can be symmetric or asymmetric. For example, the "brother of" relationship is symmetrical, for if John[1] is the brother of Bill, then Bill is the brother of John. This is quite understandable to the normal seven- to eight-year-old. The equality relationship is also symmetric, for if $A$ is equal to $B$, $B$ is equal to $A$. Likewise the inequality relationship is symmetric, for if $A$ is not equal to $B$, then $B$ is not equal to $A$. Using concrete realizations of the equality and inequality relationships (and no $A$'s and $B$'s), the older and abler pupils in the age range considered here can well understand, intuitively, that they are symmetric. But a special kind of symmetrical relationship also possesses the property of being reflexive—that is, the relationship must hold between the member and itself. Thus the equality relationship possesses the reflexive property, for $A$ is equal to $A$; but the inequality relationship does not possess the reflexive property, for it is not true that $A$ is unequal to $A$. Likewise the "brother of" relationship does not possess this property, for $A$ is not the brother of $A$. Yet the relationships of equality, inequality and "brother of" all possessed the property of symmetry.

Finally we come to relationships that possess the transitive property. Take the relationship "is heavier than." The eight-year-old well understands that if $A$ is heavier than $B$, and $B$ is heavier than $C$, then $A$ is heavier than $C$. And in the case of equality, he knows that if $A = B$ and $B = C$, then $A = C$. It must be stressed, however, that for the eight- to nine-year age group the teacher must use concrete realizations of relationships possessing one or more of these properties. Thus in the case of transitivity involving the relationship "measure the same as,"

---

[1] The set must be restricted to males. If we have "John is the brother of Mary," it is nonsense to say that "Mary is the brother of John."

an actual example to be used with the child might be, "If thirty-six inches is the measure of the length of three feet, and three feet is the measure of the length of one yard, then thirty-six inches is the measure of the length of one yard."

So the older and abler pupils we are considering can be helped to see that, say, the equality relationship has three properties: it is reflexive, symmetric, and transitive. With the aid of familiar concrete examples, he can have an intuitive grasp that for each $A$, $A = A$; that for each $A$ and $B$, if $A = B$ then $B = A$; and that for each $A$, $B$, and $C$, if $A = B$ and $B = C$, then $A = C$. These notions involve second-level abstractions, for they are derived from structuring the child's actions upon physical reality. However, if one attempts to lead the child to appreciate that the relationship of equality is an example of an *equivalence* relationship, one is attempting to get the child to put a structure on relationships possessing certain properties, which in turn have been derived directly from concrete situations—that is, from his actions upon reality. This skill comes at the level of formal operational thought, as was explained in Chapter 1.

But the older children in the age range considered here can, indeed must, if they are to understand cardinal number, have an intuitive grasp (that is, they are not able to move far from reality) that the relation "can be matched one-to-one" has three properties. First, it relates on itself, as in the case, say, of fingers matched to fingers. Second, it relates both ways so that, say, fingers can be matched to objects and objects to fingers. Third, it carries over so that fingers can be matched to objects, objects to other objects, and fingers to the second set of objects. Likewise if the nine-year-old is to have an understanding of the relation "is parallel to," he must intuitively grasp that it too has three properties. That is to say, he must be aware that a line is parallel to itself; that if one line is parallel to a second line, then the second is parallel to the first; and that if one line is parallel to a second line and the second line is parallel to a third, then the first is parallel to the third. But it will be adolescence—when formal operational thought is elaborated—before pupils will see a common structure in, say, "equality," "parallel to," and "congruent to" and understand that they are all examples of an equivalence relation.

From the point of view of the classroom, then, the teacher must think out which relationships the child is to encounter, provide situations in which these relationships may be found, and encourage the child to think about and discuss whether each relationship possesses one or more of the properties designated as reflexive, symmetric, and transitive. It is true that the child may not see the purpose of this at third-grade level, and it is also true that he will have only an intuitive grasp

*Relationships and Mappings* 125

of the properties the relationship exhibits, but by treating these ideas informally one is laying the groundwork for a grasp of the concept of equivalence relation which will be formally understood much later in school life. It is also important that pupils should be helped to appreciate that relationships may be reversed. Thus if "Mary is the mother of John," then "John is the child of Mary." Experience of reversing relations suggests an inverse relation later on and hence a lead into an aspect of mappings.

## MAPPING

We are now going to discuss another very important mathematical idea—that of mapping. This was touched on lightly in Chapter 2, but now it will be considered more carefully. Once again the groundwork is being laid in the first three grades of the elementary school which will enable important mathematical notions to come to fruition, as it were, much later. By mapping one is enabled to relate the members of one set to those of another. Relations arise by pairing the members of one set with those of another, and the first member may have more than one member of the second set assigned to it; for example, a doll can be both soft and red. But in mapping the essential element is the ordered pair, when the first member is selected from the first set, and a second member from another set and assigned to the first member. But once a member from the first set is selected, it is never again chosen. Thus since in Figure 54 an arrow goes to both soft and red, the figure does not illustrate a mapping. But the inverse relation is a mapping.

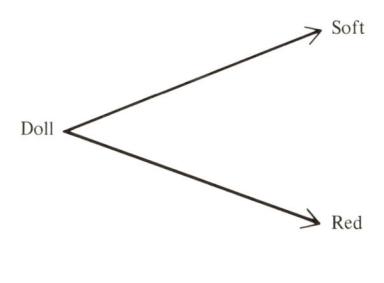

Doll → Soft
Doll → Red

FIGURE 54

We begin with some simple nonmathematical examples of mapping which will be perfectly comprehensible to second- and third-grade pupils. Let us suppose that Jack and Jim go to Atlantic City, Karen to Ocean City, Ann to Cape Cod, and Henry and Mary to Cold Spring

126        *The Growth of Understanding in Mathematics*

Harbor.[2] In Figure 55 these arrangements are illustrated as a mapping. Indeed they are illustrated as a many-to-one mapping, since in some

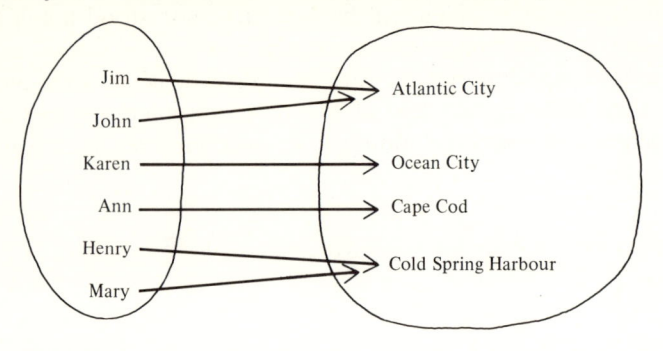

```
     Jim  ─────────┐
                   ├──→ Atlantic City
     John ─────────┘
     Karen ───────────→ Ocean City
     Ann  ───────────→ Cape Cod
     Henry ────────┐
                   ├──→ Cold Spring Harbour
     Mary ─────────┘
```

FIGURE 55

instances a member of the second set (such as Atlantic City) is assigned to more than one member of the first set (as Jim and John). Moreover Cape Cod is said to be the *image* of Ann, and Cold Spring Harbor the *image* of Henry and Mary. We can also have a one-to-one mapping over, say, "goes to," as illustrated in Figure 56. From these instances it can be seen that the arrow in mapping suggests a "going to."

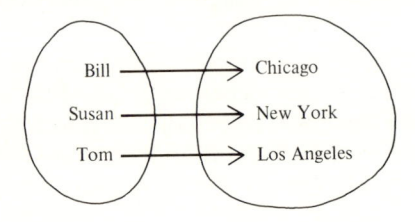

```
     Bill  ───────→ Chicago
     Susan ───────→ New York
     Tom   ───────→ Los Angeles
```

FIGURE 56

In both the above mappings the members of the first set are said to be mapped *onto* the members of the second set, since each member of the second set is an image of a member in the first set. But we can also have the situation where this is not so. For example, in Figure 57 where the mapping is under, say, "likes," Pittsburgh is not the image of any member of the first set. In this instance the members of the first set are said to be mapped *into* the second set.

There is a third case which is of great importance. Let Ralph, Pete, and Henry be members of the first set, and let their dancing partners be Margaret, Katherine, and Jill respectively (Figure 58). Note that the

[2] Use is made of the names of places on the east coast. Teachers will naturally illustrate such an example with the names of places in the vicinity of their schools.

## Relationships and Mappings

arrows point both ways, for if Ralph dances with Margaret, Margaret dances with Ralph, and so on. This situation illustrates a one-to-one

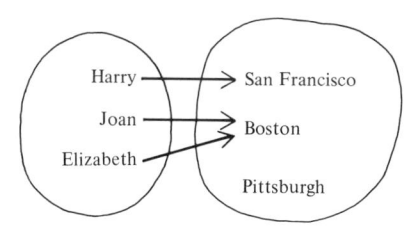

FIGURE 57

correspondence, or a mapping of the first set onto the second, and the inverse mapping from the second set onto the first. Moreover the images are interchanged.

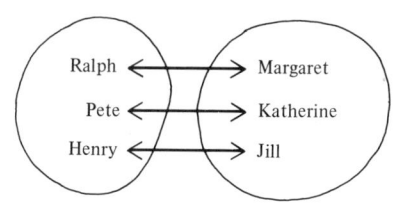

FIGURE 58

Third-grade pupils can grasp all these mappings intuitively; that is, they are understood as long as the members of the sets remain perceptible or imageable. Furthermore, they can learn that when the members of two sets can be put in one-to-one correspondence, they are called equivalent sets. Such sets, unlike equal sets, need not contain the same kind of member; the members of the first set may be, say, triangles and the members of the second set, circles.

The mappings which we have been discussing are easy to grasp intuitively, but they are not all interesting mathematically. However, from the examples the child can be helped to obtain an intuitive grasp of mappings involving numbers. Thus in Figure 59a we have under the instruction "Add" a one-to-one mapping with the members of the first set being mapped onto the second, while in Figure 59b we have a one-to-one mapping with the members of the first set mapped into the second.

We said in an earlier chapter that children need to have much experience in "making the story" of, say, 5, 8, or 10 and that a many-to-one mapping notation can be used informally to illustrate "the story" whether under addition or multiplication (Figure 60). The pairs of number bonds illustrated in Figure 60a are those that make the story of 5. The abler third-grade pupil can appreciate that $2 + 3 = 5 + 0$ is a

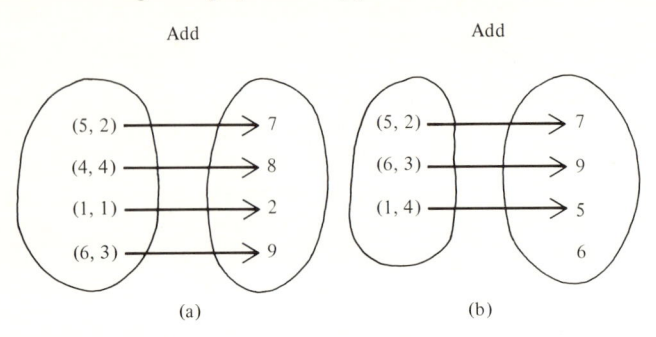

FIGURE 59

shorthand way of writing that the image of the number pair 2, 3 under addition mapping is also that of the number pair 5, 0. He also learns from the physical manipulation of members of sets, that 5, 0 can be written as 5, for 0 is found to be a neutral or identity element in respect

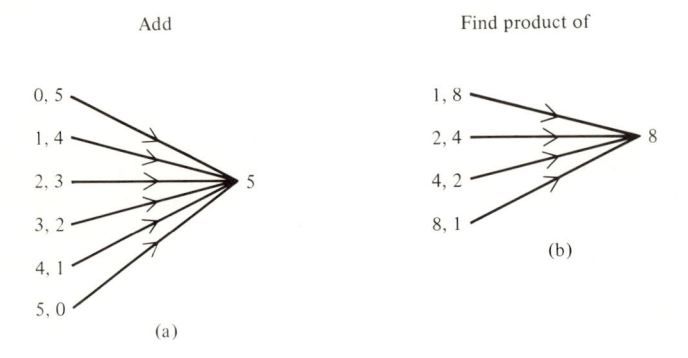

FIGURE 60

to addition since when it is added to any other number it leaves the latter unchanged. The child will not, of course, use this exact language. Nor will he formally understand that the relation:

(represents the same number as)

is an equivalence relation. To be able to do this necessitates the capacity to put a structure on abstractions that were themselves derived from actions on objects, and this is a skill that becomes available in high school. But the third-grade pupil can well understand, using sets of physical objects, that under the addition mapping:

## Relationships and Mappings

$2 + 3 \longrightarrow 2 + 3$ (reflexive property)
$2 + 3 \longrightarrow 4 + 1$ and $4 + 1 \longrightarrow 2 + 3$ (symmetric property)
$2 + 3 \longrightarrow 4 + 1$ and $4 + 1 \longrightarrow 5 + 0$ lead to $2 + 3 \longrightarrow 5 + 0$
(transitive property)

But he cannot formally understand equivalence relation, nor does he understand in a formal sense that the set of ordered pairs whose image under the mapping "add" is a given number form an equivalence class.

The more opportunities an elementary school child gets to experience situations in which examples of equivalence relations and equivalence classes are embodied in concrete realizations and discussed, the more likely it is that a formal understanding of these concepts will arise in high school. Familiarity with content seems to aid the growth of formal thinking in that particular content area. While good teaching seems to require that the teacher provide learning situations just a little in advance of what the pupil is able to do, no attempt should be made to harass or "force" the pupil. If this is done, it may be suggested that we are likely to engender anxiety or distaste in relation to mathematics, or ideas may be assimilated with distortion. Through discussions with pupils and by noting where each is, the teacher can save herself and her pupils much frustration.

All manner of operations such as "add 3 to," "subtract 4 from," "multiply by 2," and "divide by 4" (in the case of multiples of 4) can be investigated by the pupil by mapping from points on one number line to points on a parallel number line. Thus in Figure 61 the members of the set of

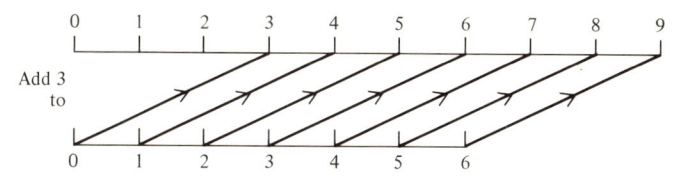

FIGURE 61

the counting numbers from 0 to 9 (domain) are mapped, under the operation of addition, onto the set of counting numbers 3 to 9 (range).

## MAPPINGS AND GRAPHS

Earlier in this chapter it was pointed out that the essential element in mapping is the ordered pair, the first member being selected from the first set and a second member from another set, assigned to the first member. Readers will, of course, appreciate that in a mapping we are dealing with a special kind of mathematical relationship, namely a mathematical function. Thus while one way of representing a function is by means of the mapping notation, another way is by means of a graph which fulfills a certain criterion. For the purpose of the present discussion, it will be assumed that the child is able to locate a point in two-dimensional space (the growth of this skill will be discussed in Chapter 8).

If one looks again at Figure 61, it will be seen that the mapping could be illustrated by a graph (Figure 62). To each member of the domain

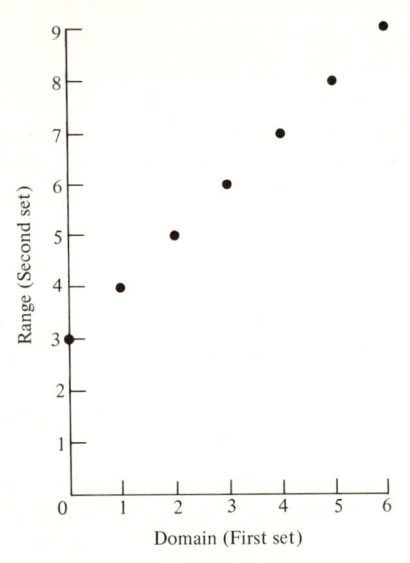

FIGURE 62

(first set) there is one, and only one, member of the range (second set). It thus represents a mapping or a function. The graph is, of course, strictly a set of discrete or separated points. Readers will also appreciate that if the set of real numbers is used, the graph obtained is the normal continuous straight line given by $y - x = 3$.

But neither situation represented in Figure 63a and 63b represents a mapping or function, because it is not true that for every member of the first set (domain) there corresponds one, and only one, member of the second set (range).

## CONCLUSION

Using suitable examples, and either the mapping notation or a graph, we can illustrate a very important mathematical idea, namely the rela-

*Relationships and Mappings* 131

tionship between the members of one set and those of a second set. By the third grade, pupils can grasp this idea intuitively. However, it is

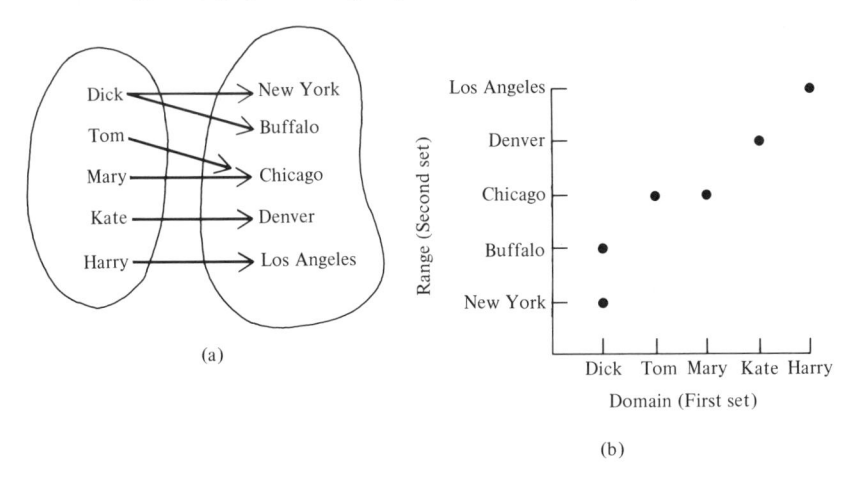

FIGURE 63

important that the teacher maintain the pupils' motivation in respect to the ideas we have been discussing. It is possible for these to become detached in the child's mind from the other mathematical ideas which he is considering at the same time unless care is taken. As we saw in the first chapter, mathematics is, for children, essentially a tool with which to explore the world. Moreover, it will be appreciated that both the mapping notation used here, and the graph, are *merely* types of diagram to illustrate the fundamental idea of the relationship between members of two sets or between members of the same set. The groundwork begun here will come to fruition later, and this knowledge will fortify teachers as they carry out the kinds of activities suggested while realizing that their pupils' understanding is limited. Readers particularly interested in the growth of pupils' ideas of a mathematical function in junior high school should consult the work of Thomas (1969).

The importance of looking at the ways in which members of sets may be related cannot be overemphasized. This idea is of first-rate importance to mathematicians in organizing and applying their work.

# 7
# Further Work on Number

**THE NUMBER LINE**

In Chapter 3 addition was introduced through joining together two disjoint sets of objects. This approach has great intuitive appeal for pupils, and we suggest that it is the best approach to the topic. However, we are now going to introduce the idea of the number line so that pupils will be able to think of the operation of addition in terms of either approach.

The number line is generally considered as a representation of the real numbers, but for the present we are going to restrict its use to the natural numbers. Later we shall discuss the question of introducing nine-year-olds to the set of integers. For the time being, at least, each mark on a straight line can correspond to a natural number, and if we are concerned only with the ordering of numbers or counting up the number of spaces between the points, the latter need not be equidistant (Figure 64a). On the other hand, once the child understands measure-

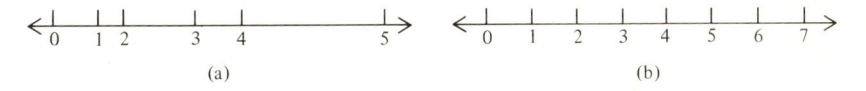

FIGURE 64

ment of length, the numbers can be spaced out at equal intervals and the lengths measured between numbers and combined (Figure 64b).

In the latter instance there is clearly some analogy between the way in which points are located on the line and the way the counting numbers are related to one another. It is hoped that children will acquire some intuitive understanding of this analogy as they use the number line, and also see how the operations of addition and subtraction are related. When introducing the number line teachers will, no doubt, draw attention to the fact that in everyday life and in science lessons, pupils meet examples of the physical realizations of the number line. For example, they use thermometers, scales on the sides of measuring vessels, and the height scale against which pupils measure each other's heights.

In both the examples shown in Figure 64, the zero point was at the left side of the line. Pupils need to be reminded that the line is very long indeed (the term "infinity" will mean little to them) and that the line drawn on paper shows only a short portion. The portion of the line indicated can represent the numbers, say, 9 to 14 (Figure 65), for there is

$$\longleftarrow\!\!\underset{9}{|}\ \underset{10}{|}\ \underset{11}{|}\ \underset{12}{|}\ \underset{13}{|}\ \underset{14}{|}\!\!\longrightarrow$$

FIGURE 65

no need for the first figure on the left side of the line to be zero. The attention of the child must also be drawn to the fact that there are arrows at each end of the line which point in opposite directions. It will be clear to the eight-year-old that the arrows merely remind him that a move to the right on the line means the numbers are increasing in size, and that the numbers get smaller as we move to the left.

A pupil should construct his own number line, making the intervals between the numbers constant but of a convenient length. He can then carry out tasks given by the teacher, such as moving a counter a given number of places to the left or right. For example, his instructions might be: "Start from 6 and move three places to the right"; "Start from 10 and move five places to the left." The child carries out these tasks and on each occasion records the result appropriately. For example, the actions can be symbolised as $6 + 3 = 9$. Moreover, as stated earlier, the beginning number on the left of the line need not be zero, while the line itself should not always be drawn in the horizontal position. Sometimes it should be drawn at an angle to the horizontal and sometimes vertically. In the latter position the number line resembles the scale against which the child measures his height.

If one so wishes, one can by placing, say, counters in the spaces between the points on the line (Figure 66) help the pupil to consider addition in terms of joining the sets of spaces on the number line instead

*Further Work on Number* 135

of joining sets of disjoint objects. By placing, say, three plain counters and four with a cross on them in the spaces on the number line (Figure

FIGURE 66

66)—starting with the space immediately to the right of 0 and leaving no blank spaces—the number on the line to the right of the last counter indicates the sum of the disjoint sets of spaces. Not all will wish to include this step, it being felt that pupils can proceed directly to the type of activity suggested in the next section for introducing addition on the number line. Indeed, teachers will realize that some pupils get confused over spaces and marks (points) and will ponder carefully if they wish to use the set of spaces in the way indicated above.

**Addition**

An example of the type 6 + 4 can be worked on the number line as follows. Starting from a zero origin, the child moves his counter to number 6 in one move (Figure 67) and then moves it on a further four places,

FIGURE 67

giving the answer of 10. When larger numbers are added (for example, 15 + 9 or 36 + 14) the number line can start at 15 or 36 as the case may be, and the counter is moved to the right as before.

Pupils need many examples to work on the number line, and these must be prepared by the teacher or provided via textbooks or worksheets. They will, of course, cease to use the number line of their own accord when they no longer feel the need for it. When asked to add 79 and 42, they will then either set the numbers down in vertical format and add them, or set them down horizontally and work, as, say:

$$79 + 42 = 80 + 20 + 21 = 100 + 21 = 121$$

Other exercises which can usefully be carried out on the number line include adding on in 2's, 3's, and 5's. Teachers will realize that vertical addition, like the movements on a number line, can be performed to some extent by rote learning. The setting out in horizontal format and the rearrangement of the numbers shows a greater understanding of number relationships on the part of the child. This point was also made in Chapter 3.

However, before leaving the number line, pupils may be introduced to a simple slide rule as an adjunct to the teaching of addition of number. They can make for themselves one number line on the lower side of one strip of thick cardboard, and another number line on the upper side of another strip of such card (Figure 68). The answer to the exercise,

| 1 | 2 | 3 | 4 | 5 | 6 | 7 | 8 | 9 | 10 | 11 | 12 | 13 | 14 | 15 | 16 | 17 | 18 |
|---|---|---|---|---|---|---|---|---|----|----|----|----|----|----|----|----|----|
|   |   |   |   |   | 1 | 2 | 3 | 4 | 5  | 6  | 7  | 8  | 9  | 10 | 11 | 12 |    |

FIGURE 68

say, 6 + 11 can be obtained by a pupil by placing the zero mark on the lower strip against the 6 mark on the upper strip and reading off the number on the upper strip corresponding to 11 on the lower. Subtraction can also be carried out using the slide rule.

**Subtraction**

In Chapter 3 we discussed subtraction in terms of the removal of physical sets. While this approach may have great intuitive appeal to pupils, it does lead to difficulties later when we wish to consider examples of the type 12 − 17. The method of "adding on" was accordingly recommended. However, the idea of the removal of subsets will again be considered here as a method of handling subtraction, for the number line does help some of the abler nine-year-olds to have a very limited and intuitive grasp of negative numbers as we shall see later.

Whereas addition involved moving to the right on the number line, the child can also appreciate by seven to eight years of age that in subtraction we have to move to the left, for in doing so we "take away" some of the spaces which we covered in moving to the right. Thus the example 7 − 4 can be worked on the number line by the child moving right on the number line to 7 (no counting of units is required) and then moving back four units to the left (see Figure 69). The number line can also be used when larger numbers are involved; for example, 22 − 13.

**Measurement and the Number Line**

So far we have been dealing with number divorced from any measures. The number line can, of course, be used to find the sum or the difference of two measurements. Thus if two parcels weigh eight lbs

*Further Work on Number* 137

and eleven lbs respectively, we can find their combined weight on the number line. Or, using a tape-measure, the child can find the length and

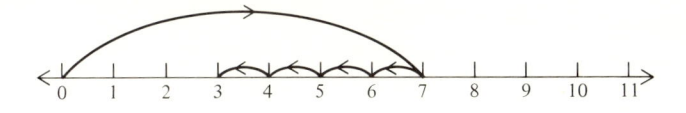

FIGURE 69

width of a room in feet, and find how much longer the length is compared with the width. If the highest temperature recorded during the day is 48°F and during the following night 33°F, the pupil can find, using the number line, by how much the temperature fell. Examples of this type are very valuable.

## THE PROBLEM OF THE INTEGERS

In some texts it is implied, without perhaps being explicitly stated, that the elementary school child—and even Grade 3 pupils—will be able to have some understanding of the set of integers (. . . $-2$, $-1$, 0, 1, 2, . . .). This point needs to be looked at very carefully.

It is perfectly true that many real life situations can be used to emphasize the need for negative integers. For example, heights above sea level can be regarded as positive, and depths below sea level as negative. Again temperatures above zero on the Centigrade Scale can be looked upon as positive and those below as negative. But even the abler Grade 3 pupils will have only an intuitive grasp of negative integers, for these cannot be abstracted from a physical set, nor are they intuitable, that is, perceptible or imaginable. For these young pupils, negative integers will always be contaminated by, or linked to, some concrete realization.

Teachers must, therefore, consider very carefully which Grade 3 pupils should be introduced to the set of integers. In this connection the number line can be helpful, for on this the integers can be referred to as directed numbers, because they tell us both "how many" and "in which direction." We can *try* to ensure that the positive integers are not confused with the counting numbers by writing integers to the right of zero as, say, $^{+}1$, $^{+}2$, $^{+}3$, and so on, and integers to the left of zero as $^{-}1$, $^{-}2$, $^{-}3$, and so on (Figure 70).

The number line can then be used to demonstrate, in the sense of providing an analogue, the operations involved in, say, $^{+}5 + {}^{+}3$ and $^{+}5 - {}^{+}3$ by moving the required number of units to the left or right as the examples demand. But the Grade 3 pupil will be taking 5 and $^{+}3$ as counting numbers and not as members of a subset of integers isomorphic to the counting numbers under addition. When employing members of the set of negative integers (these will be thought of in

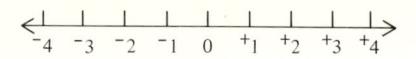

$$\leftarrow\!\!\underset{^-4\ \ ^-3\ \ ^-2\ \ ^-1\ \ 0\ \ ^+1\ \ ^+2\ \ ^+3\ \ ^+4}{\mid\quad\mid\quad\mid\quad\mid\quad\mid\quad\mid\quad\mid\quad\mid\quad\mid}\!\!\rightarrow$$

FIGURE 70

terms of some concrete realization such as "to the left of zero" or "below sea level") we can demonstrate, say, $^-6 + {}^+2$ by moving six units to the left of zero and then two units to the right. It is also easy to provide a demonstration, by analogue, of $^-6 + {}^-3$. The example $^-5 - {}^-3$ is a little more difficult, but the child can find an answer by writing $^-5 - {}^-3 = \Box$ and rewriting the equation as $^-5 = {}^-3 + \Box$. The pupil will at this point sense that $^-2$ must be put in the placeholder. We can also demonstrate $^+6 - {}^+8$ by putting $^+6 - {}^+8 = \Box$ and rewriting the equation as $^+6 = \Box + {}^+8$. Thus $^+6 - {}^+8$ may be regarded as the movement needed after a move of $^+8$ (which is to the right of zero on the number line) to yield a result equivalent to a movement of $^+6$ from zero, that is $^-2$.

These ideas are very difficult for third-grade pupils. Some will carry out the kind of examples we have indicated in rote fashion, and a few will have an intuitive insight into what they are doing. Piaget's work, together with all subsequent experimentation, suggests that it will be adolescence before the pupil can formally elaborate the concept of the set of integers. That is to say, the ordinary pupil will be around fourteen or fifteen years old before he can formally grasp that there is a set of integers (. . . $^-2$, $^-1$, 0, $^+1$, $^+2$, . . .) in which for every integer there corresponds another such that their sum is zero, and that the subset of positive integers is isomorphic to the set of natural numbers. We shall understand the young child better, and be more sympathetic in regard to his difficulties, if we keep these points in mind. Often the teacher of young children is laying a foundation, and the results of this labor, in the form of pupils' understanding, may come years later. Teachers themselves will, of course, appreciate that integers are needed basically to solve equations of the type $x + a = b$, where $a$ and $b$ are natural numbers, and to make available a solution for any pair of natural numbers.

## CLOCK ARITHMETIC

In Chapter 3 it was suggested that subtraction should be introduced by an intelligent trial-and-error approach, with emphasis on the idea

*Further Work on Number* 139

that the difference between two numbers is the number which has to be added to the second number to obtain the first. To foster this idea, teachers may find clock arithmetic (systems with a limited number of members) helpful. Consider the set of counting numbers 0, 1, 2, 3, 4, 5, the table given in Figure 71a, and the "clock face" given in Figure 71b.

| + | 0 | 1 | 2 | 3 | 4 | 5 |
|---|---|---|---|---|---|---|
| 0 | 0 | 1 | 2 | 3 | 4 | 5 |
| 1 | 1 | 2 | 3 | 4 | 5 | 0 |
| 2 | 2 | 3 | 4 | 5 | 0 | 1 |
| 3 | 3 | 4 | 5 | 0 | 1 | 2 |
| 4 | 4 | 5 | 0 | 1 | 2 | 3 |
| 5 | 5 | 0 | 1 | 2 | 3 | 4 |

(a)

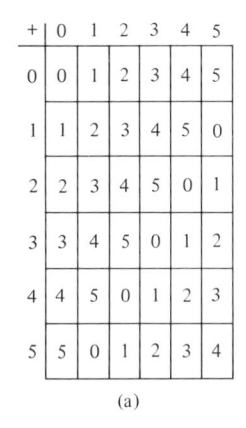

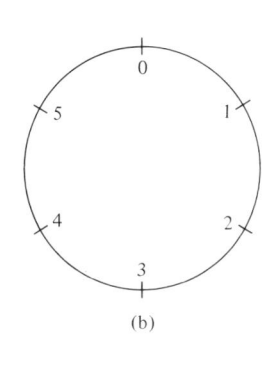

(b)

FIGURE 71

By studying the table or clock the child can be shown that, on adding in hours, the statement $3 + \square = 2$ has just one solution, namely 5. Similarly the pupil can establish that if instead of 3 and 2, any other numbers are selected from the set of counting numbers 0, 1, 2, 3, 4, 5, there is, in each instance, just one solution. He obtains this solution, of course, by finding out what number has to be added on to, say, the 3 to yield 2. This process of finding solutions by adding on is, as we saw earlier, another way of looking at subtraction. By examining the table or clock the child can establish for himself that, in this instance, $3 + 3 = 0$ (finding the additive inverse). He can now find the number to be put in the placeholder in the statement $3 + \square = 2$ in another way. If he adds 3 to $3 + \square$ he obtains $3 + 3 + \square = 2 + 3$, or $\square = 2 + 3$ since $3 + 3 = 0$. This kind of example must be repeated using different numbers within the set 0, 1, 2, 3, 4, 5, and with different sets of numbers.

This process of adding on the additive inverse is what we call subtraction, and is usually indicated by the "—" sign. Thus $4 - 2$ is the instruction to find the additive inverse of 2 and add it to 4. The additive inverse of 2, within the set of numbers 0, 1, 2, 3, 4, 5 is 4, and $4 + 4 = 2$. Thus $4 - 2 = 2$. Similarly $2 - 4$ is the instruction to add the additive inverse of 4 to 2. The additive inverse of 4 is 2, and $2 + 2 = 4$ so $2 - 4 = 4$. Through working many such examples involving different sets of the natural numbers, some pupils may see that there is a similarity between the process involved here and the removal of a subset of physical objects, or "take away" from a set initially containing more. Moreover children may realize that the additive inverse can be found, and subtraction carried out, in *all* instances; even in examples such as $2 - 4$ that have no link with the removal of a physical set. To carry out the operations discussed here and to have an intuitive grasp of subtraction in this sense requires flexible concrete operational thought.

## PROPERTIES OF THE SET OF NATURAL NUMBERS

Readers will appreciate that mathematicians have found certain properties of the set of natural numbers (themselves the properties of physical sets) to be so fundamental that they have chosen these properties to be the defining properties of a number system. Both addition and multiplication of natural numbers are closed, commutative, and associative, and multiplication distributes over addition. In the case of the natural numbers there are also the identity element properties, although these, unlike closure, commutativity, associativity, and distributivity, are not essential for a number system. In a moment we shall discuss the properties of the natural numbers in a little detail, but it must be emphasized, in advance, that the former will become explicit only after discussion between teacher and child and perhaps between children themselves, and as a result of much experience with physical sets and subsequent recordings. It is extremely important that the child come to understand these properties, for they are used to explain methods of computing with numerals for natural numbers.

To illustrate this point, consider the product of 32 and 3. The child may record the computation as

$$\begin{array}{r} 32 \\ \times\, 3 \\ \hline 96 \end{array}$$

but the process depends upon the commutative, distributive, and associative properties of natural numbers. Thus:

$$\begin{aligned}
32 \times 3 &= 3 \times 32 &&\text{(commutative property)} \\
&= 3 \times [(3 \times 10) + 2] \\
&= 3 \times (3 \times 10) + 3 \times 2 &&\text{(distributive property)} \\
&= (3 \times 3) \times 10 + 6 &&\text{(associative property)} \\
&= 9 \times 10 + 6 = 96
\end{aligned}$$

*Further Work on Number* 141

Again it is impossible for children to understand the processes involved in the multiplication and division of the rational numbers without having a grasp of these properties. In the case of the division of rational numbers, children have to learn a rote trick such as "turn the divisor upside down and multiply." Finally, an understanding of these properties gives the pupil, later on in high school or college, an understanding of the defining properties of an abstract number system. Indeed the importance of these properties of the set of natural numbers cannot be overemphasized. We now discuss each of these in turn.

## Closure

The child finds through numerous examples involving sets of physical objects that the image of, say, 3, 2 or 7, 1, and so forth, under the operation of addition or multiplication, is itself a number. This is normally understood by seven- to eight-year-olds.

## Identity

By around eight years of age pupils can, in situations involving actual objects, grasp that under the operation of addition $a + 0 = a$, and under the operation of multiplication $a \times 1 = a$, using, of course, examples involving numbers and not letters. This understanding comes rather earlier in addition than multiplication. Pupils must then have experience of working examples of the type:

$$6 + \square = 6; \quad \square + 5 = 5; \quad 9 + 0 = \square$$
$$\text{also } 8 \times \square = 8; \quad \square \times 3 = 3; \quad 2 \times 1 = \square$$

## Commutativity

Through partitioning a set of objects in different ways—say, a set of nine objects into a subset of four and a subset of 5—the child will become aware that in addition the order in which the numbers occur does not matter; that is, addition has a commutative property. He can also establish the property in multiplication by laying out, say, four rows each of five objects and rearranging the array as five rows each of four objects. Pupils should also have experience of working examples of the type:

$$9 + 3 = \square + 9; \quad \square + 5 = 5 + 4$$
$$7 \times \square = 6 \times 7; \quad 8 \times 2 = 2 \times \square$$

## Associativity

The pupil can set up, say, three rods each of different length and color (Figure 72) and immediately underneath set up replicas of the

| 3 units | 2 units | 5 units |
|---|---|---|

| 2 units | 5 units | 3 units |
|---|---|---|

FIGURE 72

same rods but with the order changed. The child can satisfy himself that the ends of the series of rods are in alignment. From this type of activity (sets of colored counters of, say, two, five, and three members placed end to end and touching one another can similarly be used) the child can establish that addition is associative. Putting the example into written form, we can put brackets around the 2 and 5 to indicate that we must first find the image of these. Thus $(2 + 5) + 3 = 7 + 3 = 10$. On the other hand, if we first find the image of 3 and 2, we have $(3 + 2) + 5 = 5 + 5 = 10$. Thus $(2 + 5) + 3 = (3 + 2) + 5$. Having made the discovery using materials that when numbers are added it does not matter which two are added first, the parentheses can be dropped.

To demonstrate the associative property of multiplication, the child can build a block of dimensions, say, $4 \times 3 \times 2$ unit cubes. He can first find the number of cubes showing on one face of dimensions, say, $4 \times 3$ units, and then multiply 12 by 2 to give the total number of cubes. Similarly he can calculate the number of cubes showing on the face of dimensions $4 \times 2$ units, and multiply 8 by 3 to yield the total number of cubes. Similarly he can calculate the number of cubes showing on the face of dimensions $3 \times 2$ units, and multiply 6 by 4 to yield the total number of cubes.

Pupils need opportunities to work, among others, examples of the following types:

$$9 + 3 + 2 = \Box + 9 + 2 \qquad \Box + 7 + 1 = 1 + 5 + 7$$
$$4 \times 6 \times 8 = 6 \times \Box \times 4 \qquad 9 \times \Box \times 3 = 2 \times 3 \times 9$$

## Multiplication Distribution over Addition

To demonstrate this property, recourse can usefully be made to colored rods once more. Consider the example $3(2 + 4)$. Rods to illus-

*Further Work on Number*  143

trate the operations involved can be laid out either as in Figure 73a or 73b. In either layout the child can satisfy himself that $3(2 + 4) = 3(6)$

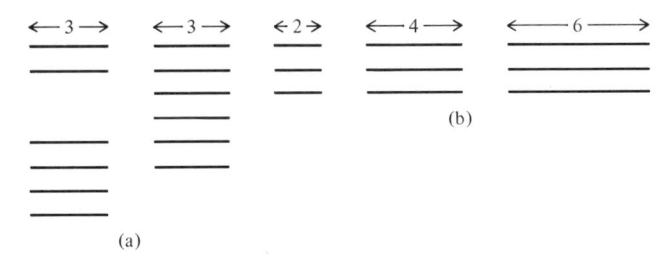

FIGURE 73

$= 18$. In order to illustrate, say, that $(3 \times 2) + (5 \times 2) = 8 \times 2$ the rods may be laid out as in Figure 74a and 74b.

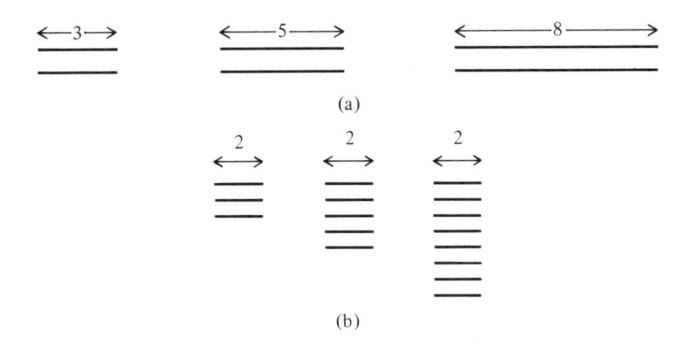

FIGURE 74

To revert to the first example, $3(2 + 4)$, the child can find the image of 2 and 4 under the operation of addition, and then the image of 3 and 6 under the operation of multiplication. He can also find the image of 2 and 3 under the operation of multiplication, the image of 4 and 3 similarly, and the image of the outcomes under the operation of addition.

Pupils need to work, among others, examples of the following types:

$$(5 \times 6) + (5 \times 3) = 5 \times \Box$$
$$(3 + \Box) + (3 \times 3) = 3 \times 13$$
$$(\Box \times 7) + (16 \times 2) = 9 \times 16$$
$$(15 \times 6) + (15 \times 5) = \Box \times 11$$
$$(\Box \times 2) + (\Box \times 5) = 8 \times 7$$

Brown (1969) has shown something of the growth of the child's understanding of the properties of the natural numbers. He has also indicated that the presentation of nonexamples of these properties, along with examples, is a good test of a pupil's understanding of the properties, for he can then spot the nonexample. Thus in working examples of identity, commutativity, associativity, and distributivity respectively, exercises such as those indicated below should be included:

$1 + \square = 5, 4 \times \square = 8$ (nonexamples of identity)
$\square + 5 = 8 + 1, \square \times 2 = 4 \times 4$ (nonexamples of commutativity)
$5 + 3 + \square = 2 + 4 + 6$
$3 \times 2 \times 1 = 1 \times 5 \times \square$ (nonexamples of associativity)
$(10 \times 4) + (\square \times 7) = 9 \times 6$ (nonexample of distributivity)

These nonexamples should be interspersed with the examples of the appropriate property. After working both types of exercise the child can be questioned as to which did not show the property in question.

Pupils should, of course, also be given the opportunity to establish that, for example:

$$10 - 3 \neq 3 - 10, 10 \div 5 \neq 5 \div 10$$
$$(8 - 3) - 1 = 5 - 1 = 4, \text{ but } 8 - (3 - 1) = 8 - 2 = 6$$
$$(9 + 6) \div 3 = 15 \div 3 = 5$$
$$(9 + 6) \div 3 = (9 \div 3) + (6 \div 3) = 3 + 2 = 5$$
$$\text{but } 20 \div (2 + 3) \neq (20 \div 2) + (20 \div 3)$$

We have already indicated that the property of closure is generally understood by seven to eight years of age and that of identity by eight. Brown's work also suggests that commutativity and associativity are understood by eight to nine years of age with the property being understood somewhat earlier in the case of addition than in the case of multiplication. On the other hand, his work clearly suggests that distributivity is understood by few children of average ability under ten years of age. Again an understanding of these properties comes earlier using physical apparatus than in written form.

## FRACTIONS

There is general agreement that fractions should be introduced to children as parts of a whole, using, say, piece of string, piece of paper, round of plasticine. In everyday life the terms "half of," "quarter of" are certainly a part of their vocabulary. Nevertheless it is necessary for the teacher to remember that the construction of part-whole relation-

## Further Work on Number

ships is a slow business, as Piaget, Inhelder, and Szeminska (1960) have indicated. The use of a verbal term does not always indicate that the term is understood.

To illustrate this construction give to the child a "cake" of plasticine. He is told that two dolls present are "going to eat up the cake but each has to have exactly the same as the other" and asked to cut the cake accordingly. Around four to four and a half years of age, there is often general fragmentation of the cake with many more than two pieces cut; or each doll gets only a small slice, leaving a large part of the cake undivided; or the cake is shared out in unequal proportions.

At the next stage the problem of dichotomy is solved when the wholes are small, but when the whole is larger the task is more difficult. Subjects have difficulty, too, in carrying out two successive dichotomies, that is, division of the whole into quarters. At this stage cutting a round "cake" into three parts is very difficult: some subjects cut three little slices, leaving a large part of the cake undivided, while others carry out two dichotomies and leave out the last quarter. Trisecting a paper rectangle is somewhat easier, but the trisection of a square remains difficult and, in keeping with the trisection of the cake, the trisection of a paper circle is very hard. Moreover children at this stage do not realize that the sum of the parts must equal the whole.

During the following stage dichotomy is always resolved, and trichotomy gradually resolved. But the conservation of the whole is still only realized intuitively and not operationally.

The final stage can be subdivided. In the first part trichotomy is carried out by means of an anticipatory plan, and there is an *a priori* understanding of the relationships between the fractions to be realized and the original whole. There is also operational conservation of the whole, that is, the sum of the parts being equal to the whole is understood as a necessary relation.

Fractions can be introduced as parts of a whole in innumerable ways, using either apparatus constructed by the teacher or purchased. Of particular value, perhaps, is the fraction board (Figure 75) although valuable work can be done in connection with fractions using paper-folding and tearing. While fractions may be introduced very informally in Grade 2, the use of the fraction board is perhaps best left until Grade 3. Pupils also need much practice in shading halves, quarters, thirds, or eighths of shapes which can be partitioned in "regular" patterns so that the fractions can be easily seen as such. They also need to investigate families of fractions such as 1/3, 2/6, 3/9.

Having introduced fractions as parts of wholes, we can also help children to look at fractions as sub-units. For example, the fractions

1/2, 1/4, 3/4, and so on, can signify subunits for measuring purposes applied to, say, lengths, weights, capacities. While the pupil begins with

|  |  |  |  |  | 8/8 or 1 |  |  |  |
|---|---|---|---|---|---|---|---|---|
|  |  |  | 4/8 or 1/2 |  |  |  |  |  |
| 2/8 or 1/4 |  |  |  |  |  |  |  |  |
| 1/8 | 1/8 | 1/8 | 1/8 | 1/8 | 1/8 | 1/8 | 1/8 |

FIGURE 75

whole units (as the foot or the meter) he soon finds that the quantity to be measured is comprised of a number of whole units but that there are also a number of "bits and pieces" left over. So we explain to the child that man came to use subunits, that is, he divided the units into, say, halves, quarters, eighths, tenths, and so forth. Again, as there are often a number of these subunits left over, man came to write three quarters as 3/4, five eighths as 5/8, and so on. The top number tells us the number of parts and the bottom the kinds of parts. To begin with, children need much experience in measurement and recording involving halves, quarters, and thirds. In respect of the measurement of length they need, at first, simplified rulers which are marked in half- and quarter-inches, or centimeters and half-centimeters. Later children can measure in eighths or tenths of an inch, or tenths of a centimeter, although many school educable retarded pupils find great difficulty in doing this even in adolescence. When recording in tenths, it is useful to introduce a new method of recording illustrated in Figure 76. This provides an obvious lead-in to decimal notation.

| 100 | 10 | 1 |  | 1/10 |
|---|---|---|---|---|
|  |  | 3 | • | 2 |
|  | 1 | 5 | • | 7 |

FIGURE 76

While pupils look upon fractions as parts of a whole or as subunits, the operations of addition, subtraction, multiplication, and division as such applied to fractions are best omitted. It is better to find, say, 1/2

*Further Work on Number* 147

of 1/2 of one foot than try to teach children to multiply 1/2 by 1/2. Finding fractional amounts of a whole number of units is also valuable; for example, 3/4 of twelve inches. If we attempt to teach the four operations applied to fractions at this stage, we are likely to give the child a series of "tricks." Later when the child has some intuitive grasp of the set of positive rational numbers and can appreciate the properties of the natural numbers, then the four operations as applied to fractions can be approached with some understanding. Indeed in this book no attempt will be made to treat the addition, subtraction, multiplication, and division of fractions or mixed numbers, although below we do indicate, briefly, how pupils in Grade 3 may be introduced, informally, to rational numbers.

## RATIONAL NUMBERS

Readers will appreciate that it took man a long time to divorce fractions from parts of rational numbers, and look upon them as pure numbers. Teachers may wish to introduce rational numbers, very informally, to selected pupils in Grade 3. It is suggested that this may be done using the number line, although children in this grade—and indeed most pupils for many more grades—will only have an intuitive grasp of such numbers.

Figure 77 represents part of a number line. Some points on the line represent whole numbers, others indicate fractional or rational numbers. In informal discussion a pupil can be shown:

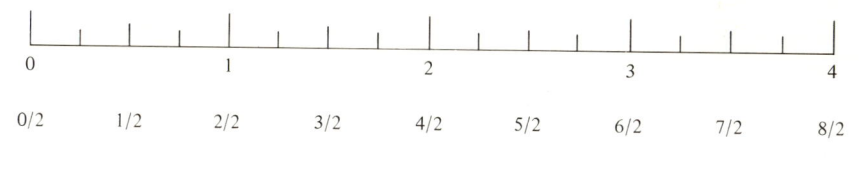

|   |   |   |   |   |   |   |   |   |
|---|---|---|---|---|---|---|---|---|
| 0 | 1 | 2 | 3 | 4 |
| 0/2 | 1/2 | 2/2 | 3/2 | 4/2 | 5/2 | 6/2 | 7/2 | 8/2 |
| 0/4 1/4 | 2/4 3/4 | 4/4 5/4 | 6/4 7/4 | 8/4 9/4 | 10/4 11/4 | 12/4 13/4 | 14/4 15/4 | 16/4 |

FIGURE 77

1. That a whole or natural number can also be expressed as a fractional or rational number. (The fraction board is also a help in this connection.)
2. The set of natural numbers is a subset of the set of rational numbers.
3. A rational number can be thought of as an ordered pair of numbers (that is, order is important) in which the second number is

never zero. (Expressed formally as $a/b$ with $b \neq 0$.) Rational numbers are, of course, needed to solve equations of the type $bn = a$, in which $a$ and $b$ are integers and $b \neq 0$.

It will take pupils a long time to regard fractions as a pair of ordered numbers; even Grade 6 pupils will, in the majority of cases, still understand this in an intuitive concrete manner.

Using the number line, we can also demonstrate:

1. The order of points on the number line is the same as the order for the natural or whole numbers. Earlier we saw that in the case of the natural numbers, "to the left of" can be thought of as corresponding to the relation "less than," since as we move to the left the numbers represented by the line become smaller. The Grade 3 pupil can see that the relation "to the left of" still corresponds to the relation "less than" in the case of rational numbers.
2. Every natural number has a successor; for example, the successor of 9 is 10. On the other hand, a rational number has no immediate successor; for example, if 3/4 is a rational number next to 1/2, then their average is 5/8, which is itself a rational number nearer to 1/2 than 3/4 is. Thus the assumption that 3/4 is the rational number next to 1/2 is incorrect.
3. Because of the point just made, the members of the set of rational numbers are close together, or the set is said to be dense. So, unlike the natural numbers, they have a density property. The selected Grade 3 pupil will grasp intuitively that the members of the set of rational numbers are very close together on the number line and that by making the bottom numbers larger (making the fraction smaller) we can insert more and more numbers.

In conclusion, I wish to repeat that this discussion with selected pupils proceeds informally. Here, as elsewhere in mathematics, the teacher is planting an idea, the results of which will not be fully evident until years later.

## SOME NUMBER PATTERNS

It was pointed out in Chapter 1 that mathematics is the study of structure or of systematic patterns of relationships. The importance of the

*Further Work on Number* 149

teacher making children aware of relationships whenever possible cannot be overemphasized. Thus to conclude this chapter we look at a very few number patterns suitable for study by pupils in the age range considered in this book. It is hoped, of course, that readers will introduce children to many more activities of the kind considered here. In all such activities there is a need for informal discussion followed by recording, and only when correct ideas have been established by pupils should the relevant technical terms be employed. Thus the child should:

1. Lay out, say, rectangular blocks as in Figure 78, thus leading to the idea of triangular numbers.

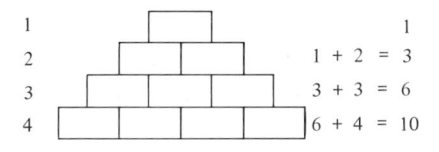

   1
   2
   3
   4

   1
   1 + 2 = 3
   3 + 3 = 6
   6 + 4 = 10

   FIGURE 78

2. Draw a number square of side, say, 5 and select:
   a. sequences of numbers which differ by 2, by 3, by 4, by 5, by 6;
   b. sequences of odd numbers, and of even numbers;
   c. squared[1] numbers, such as $2^2, 3^2, 4^2, 5^2$;
   d. rectangular numbers, such as 4, 6, 8, 12, 14, 15, and so on, which are comprised of factors.
   
   The exercise can be repeated with a 10 square.
3. Construct mappings of multiples of 3, 4, and so on, using two number lines as indicated in Chapter 6.
4. Establish that:
   a. the sum of an odd or even number of even numbers yields an even number. Thus $2 + 4 = 6$; $4 + 12 + 8 = 24$;
   b. the sum of an odd number of odd numbers yields an even number, and the sum of an even number of odd numbers yields an even number. For example: $3 + 7 + 1 + 13 = 24$; $9 + 11 + 5 = 25$.
5. Find, using counters or other suitable objects, that if we commence with 1, add the next odd number, 3, and to the total add the next odd number, and so on, a square number is always obtained (Figure 79).

[1] The pupil has to be introduced to the notation of $2^2$ indicating $2 \times 2$, $5^2$ indicating $5 \times 5$, and so on.

6. Have his attention drawn by the teacher to the fact that certain products have only two ordered pairs of factors. In this way the

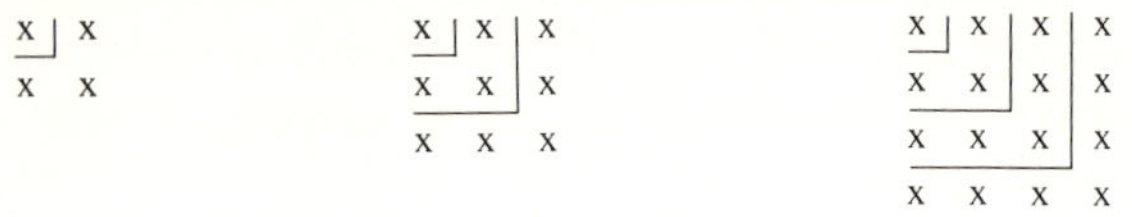

```
x | x          x | x | x          x | x | x | x
x   x          x   x | x          x   x | x | x
               x   x   x          x   x   x | x
                                  x   x   x   x
```

$1 + 3 = 4$      $1 + 3 + 5 = 9$      $1 + 3 + 5 + 7 = 16$

    $= 2^2$               $= 3^2$                    $= 4^2$

FIGURE 79

child can be introduced to the idea of *primes*. From his experience of mapping under the rule "is the product of," he will be able to write down the following products[2] and related ordered pairs of factors:

1. (1,1)
2. (2,1) (1,2)
3. (1,3) (3,1)
4. (1,4) (2,2) (4,1)
5. (1,5) (5,1)
6. (1,6) (2,3) (3,2) (6,1)
7. (1,7) (7,1)
8. (1,8) (2,4) (4,2) (8,1)

It will become apparent to the pupil that certain products have only two ordered pairs of factors. In the above list of products these are 2, 3, 5, and 7; these and other numbers which have only two ordered pairs of factors are, of course, known as primes. The child can see, with small numbers, that factoring into primes is unique whereas other factorings are not. Thus the factors of 17 are (17,1) and (1,17), whereas the factors of 18 are (6,3), (3,6), (9,2), (2,9), (18,1) and (1,18).

Prime numbers between, say, 1 and 100 can be found using the Sieve of Eratosthenes—a piece of apparatus which children find much enjoyment in using. A large piece of flannelboard can be hung at some convenient place on the wall, and onto the flannelboard are attached all the numbers from 2 to 100 in sequence. Since 2 is a prime number, it is left; but the child removes all multiples of 2. The next prime is 3; that is un-

[2] Only the products 1 to 8 are given here as illustrative. The child may well work with products of 12, 15, or higher.

*Further Work on Number* 151

touched, but all multiples of 3 are removed. Since 4 has already gone, the next prime is 5; that stays in position, but all multiples of 5 are taken down. Number 6 has already been removed, so the pupil has now only to leave 7 in position and remove all multiples of 7. The pupil should, of course, be questioned as to why it is unnecessary to go beyond multiples of 7. The numbers can be placed in position again, and the apparatus is ready for the next child or small group of children to work with.

One direct result of having established some understanding of prime numbers is that the child can tell at once and without finding the products that $3 \times 5 \times 9$ is not equal to $2 \times 7 \times 11$. On the other hand, one has to work out the product of $6 \times 14 \times 9$ and the product of $4 \times 18 \times 9$ to establish if the products are the same.

7. Establish (with aid of teacher) that:

$$1^2 + 2 \times 1 + 1 = 4$$
$$2^2 + 2 \times 2 + 1 = 9$$

and explore similar patterns, the child knowing to make clear his findings. This work can be aided by pegs, counters, or other suitable material as illustrated in Figure 80.

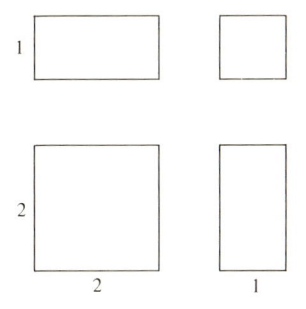

FIGURE 80

# 8
# Pictorial Representation

It was shown in Chapter 4 that a child builds up a frame of reference enabling him to "see" objects within a Euclidean grid of horizontal and vertical coordinates. Piaget asserts that the child is unable to locate a point in two- (or three-) dimensional space until such a coordinate system is elaborated. Accordingly this chapter will open with a discussion of the development of the child's ability to locate a point in two-dimensional space. This ability underlies much pictorial representation in mathematics and science.

Piaget, Inhelder, and Szeminska (1960) provide an interesting task which enables us to study this development. In essence the child is given two rectangular sheets of plain white paper measuring approximately fifteen inches by twelve inches. The first, $P_1$, is placed at the top right corner of a piece of hardboard, and a second sheet of the same size but of plain semitransparent paper, $P_2$, is placed at the bottom left corner of the sheet of hardboard, as indicated in Figure 81.

The distance between the corners nearest to one another is about eight inches. On the sheet $P_1$ a red dot is drawn about halfway between the center of the sheet and its top right corner. The child is asked to draw a dot $D_2$ on the other sheet in exactly the same position on the lower sheet as dot $D_1$ is on the upper sheet, so that if the lower sheet is superimposed on the top one, $D_2$ would fall on $D_1$. Since sheet $P_2$ is semitransparent, the coincidence of the dots can be confirmed by placing the lower sheet over the upper sheet. A ruler, strips of cardboard, and lengths of string are provided. If necessary, it is suggested to the child that he use them, but he is not shown how to do so.

Three broad stages can be found in the children's attempts to solve this problem. Up to five or six years of age, the point $D_2$ is located by

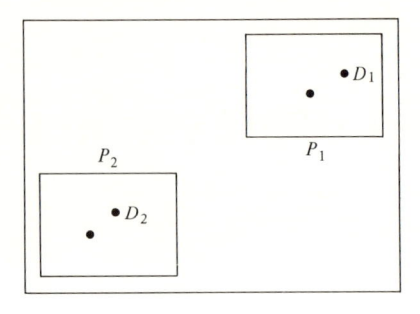

FIGURE 81

visual estimate. However, sometimes it is drawn on the wrong side of the center of $P_2$. On placing $P_2$ over $P_1$ the child sees his error, but he fails to realize the necessity of measurement. If he uses the ruler or lengths of string, it is only as an aid to perception and not as a means of measuring. In the second stage the pupil begins to realize the need for measurement, although only linear measurement is possible for him. Starting from the top right corner of $P_1$ he will place the ruler in position, make some estimate of the inclination of the ruler to the horizontal, and attempt to maintain this inclination as he carries his ruler across to $P_2$. The child now has some awareness that two dimensions are involved, but, as stated above, measurement remains linear.

At the beginning of the third stage, there is an increasing realization of the importance of the angle of inclination, and also slow decomposition of the inclination into two separate measurements. But there is still much trial and error behavior. For example, the child may attempt to draw horizontal and vertical lines to position $D_2$, or to take into consideration one of the sides of the sheet and an oblique line at the same time. By the end of the stage, however, the pupil measures the height of the point above the base of the sheet and its distance from a side, and the measurements are coordinated at once. Also, he can explain what he is doing. In my experience there is much variation in the age at which pupils pass through stage three. Some children reach the early part by six years of age, others much later; many pupils only complete the stage by the eighth or ninth year.

*Pictorial Representation* 155

## THE MATHEMATICAL VALUE
## OF PICTORIAL REPRESENTATION

The mathematical value of pictorial representation in the age range considered here is great. First, it provides children with experience in collecting and sorting data prior to representing the data in graphical form. Such data may range from the number of boys and girls in the class at any one moment to the air temperatures over a period of one month. Second, it provides a visual means of portraying mathematical relationships; some children may see relationships in this way which might escape their grasp if presented in other ways. Since mathematics is essentially the study of systematic patterns of relationships, any activity which helps pupils to recognize relations is to be welcomed. Third, and because of the point just made, pictorial representation gives many opportunities to discuss the relationships displayed and to use the appropriate vocabulary—for example, "is less than," "is warmer than," "takes more time than."

A fourth point is that graphical representation can be linked with mapping, as we saw in Chapter 6. Thus suppose that Jack, Fred, and May go to Mexico, Karen to Alaska, and Susan and Tom to Canada. These movements can be represented in two ways (Figures 82a and 82b). The relationship between members of one set and those of another (or between members of the same set) is so important a notion that it seems likely to be of help to pupils if the relationship is recorded in as many ways as possible.

Fifth, pictorial representation provides an opportunity for the teacher to discuss with pupils the difference between continuous and discontinuous variables. Thus in Figure 82c the data of Figures 82a and 82b are put as a frequency diagram. Three children went to Mexico and one to Alaska, but there is no continuity between Mexico and Alaska, and we cannot meaningfully join the points of the graph. On the other hand, if we take the air temperature (in the shade) at 0800 hours and find that it is 67° F, and again at 1200 hours and find that it is 79° F, we know that the change of temperature with time is continuous. If therefore a plot was made of temperature against time, it would be in order to join the points. This example also raises the question of whether points should be joined with straight lines or whether as smooth a curve as possible should be drawn to connect them. Naturally the discussion around these issues must be in language the children can understand.

The collection of data for graphical representation permits the suggestion of a sixth value for graphical work. It draws attention to the distinction between measures that can be ascertained precisely in everyday life and those that cannot. For example, the pupil can count the number

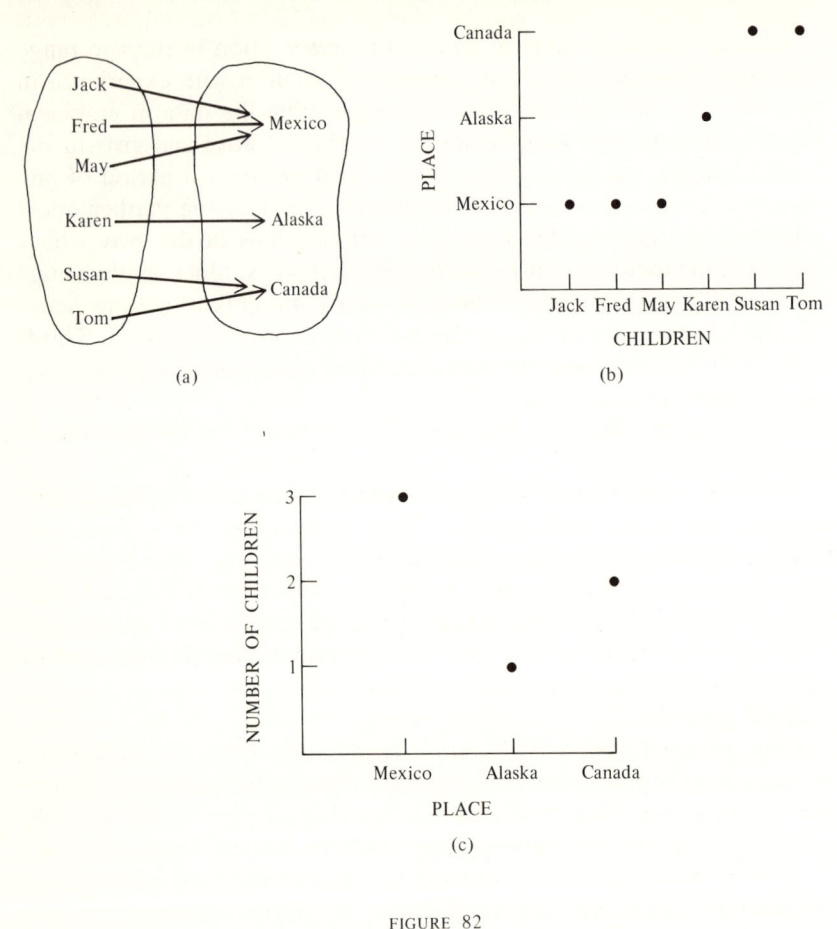

FIGURE 82

of objects precisely and record these on a graph. But when we weigh a child on a pair of scales to the nearest pound, and find the reading is 70 pounds, we only know that this figure lies somewhere between $69\frac{1}{2}$ and $70\frac{1}{2}$ pounds.

Seventh, the graphical representation of data takes different forms according to the nature of the data collected. Some data yield a symmetrical form. These different forms should be discussed with pupils, since the symmetrical form in particular is of such importance in later work in mathematics.

# Pictorial Representation

Finally, the ability to interpret a graph is just as important as the ability to construct it, or even more so. Indeed it is vital for the citizens of today and tomorrow to be able to interpret pictorial representations of data and make inferences from them. As adults they will need to interpret graphs relating to, say, earnings, prices, employment, exports, population, and so forth, and the interpretation of graphs ("what they tell us") needs to be commenced at an early age.

Pictorial representation of mathematical data has, of course, other uses outside the age range considered here. But during the years which we are now concerned with, and later, discussion with individuals and with small groups of pupils is vital for both the construction and interpretation of graphical representation.

## SOME SUGGESTED STAGES IN PICTORIAL REPRESENTATION

It will be apparent from what has been said that we cannot suddenly introduce the kindergarten pupil to the line graph. We saw at the beginning of the chapter that the ability to locate a point in two-dimensional space is not possible for the majority of five-year-olds. Thus a beginning must be made with the collection of actual materials. For example, two pupils, working together, may each take a few handfuls of colored cubes, counters, or other suitable objects from a box. After counting up, say, all the yellow ones taken, it could be that Jack has five such cubes and Tom has two. These cubes are then placed vertically or horizontally as shown in Figures 83a and 83b respectively, so that each can see how many yellow ones were collected. In Figure 83a the table is used as a base, and in Figure 83b the edge of the table is used as a base line. Or one child may select a handful of colored objects, take out, say, the red ones and yellow ones collected, and place these either vertically from the top of the table or horizontally from an edge.

So far only two sets of data have been used. The work can now be extended by considering objects of a greater number of different colors and/or drawings of objects instead of objects themselves. Combining both progressions here, one could have a child select several handfuls of rings in, say, six colors. Those of each color are placed on dowel rods standing vertically, and the pupil makes a drawing (Figure 84) of the arrangement using a short horizontal line to represent each ring. The drawing is obviously much like the actual physical arrangement of objects with the short horizontal lines and rings being in one-to-one correspondence. Once a pictorial representation of data is made, a heading *must* be placed by the child to indicate the nature of the data

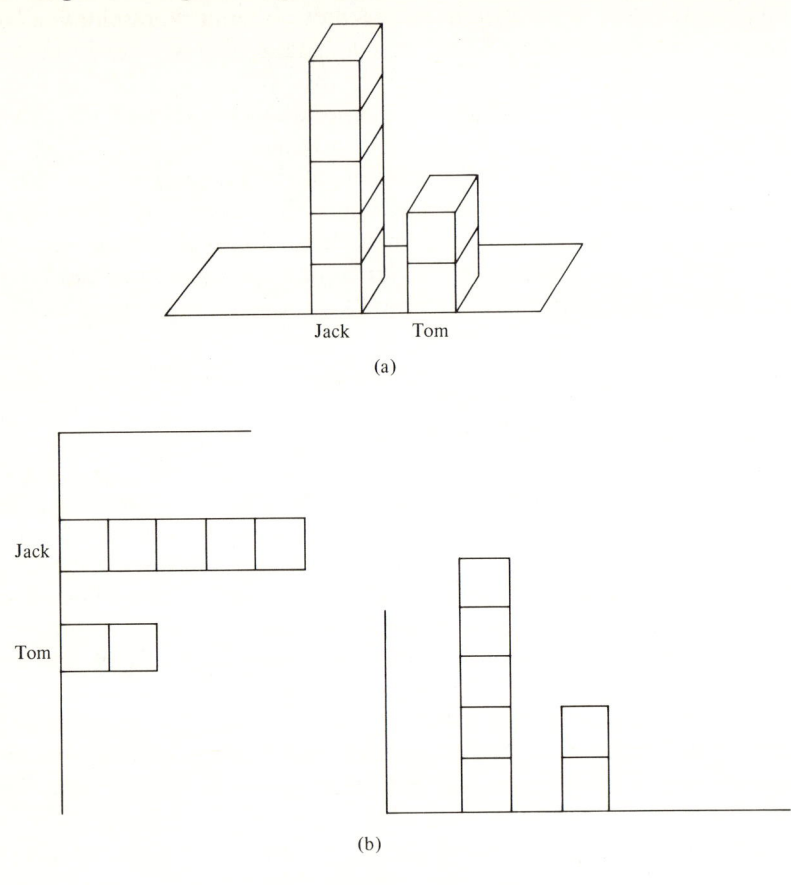

Jack    Tom
(a)

Jack

Tom

(b)

FIGURE 83

collected. In this case the heading might be "Drawing to show the numbers and colors of rings taken."

In each instance there must be ample discussion with the child to bring out the salient features of the data and its representation, as the understanding of these will depend to a considerable extent on such discussion. There will be ample opportunity to illustrate the appropriate use of relational terms like "more than," and instances where the terms "more," "less," "fewer" apply. Although the examples listed here have involved objects such as rings and cubes, the data collected could involve, say, numbers of leaves of different types, numbers of children

*Pictorial Representation* 159

with different colored eyes, numbers of children with different size shoes, or numbers of pets kept.

The next major step forward occurs when representation is made by

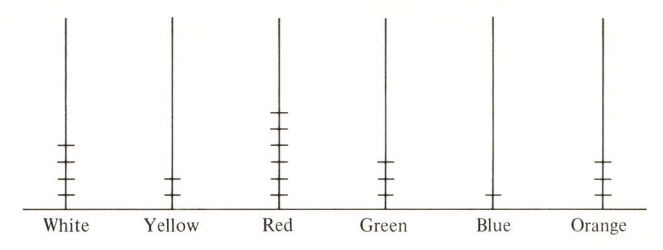

FIGURE 84

pictures or, say, colored squares of paper (the reverse side of which will adhere to other paper when moistened). The pictures or squares are both in one-to-one correspondence with the items of data collected, but in the latter instance the squares of colored paper do not look like the items. For example, a child may have collected data about the kinds of pets kept at home by boys and girls in the class. It could be that among the boys there were eight different kinds of pets kept but among the girls only five. This information could be recorded by means of squares of paper, as indicated in Figure 85. Much experience needs to

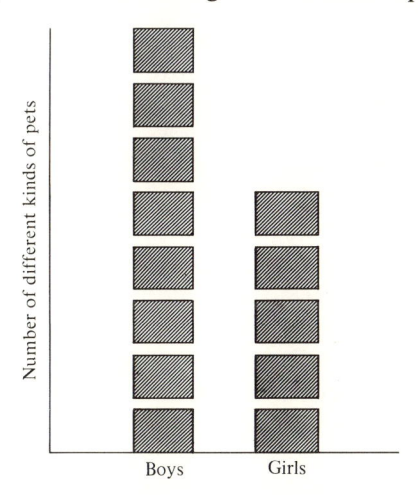

FIGURE 85

be given pupils using either squares of paper or through drawing some other symbol, and there should be no hurry in moving the child on to the use of squared paper. Moreover it might be best to keep to few values of the variable when use is first made of such paper. Thus a child might consider the scores at Ring Toss obtained by three pupils—Carl, Debbie, and himself. He indicates their scores by shading in the appropriate number of squares (Figure 86a).

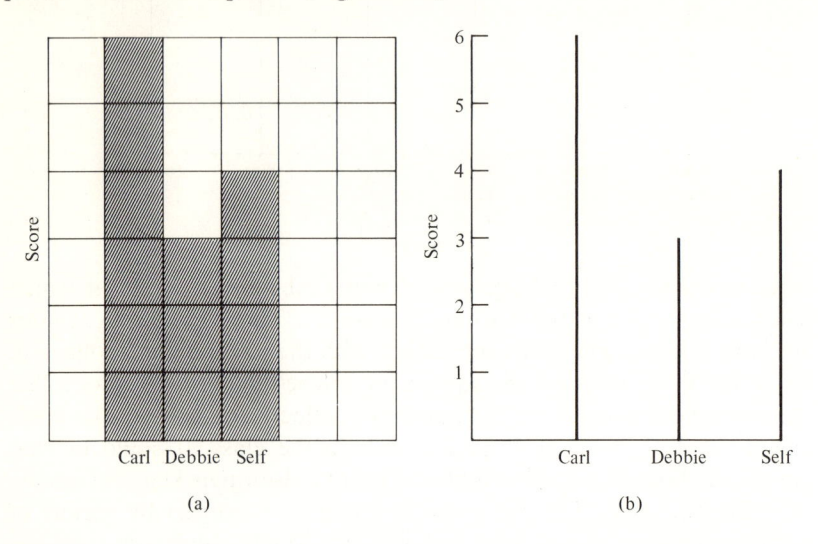

FIGURE 86

The third major stage involves a move towards more abstract representation. For example, vertical (or horizontal) lines can be drawn to indicate, say, the scores made at Ring Toss, so that the pictorial representation of Figure 86a would be replaced by that of Figure 86b. A development within this stage would be, say, the collection of heights or weights of pupils in the class, or the ascertainment of the outside temperature at hourly intervals from 0900 hours to 1500 hours one one day of a week. The temperature data could be recorded as in Figure 87a, where the vertical lines represent the lengths of the columns of mercury measuring temperature, or as in Figure 87b, where the tops of the vertical lines are replaced by small crosses.

The collection of these kinds of data brings the attention of the pupil to two issues. First, the horizontal or vertical scale need not begin at zero. Second, it raises the issue of continuous and discontinuous quantities. While it is very helpful to join the tops of the lines in Figure 87a and the crosses in Figure 87b by straight or curved lines (this might be a matter for further discussion), it would not be as useful to do so in other instances. Suppose, for example, one had plotted the outside air tem-

# Pictorial Representation

peratures at 1000 hours each day for a week. Joining the plots in this instance would tell us nothing about the temperature at, say 2200 hours

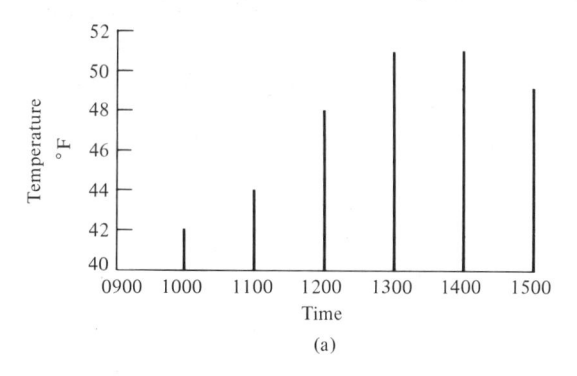

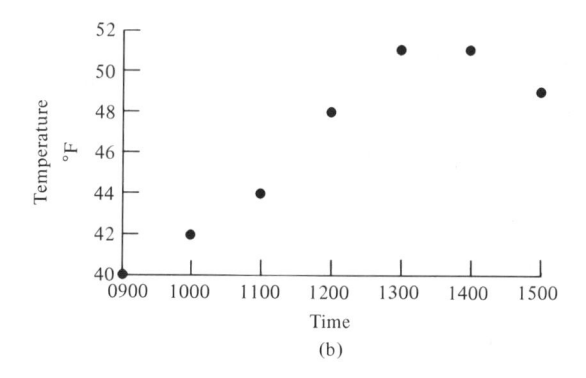

FIGURE 87

on any night but only how temperature changed at 1000 hours on successive days, whereas a joining of plots in Figure 87b does enable us to estimate the temperature at 0930 or 1115 hours. Similarly if we plot the heights of children, there is little value at this age in joining the points. Later on, of course, when a graph is made of the heights of large numbers of pupils, a joining of the points will show us how height is distributed among such pupils; this is very important when we are discussing, seriously, the shapes of distributions. As examples of continuous variables, pupils may usefully draw a graph of some of the multiplication tables. In all graphical work the teacher must suggest suitable data at first; later pupils should be encouraged to collect their own. Likewise the teacher must select the scale at first; later pupils choose their own.

So far the emphasis has been on the construction of graphs. But we are also concerned with their interpretation, which is as important as their construction. The pupil needs to be questioned about the information which can be obtained from the pictorial representation, especially that which is concerned with relationships between the variables, and the deductions, however simple, which can be made from the representation. Indeed it is an extremely useful exercise for pupils to write a paragraph or two in their exercise books indicating their main findings in the case of each graph they construct. For example, a third-grade pupil might write about the data represented in Figure 87 as follows:

"The temperature rose slowly until 1100 hours, and then it increased more quickly. After 1300 hours it did not rise much more, and the temperature began to fall after 1400 hours. The largest rise in any one hour was 4° F, and the difference between the highest and lowest temperatures we recorded was 9° F. This graph shows that the warmest time of the day was about 1300 hours or soon after."

While graphical exercises found in textbooks and on worksheets have their place with older pupils, the motivation and understanding of younger children demands that priority be given to data which they collect themselves.

In this chapter emphasis has been placed on the growth of children's understanding of the construction and interpretation of pictorial representation. No emphasis has been given to block graphs, line graphs, pic diagrams, and isotypes as such. Teachers will be aware that when pupils are using block graphs, it is the intervals on the axes with which pupils are concerned, whereas in constructing line graphs it is the points on the number line ($x$ or $y$ axis) which are relevant.

## SIMILARITIES AND PROPORTIONS IN GEOMETRIC FORM

There is now published evidence in both the U.K. and the U.S.A. to support general classroom experience that proportionality in nongeometric forms is not well understood until fourteen or fifteen years of age in pupils of average intellectual ability and around twelve years of age in very able ones. It is easier to study the growth of the concept of proportionality in geometric than in nongeometric forms, for long before the child can think about similar figures, he can directly perceive whether figures having certain dimensions show the relationship of similarity. Figures are, of course, mathematically similar if corresponding angles are of the same size and if corresponding sides of the two figures are in the same ratio. What we hope to be able to do is to help the

## Pictorial Representation

pupil to obtain an intuitive understanding of similarity in geometric form by providing appropriate activities. First, however, we turn to a brief discussion of the stages through which a child passes in understanding similarity.

Piaget and Inhelder (1956) have provided a number of experiments which enable us to study this growth of understanding similarity, only one of which will be mentioned here. The study is prefaced by the child being given a number of different rhombuses to be arranged in pairs having the same shape. One rhombus of each pair is clearly larger than the other member, and the shape of one pair is unmistakably different from that of another pair. When there is this marked difference in shape, it is easy for children of all ages to put them in pairs, and this helps them to grasp the point at issue. The pupil is then presented with a rectangle—say, one inch by one half inch—and is asked to draw a "box," "square," "rectangle," or whatever else he cares to call it, "the same but larger" on another sheet of paper. One can either avoid suggesting any particular size, *or* one can fix the length of the longer side at two, three, or four inches.

The following stages may be observed in the increase of understanding. Children under about five years of age seem unable to make anything of the task. In the second stage, the child's drawings tend to exaggerate the length of the rectangle he wishes to enlarge, because for him the essential of a rectangle is its elongated shape. If his drawing is put alongside an enlargement which is correctly proportioned, he thinks the latter is too high and may even wish to cut down its height. No attempt is made to measure, and although the rhombus could be correctly paired, the idea of similarity remains meaningless.

The third stage begins between seven and eight years of age. The pupil now begins to measure, but his drawings still exaggerate the length of the rectangle. If he is shown a series of larger rectangles, his perceptual estimates of similarity are in advance of his drawings, and the former appear to guide the latter. The child now centers alternately on length and width and appears to be trying to take into account both dimensions simultaneously and so arrive at a conscious comparison. In the latter part of this third stage—which may extend near to the end of the elementary school period—both length and height are increased in an effort to obtain the correct ratio, but an equal amount is added to each. Consequently he often finds his perceptual estimates at variance with the results of his calculations on which his drawing is based, and he may alter the drawing to suit his perceptual impression. Finally, at the end of the elementary school period or in high school, the pupil begins to recognize the tru nature of proportionality. Thought now influences perception rather than vice versa (as was the case earlier) and the enlarged similar rectangle can be accurately constructed.

The child begins to have an intuitive understanding of mathematical similarity even before he enters kindergarten. For example, the girl realizes that the dressed doll is something like herself and other little girls, and the boy appreciates that the toy automobile is something like the real ones on the streets as far as shape is concerned but not in size. And when in kindergarten pupils begin to work in clay or plasticine and try to model, say, animals, people, or fruits, they try to make these objects much like the real things in respect of shape. At this age the child has some vague intuitive grasp of similarity; adults need to take advantage of his keen delight in modeling and carefully point out the likenesses and differences between his construction and the real thing to maintain and develop this intuitive understanding. A comparison of the features of a doll's house with those of a real house is another useful exercise at this stage.

Late in kindergarten, and in Grade 1, new activities can be introduced. A set of nesting cubes provides a useful example of mathematical similarity, while the collection of, say, leaves or flowers of the same kind but different in size provides another opportunity to discuss similarities and differences. Again pupils in these age groups sometimes attempt to build "maps" of houses, streets, rivers, fields, and so forth, on the classroom floor. Bricks may represent, say, houses, and pupils may ask an older child or the teacher to draw in the streets by means of chalk lines. This type of spontaneous activity should be made use of, for here again we have a situation which embodies features of mathematical similarity, especially if the map represents well known features in the neighborhood of the school or home so that the features on the map and on the ground can be immediately compared. A little later a small group of pupils may wish to make a better map by taking a large sheet of paper and by painting in the main features (houses, roads, rivers) which they wish to represent.

In the case of second- and third-grade pupils, mathematical similarity can be introduced through rather more directed activities, although these should always be supplemented by suitable examples which occur in everyday life to reinforce the more structured activities. Thus a child may be provided with sets of triangles, rhombuses, and other polygons some of which are similar and some are not. He is asked, in respect of a shape of a given number of sides, to put together those that are alike in shape but not in size. Another very helpful activity involves the use of graph paper. The pupil draws a square on a side of one unit, making

*Pictorial Representation* 165

the bottom left corner the origin (Figure 88a). A square with two units on a side is then drawn, followed by one of three units on a side, and so

(a)

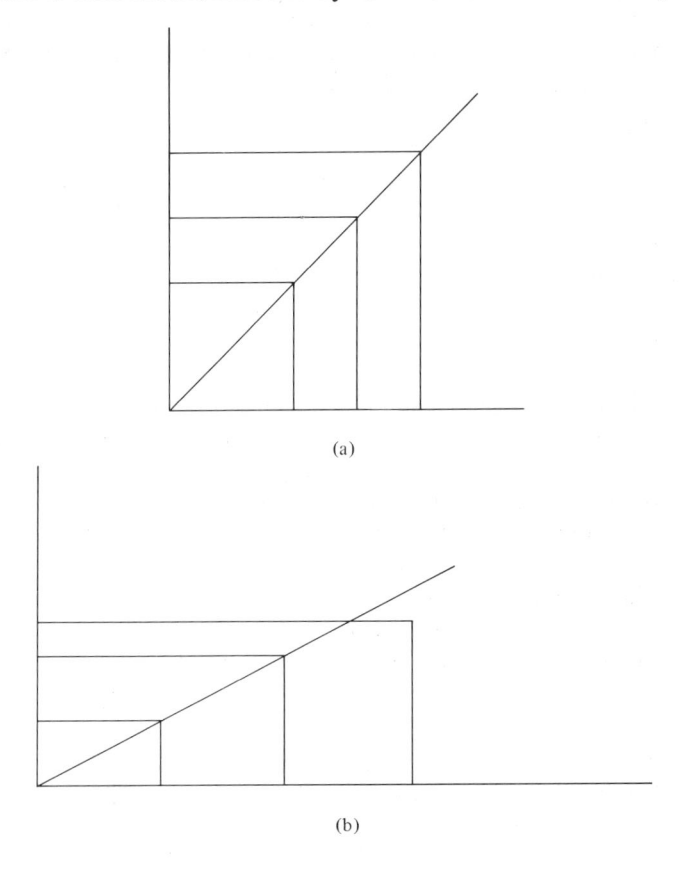

(b)

FIGURE 88

on, so that the bottom left corners of all the squares coincide. If a diagonal from the origin is drawn, this too helps to give the pupil an intuitive grasp that the squares are similar—that is, the squares are recognized as similar at the perceptual level.

The exercise can then be extended to the construction of rectangles as indicated in Figure 88b. The first rectangle can be, say, two units long and one unit high, the next four units long and two units high. But the child should also be instructed to draw a rectangle, say, six units long and two and a half units high. All rectangles are, of course, drawn with their bottom left corners at the same point. On drawing the diagonal to the first two rectangles from the origin, and producing this to cut the side of the nonsimilar rectangle, the child is again helped to recognize, intuitively, examples and nonexamples of similarity. From these and similar activities the child learns that the smaller rectangle (or square) is an exact replica, reduced in size, of the larger similar rectangle (or square).

The above type of exercise naturally leads into the topic of drawing to scale—a topic worthy of introduction to Grade 3 pupils. But at all times the child should decide on the scale he will use, after discussion with the teacher if necessary. Some suggestions for suitable activities, given in rough order of progression of difficulty are:

1. Given a line, say, eight or twelve inches in length, draw it to half scale.
2. Given a rectangle of suitable dimensions—say, twelve inches by six inches—draw it to half scale. This is called making a plan of the rectangle. In this and the previous exercise, the objects provided are of such dimensions that the scale to be chosen— one unit on the plan to represent two units on the object—makes the task relatively easy.
3. Make a plan of an exercise book to half scale. Now the pupil has to decide on the scale he will use.
4. Make a plan of a table top. Here a suitable scale may be one inch standing for one foot, but it is for the pupil to establish this.
5. Make a plan of part of the playground or school garden. In this activity 1/8 or 1/10 of an inch may be an appropriate scale. However, the drawing of lines to eights and tenths of an inch is a difficult task for some third-grade pupils.

In all these activities the notion of mathematical similarity will constantly be before the pupil, as it will when discussing, say, the photograph.

Children may then proceed to make simplified maps of the school grounds and of the district immediately around the school if the latter task is a suitable one. With selected pupils one may carry out the reverse task. They can be presented with simplified maps of the school or immediate environment, then measure the distance between two points on the ground, find the distance on the map between the representation of the two points, and so determine the scale used. The term *representative fraction* may be introduced.

# 9
# Weight, Mass, Time, and Volume

The setting up of correspondences, adding, multiplying, within systems of classes and relations, are regarded by Piaget as examples of logical operations. Compared with these he regards infralogical operations as those involving quantity, measurements, space, and time, for here we are dealing with entities whose contents are continuous in character and which depend upon spatio-temporal proximity. However, infralogical operations can be regarded as formally similar to logical ones, and they develop at about the same time, although, as we have just said, they have some attributes which are essentially different from those of logical operations. A number of mathematical ideas involving infralogical operations have already been discussed; a brief discussion of some others will follow. In my view, some (but not all) of the infralogical operations are more dependent upon specific experiences than are logical operations. In other words, the development of logical operations is perhaps a somewhat truer guide to the quality of the child's thinking skills than are the infralogical operations.

## WEIGHT AND MASS

The weight of a body is, of course, that property which it possesses in virtue of the earth's gravitational pull; that is, weight is a force. Thus weight is not the same as amount of matter or mass—that property of the body which determines its acceleration or deceleration when a given force is applied to it. It is now very much easier to make children aware of this distinction between weight and mass than it was a few years ago. Whereas the amount of matter in an astronaut's body is the same whether on earth or out in space, the weight of his body will diminish as the space vehicle carrying him recedes from the earth. Almost all pupils will have seen on television the effects of weightlessness in space, and will be aware that an object "weighs" less on the moon than on the earth.[1] In summary we can say that the mass of a body is always constant[2] and does not depend upon the position or location of the body in space, whereas the weight of a body—or the pull of gravity on it—does vary with the body's location.

However, young children even before they come to kindergarten will have heard the words "lift," "pull," "push," "light," "heavy" used. But they cannot have any appreciation of what these words mean until they have picked up objects and through their muscles felt the effects of the gravitational pull. This point must be emphasized. It is through lifting objects that children experience the pull of the earth and hence their notions of weight or of the earth's pull. Hence pupils need to engage in activities of the following kinds:

1. With eyes closed, the child picks up a number of objects in turn and then puts them in order of weight. He commences with two objects and increases the number until he has four or five.
2. A number of pairs of objects are examined, and the pupil writes down which member of each pair he considers is the heavier without lifting them. He then picks up each member and checks his result.
3. A pupil mimes a number of scenes: in one he carries a heavy sack on his back, in another he carries a feather.

Once the child has derived a concept of weight through muscle sense, then he must be introduced to the use of scales, for this piece of equipment will enable him to determine which of two objects is the heavier without having to lift them and rely on his own judgment. The movement of the pans shows us the one on which the earth exerts the greater force. However, to begin with, standard masses are not used. Rather pupils should find out how many nuts are required to balance a number of nails, or the amount of sand which weighs the same amount as a given stone, or the number of seashells needed to balance some lead shot. Such activities lead the child to find out a great deal about substances;

---

[1] There is good reason to try to get children to develop intuitive notions of weight and mass. This can save much frustration later when mechanics is introduced.
[2] This is, of course, true in a classical or nonrelativistic sense.

for example, he learns that many shells are needed to balance few lead shots, and in general a great deal more of one substance may weigh as much as much less of another substance. This finding gives an immediate lead-in to the need for standard masses, for, as readers will realize, pound and kilogram are units of mass, not of weight.

Pupils should also be introduced to the spring balance. Further, by placing various masses on the bottom end of a piece of elastic suitably anchored at the top end, the pupil gets an immediate and impressive indication of the effects of the earth's gravitational pull. By placing the elastic against a vertical scale, selected older children within the age range considered can draw a graph showing the extension of the elastic against the mass placed at the lower end.

Other activities should involve the use of kilograms as well as pounds, obtaining one's own personal mass, the weighing of parcels and of containers both full and empty, the floating and sinking of objects in water in order that the child can derive the notion of "heavy for its size" or "light for its size," the construction of conversion graphs as required from, say, pounds to kilograms or vice versa. It should be noted that while we can correctly say "The mass of the butter is one kilogram," we can also speak of weighing a parcel, since here we are speaking of the relative pulls of the earth on a parcel and on a mass in the other scale pan.

We must, of course, take note of the fact that until around eight to nine years of age, many children will deny the conservation of weight (invariance of the pull of the earth on the object) under certain spatial changes; for example, when a ball of clay is rolled into a sausage shape. It was indicated in Chapter 1 that if a five-year-old is shown two bottles of soda which he regards as each containing the same amount of liquid, and the contents are poured into two other vessels of very different shapes, he will most likely deny conservation of quantity. The same is broadly true if a ball of clay or plasticine is rolled into the shape of a sausage. But from Grade 2 upward there is an increase in the percentage of pupils who will conserve the amount of substance regardless of the perceptual difference between the ball and the essential shape of the sausage, provided that nothing is added to or taken from the clay or plasticine. Logical necessity demands that the amount of plasticine remain the same.

If now the child deforms the ball into a sausage, and we question the pupil about the weight of the ball and sausage, the five-year-old will likewise deny conservation of weight. Indeed, conservation of weight comes a little later generally than conservation of quantity, although the separation in time is very little in the case of able children. Moreover in odd instances, conservation of weight may even be acquired before conservation of quantity. However, specific experience does seem to affect the onset of conservation of weight. For example, Lovell and Ogilivie (1961) showed that if a piece of plasticine is cooled and becomes hard, many pupils who will conserve weight when a ball of plasticine is rolled into the shape of a sausage will now deny conservation of weight. General experience of life indicates to children that, on the average, hard things are heavier than light things, and it may be a year or so later before a child will conserve weight in a variety of tasks. Because of this kind of finding, and from findings in cross-cultural studies where pupils have undergone experiences very different from those of children in the U.S.A., we stated earlier that it seems as if some infralogical operations are affected by specific experiences. Put the other way round, the concept of the invariance of weight depends, in part, upon prolonged and varied experience of the physical world. Pupils need to engage in appropriate activities, coupled with discussion with the teacher, to help them come to appreciate that the weight of a body is conserved, regardless of the spatial rearrangement of its parts, provided nothing is added or taken away.

**TIME**

The child's first basic notions in relation to time are built in the sensori-motor stage as, for example, when he extends his hand or otherwise adjusts his actions to catch a swinging rattle. He does not, of course, have any sense of time as he will later, but in such activities are to be found the origins of the sense of timing and the most basic notions of time. At five to six years of age the child may have a good sense of timing, as when he runs to catch a ball, and he may use words related to time, such as "tomorrow," but he is still some way from temporal operations.

Time is not an easy concept to understand. The Greek philosophers discussed its nature; Augustine in his *Confessions* (Book XI, 14) asked "For what is time? Who can readily and briefly explain this?" Today we know that space and time, in the sense in which the scientist regards them, are mental constructions that have to be elaborated (see Whitrow, 1961). Time can be regarded as the abstract of all possible sequences. It takes the child some years before he can elaborate the construction, first at an intuitive and then at a concrete operational level. Our appreciation of the quality of the pupil's understanding of time is bedeviled by the fact that he can use time words and tell the time on the clock before he can handle temporal operations.

The relationship between perception and conception is complex. It was pointed out in Chapter 4 that there is a delay of some years between the perception of space the representation of space. Likewise there is a delay between the pupil's perception of time and his conception of it. Nevertheless it seems that time perception plays a role in the conception of time, although the latter is also greatly dependent on the growth of mental operations, just as earlier we saw that the child's conception of space was effected with the onset of systematized thought at around seven to eight years of age or thereabouts. Boring (1936) has suggested that time perception has five bases. In his view the child:

1. Gets some perception of succession or how stimuli follow on one another when, for example, he runs a pencil over the teeth of a comb at different rates or runs a stick similarly across a set of railings.
2. Obtains some perception of continuity when he watches some action until it stops—for example, a slowly turning wheel.
3. Acquires some notion of temporal length from the differing perceptions involved in, say, a short and long musical note or blast on a whistle.
4. Learns to respond to the environmental signals of the present, such as a pain or hunger.
5. Acquires the capacity to perceive patterns of successive stimuli. This ability to possess a sense of rhythm may have a physiological basis.

**Some Notions of Time**

In developed societies it has long been the custom to use astronomical time, but this is not necessarily the case among less developed peoples, although the position may be changing. In the latter, events in everyday life were fixed by the rhythm of the collective life. Thus it might be said that something would be done "in the frying of a locust" (in a moment) or "in a rice cooking" (about half an hour). Such sayings reflect an intuitive grasp of time. Other peoples may have no word equivalent to "time" in the languages of developed societies, and the sequence of significant events in the tribal life may go back no more than fifty years or so. Naturally the happenings of the remote past become intermingled with mythology. Again, the events of a day may be divided into, say, *milking time* and *watering time,* while in the case of more settled communities the year might be divided into, say, *planting time* and *harvest time.* In such societies it seems that they use, as it were, moments of time embedded in a continuum of action. Time is also marked off in the young child by isolated and distinct actions, which sometimes have strong feelings associated with them. For example, a two-year-old will say "bath" to indicate a wish in which a time element is implied. Once again time seems embedded in a series of events in which space and time are not yet differentiated.

But slowly over the years there is a kind of emergent experience of temporality—a gradual reaching out by the child into past and future, an awareness of things in a state of change, the growth of a time vocabulary, and the differentiation of time from space. But his notions of time remain largely intuitive until around eight to nine years of age, as we shall see later. Thus Ames (1946) found that American children could use words like *morning* and *afternoon* by four years of age, know the name of the day by five, could tell the time on the clock by seven years of age, and could use words like *summertime* and *playtime* before the word *time* itself. Such findings suggest that the ability to use these words correctly is built up by associating their use with certain situations so that the child learns to use the word *night* when it is dark. These associations leading to the proper use of time words are very important, but the use of such words does not necessarily mean that the child has a concept of time as he will have later. Again, telling the time on the clock, although a vital skill which all children need to have, involves no more than dial reading. The reading on the clock integrated into the sequence of other events does require some concept of time, however.

One pioneer study of the child's understanding of time was that of Oaken and Sturt reported by Sturt (1925) whose work was replicated and largely confirmed by Bradley (1948). While almost all children of six years knew that it was the same day of the week all over a small nearby town, it was not until ten years of age that 85 percent of pupils realized that it was the same day of the week over all towns in England. Again, in both studies pupils were asked if their mother and their grandmother were alive in 1492 when Columbus set out for the New World. Both investigations showed that the first question was not understood by 75 percent of pupils until seven years of age, and the second question was not understood by 75 percent of pupils until nine. Indeed time perspective in children less than nine years of age is very shallow. Whereas at six years of age time can be related to the child's personal experiences (morning, afternoon), it is not until eight that there begins to be an extension of the understanding of time in relation to both

# Weight, Mass, Time, and Volume

duration and space; for example, time since an event and time elsewhere. This has important implications for teachers of history and geography.

**Temporal Operations**

So far we have discussed the child's perception of time and his intuitive notions of time. We now discuss temporal operations which enable a child to acquire a concept of time based on intuitable data. Somewhere between eight and nine years of age children begin to carry out the following operations:

1. Seriate events according to their order of succession; that is, ordering operations can be carried out.
2. Mark off intervals of time between ordered points on a time scale and "fit" smaller ones within larger ones, thus carrying out the operations of subdivision and inclusion.
3. Carry out metrical operations; that is, choose time as a unit and use it as a standard for the measurement of all other intervals. Once again we have a synthesis of subdivision and displacement, as in the measurement of space.

These operations develop at about the same time in the child. Only a brief reference will be made here to the experimental evidence which supports the above statements. Interested readers should consult Piaget (1969b), and Lovell and Slater (1960).

In one experiment the pupil is shown two cylindrical shaped vessels which hold the same amount of water, but one is much shorter and wider than the other (Figure 89). The wider vessel is placed vertically above the taller but narrower cylinder, and water runs from the upper into the lower vessel. The flow is regulated by a tap. The experiment begins with the top vessel being full and the bottom one empty. As water flows out of the upper vessel, the water level is at $I_1$ when the water level in the lower vessel is at $II_1$, and so on. The precise locations of levels $I_1$ to $I_6$ and $II_1$ to $II_6$ are indicated on the vessels by small pieces of paper. On these pieces of paper $I_1$, $II_5$, and so on, are written. A series of line drawings are given to the child showing the water levels in each of the two vessels at each stage in the experiment, and he is asked to check the correspondences between the drawings and the actual positions of the water levels as the water flows.

Three tasks then follow for the subject. First the drawings are shuffled, and he is asked to put them in a series showing the correct order of events. Second, the six line drawings are cut into two (so that the pictures of the upper and lower vessels are separated) and the twelve

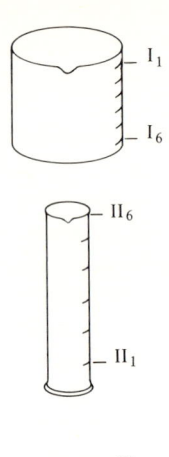

FIGURE 89

drawings reshuffled. The child is shown a drawing indicating a particular water level in the top or bottom vessel and is asked to select the drawing representing the water level in the other vessel. Third, the pupil is questioned as to whether the time taken for the water level to move from, say, $I_2$ to $I_5$ is the same as that for it to change from $II_2$ to $II_4$, and so on. Studies at Geneva and Leeds suggest that it is eight to nine years of age before the majority of children will be able to carry out these tasks successfully.

Other experiments have indicated that the equality of synchronous intervals cannot always be recognized until eight to nine years of age. For example, if two dolls are made to move across a table, starting together from the same point and finishing together at the same point, many kindergarten and first-grade pupils will correctly say that they started at the same time, stopped at the same time, and "walked" for the same time. But if both dolls start together from the same point, travel at different speeds and so finish at different points although stopping after the same period spent in moving, simultaneity of times of arrival is denied until around seven years of age, and the equal duration of the synchronous intervals is denied until eight to nine years of age.

It appears that the child's ideas of time are at first mixed with his ideas of space and spatial changes. They are also affected to some extent by the situation in which he finds himself, in the sense that correct responses can be obtained from him using some apparatus but

# Weight, Mass, Time, and Volume

not using other equipment. But it is not until instants and points in the time continuum are coordinated that time becomes an invariant quantity independent of speed of movement,[1] distance moved, or actual position. For Piaget temporal operations depend upon the growth of the pupil's thinking.

### Some Suggested Activities

Children can be helped to acquire the correct use of words involving time and to tell the time. These things are not, however, our main concern here. Rather, we are more concerned with helping pupils to elaborate temporal operations. It seems likely—although we cannot be certain—that watching or hearing any event which has a clear beginning and ending, or engaging in any activity with this characteristic, will help in this respect. For example, watching an egg-timer or listening to a musical note may be an aid. The very rhythm and routine of life probably plays a role too. Pupils go to bed and get up, feel hungry and get fed, go to school and return each day. These and similar happenings seem likely to link in the mind the succession of events and the interval which separates them. We have to try and help pupils to appreciate that while an object has the property of length, so an event or activity has a duration. Furthermore, just as we use a ruler or other piece of apparatus to measure lengths which cannot be placed side by side for direct comparison, so there is a unit of time with which we can compare the duration of events or activities. Thus duration may be looked upon as the quantity of time through which the event extends.

A discussion of the order of actions involved in the following kinds of activities is likely to help a child to order or seriate events: getting out of bed, dressing, eating breakfast, going to school; braking the automobile, stopping at the traffic lights, waiting for the light to change to green, accelerating; counting from 0 to 10, counting through 4, 5, 6, and so on; and making the "rocket countdown" 5, 4, 3, 2, 1, 0.

The appreciation of the duration of events can be helped by the following:

1. Bouncing a ball, skipping, watching a dripping tap. Here the duration extends between the bounces, skips, or drips.
2. Watching a flashing light, listening to a musical note, watching the swing of a simple pendulum (made by suspending a weight from the end of a piece of string roughly one meter long and

---

[1] Time here is classical or nonrelativistic time.

having its top end securely fastened). Here the duration may be of the flash, sound, or swing, or the duration of the interval between flashes, sounds, or the bob being in a vertical position.

In any of the events indicated in the above list, the frequency of the happening can be altered, thus giving the pupil the opportunity to note changes in duration. He should also be encouraged to note that in other important activities, such as listening to the ticking of a watch, following the second hand of a watch rotating once, feeling the pulse, listening to a telephone bell ringing, and watching the directional lights on an automobile, duration is fixed in the sense that the experimenter cannot easily change these at will. Except for the pulse rate, the times involved, although conventional, are arbitrary.

Finally there is the question of helping pupils to put durations in order of their lengths. The following kinds of activities may be an aid in this connection:

1. Have a series of pendulums with strings of differing length. The pupil puts the times of swing in order. (The teacher may have to help here, as the pupils may merely order the lengths of strings, thus getting the correct ordering without fully considering the times.)
2. The pupil counts from, say, 15 to 0, 6 to 0, 11 to 0, and puts in order the times which he takes to count through the numbers. It is better to have him count backwards, for this puts the emphasis on time durations and their seriation, and not on the seriation of numbers.
3. Putting in order of duration the times taken to hop along a line drawn in the corridor or playground, to walk along it, and to run along it.
4. Using a stopclock, the pupil notes the times it takes to write his name in full; his home address; the address of his school; and a sentence of his own choosing. These times are then put in order of duration.
5. Using a stopclock, the pupil notes the times he takes to walk 100 yards; address an envelope to his home; tie up a parcel; say the alphabet both ways; play a record; feed a rabbit. The times are again put in order of duration.

The above activities and the child's ordering of their duration lead naturally into the need for a standard unit of time. This leads back to the clock and to time-telling, but by now the child should look upon the

# Weight, Mass, Time, and Volume

use of the clock with far greater understanding. As we said earlier in the chapter, at first the child may tell the time in the sense that he can read a dial. Now he has a greater understanding of the significance of a standard unit of duration and of the clock as a measuring device.

Temporal operations have been discussed at some length, because they are of great importance and yet cause considerable difficulty. Unless a concept of time has been elaborated, the child cannot understand what is meant by speed or any other relationship involving time. Even so, the child's understanding of time in the elementary school will be confined to intuitable data. It will be high school before 75 per cent of the age group will correctly answer the question "In springtime, when we advance the clocks by one hour, do we get one hour older?" and realize that time on the clock is a purely arbitrary convention.

## VOLUME

Our treatment of volume will be brief, as children in the age range considered will have only a limited understanding of the concept. Before a pupil can have a well developed concept of volume, he must understand the three meanings given to the term:

1. Internal volume or capacity—the amount of space inside, say, a box
2. Volume as "occupied" space, or the amount of space or room which a box takes or occupies
3. Complementary volume, or the amount of water displaced by an object when the latter is inserted in the former

The work of Piaget, Inhelder, and Szeminska (1960) and also of Lovell and Ogilvie (1961) suggests that an understanding of volume, in the three senses indicated above, is not possible for pupils until around eleven or twelve years of age. But certain kinds of activities will promote the pupil's thinking in regard to the concept of volume within the age range considered here. For example, the teacher can help the child to appreciate that the internal volume or capacity of, say, a box is a measure of the material that would fill it. Thus the pupil can find its internal volume by finding the number of unit cubes that fills it (it is assumed that the dimensions of the box are such that an exact number of unit cubes exactly fills it). If, for example, the box has dimensions of, say, $3 \times 2 \times 4$ units, he must fill the box and determine the number of cubes required. But he must also be questioned as to whether a box of dimensions, say, 6 × 2 × 2 units would have the same internal volume by filling such a box with the units used in the first box. Through many examples of this general type, he can be helped to appreciate that boxes of very different shape can have the same internal volume. Even with eight-year-olds it will be found that it becomes harder for them to conserve internal volume as the number of cubes used increases and as it is possible to get greater perceptual differences between the boxes.

The building of "houses" from unit cubes helps the pupil to appreciate that an object occupies a certain amount of space or takes up room in space. Once again "houses" with very different shapes can be built from the same number of unit cubes and the child questioned to see if occupied volume is conserved.

Again, the child can build a block of dimensions, say, 6 × 3 × 2 units. The teacher then requests him to draw in his exercise book, or on a sheet of paper, rectangles of dimensions, say, 3 × 3 units or 12 × 1 units and, using these as bases, to construct blocks ("houses") which occupy the same amount of space. Tasks of this general type can be very helpful.

Finally we want to help the child to understand that when objects are immersed in, say, a cylindrical shaped glass vessel, the water level can be seen to rise. In other words, the object, perhaps a stone, now takes up some of the space previously taken by the water, so the level of the water must rise. Pupils can insert (on the end of a thread securely attached) stones or metal objects of varying size and mark the different levels to which the water rises. They will determine in a general way that the larger the object—or the greater the space it occupies—the higher the water level reaches. But it will be late in the elementary school before they understand that if a block of metal cubes of dimensions 3 × 3 × 4 units is rearranged as 2 × 3 × 6 units or as 1 × 2 × 18 units, then the water level will rise to the same in all three instances. Such understanding is, of course, basic to a grasp of Archimedes' principle.

Children in the age range considered here have to overcome many misconceptions regarding displacement volume. Individuals may think that the amount of water displaced depends upon the weight of the object and that a very heavy cube will displace more water than a lighter one of the same size; that the amount of water displaced is not the same when the object is suspended just below the surface as when it lies on the bottom of the cylinder; and that when a cube of given size is immersed very carefully in a small vessel that is full, it will cause more water to overflow than when it is equally carefully immersed in a large container. There is a great need for the child to acquire physical expe-

# Weight, Mass, Time, and Volume

rience—using the term in the Piagetian sense—in order that these misconceptions may be eliminated.

Some pupils in the second and third grades will learn that the volume (internal or external) of a cuboid may be calculated by finding the product of the lengths of the sides of the cuboid. This comes through the repeated application of a unit volume within a larger volume, just as area was found by the repeated application of a unit area within a larger area. But it will require the onset of formal operational thinking before pupils can make a direct transition, with understanding, from length to volume (see Chapter 5, where this problem was discussed in respect of area).

# 10
# Classroom Organization and Children Learning Mathematics

In conferences sponsored by UNESCO, Dienes (1965) indicated that the current experimental work concerned with the teaching of mathematics appeared to possess a number of common features. These were thought to be:

1. Emphasis on structure
2. Emphasis on meaning, understanding, and finding out, rather than the rote learning of specific techniques
3. The building up of a positive attitude to mathematics, or even emotional involvement in mathematical activities, as a basis for motivating the pupil into wanting to make progress in mathematics
4. The extension of the curriculum far beyond the conventional four rules
5. Induction to precede deduction wherever possible

These points have been borne in mind in presenting the content of, and approach to, mathematics in the preceding chapters. But before readers feel free to attempt the suggestions made in this book, there are a number of other issues to be considered.

## VARIETIES OF CLASSROOM ORGANIZATION

It is not my intention to comment on forms of school organization, as the individual teacher is not in a position to alter the form of organization within a given school. But given a teacher and a group of pupils, the teacher does have some choice in deciding the mode of teacher/pupil interaction. On some occasions the teacher stands in front of the class and imparts information to the whole group with verbal exposition. This will be the case either in kindergarten or in the early grades when the teacher is, say, reading a story or describing an object or picture. It is also the case when the class is singing or dancing and the teacher is directing the activity. In a second situation the teacher may still be in front of the class and the pupils are again treated as a single group, but they are asked questions and are expected to give and discuss many answers. Moreover, pupils may make their own contribution to the discussion from their experiences.

In a third type of classroom situation, children are seated at small tables[1] in twos, threes, or fours per table. They are working at tasks provided by the teacher although sometimes chosen by themselves; but not all pupils seated at a table may be engaged in the same task. Pupils discuss their difficulties with one another and with the teacher; they also agree on their solutions. Pupils are also free to get up from their seat to fetch apparatus or to seek further information. The atmosphere is informal, and although the teacher still supplies the direction to the work of the classroom in the sense that she should know the precise purpose of each task which is set; she may also be regarded as an expert consultant.

It is this third type of classroom situation which is most appropriate for learning mathematics, especially in the case of young children. The other forms of classroom organization have their place in some areas of the curriculum; but in mathematics, where the child has so often to derive his abstractions through reflecting upon actions which he carries out on materials, there is only a limited place for the teacher standing in front of the class, or sections of the class, and teaching through verbal exposition. Rather verbal dialogue or verbal explication must take place between teacher and child, teacher and small group, or child and child.

In both kindergarten and the first three grades it is hoped that there will be periods in which pupils freely choose to engage in activities which appeal to them and in which they become absorbed. Such periods of the day can be regarded as "children's time," and the activities in which they engage may well help to prepare them for the mathematical ideas which they will meet in other periods of the day, in which they

---

[1] When small tables are not available, pairs of desks may be placed together to give a flat surface to work on.

engage in activities promoted by the teacher in order to reach certain goals.

It is helpful if teachers in the elementary school are free to plan their school day as they wish. They are not then restricted by a rigid timetable to commencing a mathematics (or other) period at a given time and ending it at a fixed time. This happy arrangement is not always possible, and if teachers are constricted by fixed periods, they naturally have to do the best they can. In kindergarten the position will be much freer.

In summary it is suggested that in mathematics the teacher should attempt to move away from a formal classroom atmosphere in which pupils are taught as a group or as two or three groups. Instead it is hoped that there will be a move to the position in which children work individually or in small groups at tasks which have often been provided by the teacher. On some occasions, however, a mathematical task will arise incidentally out of activities not directly connected with mathematics. The teacher should seize upon such situations and exploit them to the full. Such tasks may help pupils to grasp new mathematical ideas or to practice some new skills which have been acquired.

Readers are aware of the value of individual involvement in, say, art, craft, music; this book argues the value of individual assignments in mathematics. But because mathematics is a structured and interlocked study of relations, which are expressed in symbols and governed by firm rules, then perhaps more than in other subject areas the initiation and direction of the work is the responsibility of the teacher.

## MAKING A BEGINNING

In classrooms where the teacher has been mainly teaching mathematics by verbal exposition and by demonstration, and pupils have been used to doing little more than listening, watching, and working examples involving computation from textbooks and worksheets, the change to the approach suggested here may involve some stresses for teacher and children. The teacher has to prepare a great number of activities for pupils who will perhaps be at very different stages. At the same time pupils have to learn to work singly, in pairs, or in small groups, discuss with teacher or peers, and be much more responsible for their own actions. Moreover, children must still be able to work examples from textbooks or worksheets involving straight computation or problems. There are, of course, teachers who are already working in this mode.

However, teachers who wish to make a transition should effect the change slowly. This enables both teacher and pupils to become adjusted to their new roles, and gives the teacher time to convince herself that children *do* learn by carrying out the activities set them. It may be better to begin with, say, just six pupils per day working in the way suggested, while the remaining pupils in the class carry on as before. If six pupils per day work in this way, then once a week all the children in a class of thirty or so pupils will have the experience of a more active approach to learning. Moreover, by beginning with a small number of pupils, the teacher has fewer materials to prepare, although there will be a good spread of mathematical ability and attainment across the whole class, and a range of activities will be required. On the other hand, six pupils with their activities and materials take up less space than a whole class engaged at once on this approach. Perhaps most important, this slow move to the new approach gives the teacher confidence in a transition from an approach which is known to one which is new. With greater experience and confidence the teacher can move to, say, a dozen pupils engaged in this way, and then to the whole class.

When there are a large number of children in a class or the size of the classroom is small, it may be necessary to restrict the numbers of children engaged in the activities proposed in this book, or have some restriction in the range of materials available. However, use can often be made of school corridors for mathematical activities when classroom space is limited.

Once a teacher can be seen at work along these lines, other members of staff may become "infected" as it were. However, teachers must be convinced that the approach is a good one, that pupils learn more mathematical ideas and enjoy doing so, and at the same time computational skills do not suffer.

## THE QUESTION OF LEARNING BY DISCOVERY

Much has been written about the value of learning by discovery or of finding out for oneself. Often, though, the advocates of such methods have done so in a rather unthinking manner. Two points in particular are worthy of discussion at this juncture. First, the only hard research findings to date suggest that when students are presented with a task and told to find out "what-happens-if," the learner generally feels curious, is challenged, and becomes motivated to solve the problem. In other words, students tend to continue to learn when they are forced to discover generalizations for themselves (see Kersh, 1964).

This is not to say that this is the only benefit derived from discovery learning, but hard facts about other benefits are difficult to come by.

The second point has been amply made by Ausubel (1964). It has been assumed that all expository verbal learning consists of glib verbalizations rotely memorized, whereas laboratory experience and active methods are inherently and necessarily meaningful. Ausubel points out, with much reason, that verbal exposition and problem-solving through activity can be either rote or meaningful. In both modes, meaningful learning takes place only if the idea to be established can be related, in a nonarbitrary and substantive fashion, to what the learner already knows. Thus laboratory experience and active methods are not genuinely meaningful unless such work and methods rest on a base of understood concepts and the operations involved are also meaningful. It is quite possible to acquire procedures for manipulating problems and to solve "types of problems" by rote memorization.

It has been necessary to raise these issues, because much has been written about the value of so-called discovery methods, yet few of the writers have paused to consider the strengths and limitations of such methods. Indeed, two further points must also be made. First, some knowledge has to be given verbally, both in kindergarten and earlier. For example, all his life the child has heard through the verbalizations of others that the color of grass is "green." He could never have thought this out for himself: it is a fact of life that in the English language that property of grass known as color is said to be "green" — the word being written and spoken in certain ways. Thus some information has to be given to pupils verbally.

Second, we take Piaget's position as far as mathematics is concerned, and argue that mathematical ideas are derived from "reflective abstraction." That is to say, mathematical ideas derive from the abstractions or dissociations which the subject makes from his actions on objects and not from the objects themselves. The abstraction is from the knowing activity itself and not from the objects of knowing. As we said in Chapter 1, the child reflects on his activity in an autoregulatory sense. Thus we are not going to say that the child discovers a mathematical entity, or that the teacher is using discovery methods, in the sense that the word implies something immediately to be found as a nugget of gold can be discovered in the earth or as a lizard or crab can be discovered underneath a stone.

In mathematics the "reflected" or "constructed" abstractions or structures are not identical with the structures from which they were derived. The operations involved in the concrete situation are analogical to the mental structures but are not identical with them. As we saw in Chapter 1, the ability to classify and seriate derives from the child's making the necessary abstractions as he classifies and orders materials. But we must also note that mathematical concepts are not exactly inventions; for if mathematics is closely examined, it will be seen, looking back, that all mathematical concepts have the character of necessity. At a given time one cannot be aware of all the mathematical ideas that are implicit in a mathematical structure; only in retrospect is the necessity realized. So for Piaget, mathematical construction is not an invention or a discovery, but a process *sui generis*.

The position taken in this book is that through the use of individual or small group work, and with pupils engaged in discussion with teacher and peers, there is a greater likelihood that reflected abstraction will take place. This approach does not, of course, *ensure* that mathematical constructions take place. If they do not, the pupil may learn to use certain rules in rather a blind fashion. Whether the approach suggested in this book brings about meaningful learning depends upon whether or not reflective abstraction takes place.

Before we conclude this section it may be helpful to look at the function of games in the classroom insofar as they relate to the growth of understanding in mathematics. Dienes (1960) has very usefully divided games into three broad types, although he interprets the term *game* widely to embrace experiences more generally. His game would often accord with activity as used in this book. Particular games are played or relevant experiences are given in respect of some specific mathematical idea.

First, there is the preliminary game. In this the child may, say, use Cuisenaire Rods to build a bridge. His behavior has the appearance of unorganized play; his performance has little or no structure in relation to the concept in question. This is typical of a child in kindergarten or earlier in the nursery school.

Second, there is the structured game, which has a certain directionality built into it, this directionality corresponding to the structure of the concepts whose formation it is intended to promote. In the view of Dienes, if this direction is not sensed by the child, then he needs more preliminary play or another game which displays the same structure. On the other hand, if the pupil does what he is "meant" to do with the material, then he is moving towards insight. In other words, once his thinking is beginning to give him some insight into the purpose of the game, he is more likely to be able to derive further insight by more game-playing.

Third, there is the practice game; this helps to anchor the insight more firmly in the child's experience. It may also act as a preliminary game for a later concept.

## APPARATUS

Some of the equipment and materials which will be required in the study of mathematics are listed below. It must be understood that such a list is merely suggestive. Some schools, or classrooms, may have many of the items listed and more besides; others may have far less. A range of equipment and materials can be built up as funds become available. Structural apparatus produced commercially is very useful, but teachers should not be discouraged if they are unable to purchase it; substitutes from more everyday objects will provide the opportunities which children require. It is the tasks which the teacher sets children with the apparatus, and the resulting abstractions that the child makes, which are important, and not the actual materials themselves. It is pathetic to see a classroom well stocked with apparatus, and the teacher having little or no idea as to how the materials can best be used to give relevant experience to pupils. In the list given below there are some items which it might be thought should be included in science rather than in mathematics lessons. They are included because mathematical and scientific ideas can often be usefully considered together to give some knowledge of both physical and mechanical properties of simple systems, as, for example, in the case of gear wheels. There is a great need, in my judgment, to begin the study of very simple mechanical systems in the age range under consideration. Pupils when much older, when studying mechanics, have many difficulties in envisaging real life situations, as when they have to consider the forces acting on a system.

### Items

Collections of attractive items for sorting and matching in one-to-one correspondence, such as plastic cups and saucers, knives and forks; beads, counters, nuts, shells; number strips; rope, string, drinking straws; foot rulers with alternately colored inches (for easy reading) and "no ends," foot rulers in inches, half-inches and quarter-inches with "no ends," yardstick, meter stick, and ruler marked in centimeters; surveyor's tape, trundle wheel; materials for weighing such as dried peas, flour, sand; balance scales, spring balance; various kinds of stationery (colored paper, paper circles, paper squares), cards of varying thickness, pencils, crayons; egg-timer, clock faces, stopclock; cubes of varying size, nesting cubes, wooden building bricks; variety of 3D shapes, geometric shapes (plastic); structural apparatus, erector kits; set squares, compasses; plumb line, compass, clinometer; liquid measures; thermometer, rain gauge; spirit level, gear wheels, magnets, pulleys, wires, bulbs and batteries; scale models of cars and airplanes; pendulum; scissors; squared paper; pegs and pegboard.

**CHILDREN'S RECORDING OF THEIR WORK**

Children should be encouraged to record their mathematical experiences in as many different ways as possible. The more ways they employ, the more they tend to be helped to understand what they have been doing. The following are suggestions:

1. Spoken language. Through discussion with teacher, with peers in pairs or in larger groups, the child is helped to organize his experience, carry his thinking with greater precision, and turn around his thoughts so that he can communicate, in turn, with others.
2. Drawing. A drawing is made to illustrate some mathematical experience, the drawing then being described in written language.
3. Venn diagram. This can be used to illustrate some experiences involving relations between sets.
4. A block or line graph. There must be a decision by the child about the scale to be used and oral discussion about the interpretation of the graph, as well as some written work, as indicated in Chapter 8.
5. Mapping. This is a means of expressing a relationship, as we have seen. Some data can be illustrated both as a mapping and as a graph (see Chapter 8).
6. Equations can be recorded in equation form, equivalence can be indicated by $\longleftrightarrow$, and inequalities by the signs $>$, $<$.
7. Tabulation. Data can be expressed, say, in column form.
8. Record of a solution to a problem using computation and words —for example:

    Number of pupils in the class from Monday to Friday:
    $28 + 31 + 30 + 27 + 30 = 146$

## ASSESSMENT OF PROGRESS

It is very important that teachers keep a record of each pupil's work and progress. Attention must be paid to three points. First, a record must be kept of the activities in which each pupil engages. Second—and this is vital—there must be periodic checks on the child's understanding in respect of these activities, and the findings must be carefully recorded. This necessitates individual questioning of pupils and discussion. Without this the teacher has little idea whether the pupil carries out an activity in rote fashion, through the help of other children, or with partial or complete understanding. Third, there must be a record kept of the examples in textbooks, on worksheets, or on individual assignment cards (prepared by the teacher) worked by each pupil. This gives a record of the computational practice. Concepts and computational skills must also be revised from time to time.

## PARENTS

Parents sometimes have difficulty in appreciating both the current approaches to mathematics teaching and the mathematical ideas now introduced. They often judge progress in mathematics by the amount of time spent on computational practice and the number of exercises marked by the teacher as correct. When they see perhaps less time spent on computation, they may suffer some anxiety. It is suggested that schools take parents into their confidence over these matters, using whatever methods they think best. Teachers might make clear to parents that by nine years of age, a child will generally handle computation very efficiently. Moreover pupils will have a greater understanding of what they are doing, and they will have been introduced to a whole range of new ideas which will come to fruition later on in school life.

## KNOWLEDGE OF CHILDREN
## AND KNOWLEDGE OF MATHEMATICS

The first chapter of this book gave a brief sketch of Piaget's developmental system in order that readers might have a better understanding of the relative difficulty of various mathematical ideas for children of different ages. I should like to repeat that teachers must know the broad outline of children's intellectual development and be aware of a particular child's level of understanding.

But in order to give direction to children's work, the teacher must also be aware of the structure of the subject matter. The teacher has always to help the child to move from where he is, and help him to learn about new ideas. Naturally the teacher can only do this if she knows what she is doing and where she is going. She will make effective use of equipment and materials only if she knows precisely how to use them to help the pupil make the necessary abstractions or practice some new skill. Thus the teacher of young children must know some mathematics as well as know something of children's intellectual growth. This important point is often overlooked. Without some knowledge of the subject matter she will not know the precise direction in which to move or what mathematical experiences can be obtained from given materials. The position was well put by Cremin (1961) who argued that the demand on the teacher was twofold: thorough knowledge of the discipline, and an awareness of the common experiences of childhood that can be utilized to lead children toward that understanding which is represented by this knowledge.

## A DIFFICULTY WHICH MIGHT FACE SOME READERS

Some of the mathematical ideas introduced in this book may be relatively new to readers, who may wonder why they should be introduced to young children whose understanding of them will be limited. The answer is that the ideas are extremely important and of great practical consequence. It is hoped that the introduction of these ideas in an interesting and informal way will make children familiar with them, help pupils to have good attitudes to them, and so make them feel more "at home" with the ideas when they meet them again more formally later.

To illustrate the importance of the ideas introduced, let us consider the idea of mapping—an idea fundamental in mathematics today. Conformal mapping of one complex variable upon another can significantly relate very diverse entities: for example, the shapes of seemingly distinct forms of shellfish; or the Fibonacci numbers 0, 1, 1, 2, 3, 5, 8, 13 . . . (of which each number is the sum of the two preceding ones) and the number of petals on a flower, for the Fibonacci series plays an outstanding role in the description of flowers as far as the number of petals is concerned.

Using an entirely different type of example, a one-to-one mapping can provide a means of investigating infinite sets. Consider the two infinite sets:

$$A = (1, 2, 3, 4, 5, \ldots)$$
$$B = (2, 4, 6, 8, 10, \ldots)$$

It is possible to map $A$ onto $B$ as, for example:

$$\begin{array}{cccccccc} A & 1 & 2 & 3 & 4 & 5 & \ldots & n & \ldots \\ & \downarrow & \downarrow & \downarrow & \downarrow & \downarrow & & \downarrow & \\ B & 2 & 4 & 6 & 8 & 10 & \ldots & 2n & \ldots \end{array}$$

The images of 1, 2, 3, 4, 5 are respectively 2, 4, 6, 8, 10, and so forth. If $n$ belongs to $A$, the mapping may be put as $f: n \rightarrow 2n$ where $2n$ belongs to $B$. The inverse mapping may also be considered. The image of any member, $2n$, of $B$ is $n$ in $A$, where $n \neq 0$ and $n$ is a natural number. Thus a one-to-one correspondence exists between the members of $A$ and the members of $B$. But $B$ is clearly a subset of $A$, and our example illustrates that the infinite set $A$ is in one-to-one correspondence with a part of itself.[2]

This unique property of an infinite set may be illustrated by a geometrical correspondence. Let $AB$, $A_1B_1$, be two given lines of unequal length (Figure 90). Let $AA_1$, $BB_1$ meet in $T$. Let $X$ be any point on $AB$.

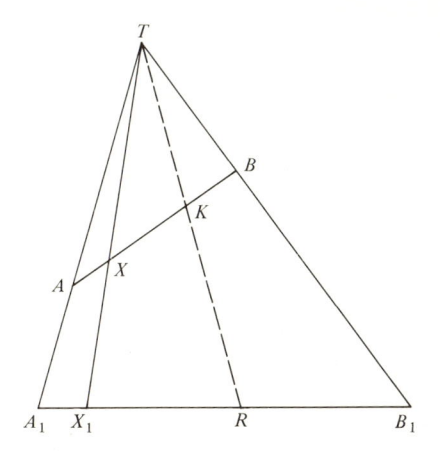

FIGURE 90

The line $TX$ meets $A_1B_1$ in a unique point $X_1$. Let $X_1$ be the image of $X$. Repeat this construction for each point $X, Y, Z \ldots$ of $AB$. Then

---

[2] It is not demonstrated here, but it is easy to show that if a set has a limited or finite number of members, it cannot be put into one-to-one correspondence with a part of itself.

there is a series of unique images $X_1$, $Y_1$, $Z_1$ ... on $A_1B_1$. Thus each point on $AB$ has one image on $A_1B_1$. Let us assume, since $A_1B_1$ is longer than $AB$, that $R$ is a point on $A_1B_1$ that is not the image of a point on $AB$. Join $TR$. Then $TR$ meets $AB$ in a single point $K$, say. But as $K$ is on $AB$, it has a unique image $K_1$ on $A_1B_1$ according to our geometrical construction. Hence $K_1$ and $R$ are names for the same point. The assumption that $R$ was not the image of a point on $AB$ leads to a contradiction (that it is the image of $K$) and so this assumption is false. Since this geometrical procedure is reversible (join $TX_1$ to cut $AB$ in $X$) the image of $X_1$ is $X$. We can thus say that the points of $AB$ are in one-to-one correspondence with the points of $A_1B_1$. But as $AB$ may be regarded as a length cut from $A_1B_1$, $A_1B_1$ is in one-to-one correspondence with a part of itself. From this point of view the whole is no greater than many of its parts. In other words, there are as many points on a line as there are on a line that is one-half or one-third or one-fourth, and so on, of its length.

The distribution of points on a line segment is said to be "everywhere dense," that is, between any two points there are an infinite number of points. Because of this property, points on a line taken in order represent the real numbers—giving the number line. There is a one-to-one correspondence between the real numbers and points on the number line. A number is represented by the position of a point, and conversely a point represents a number.

## A CONCLUDING COMMENT

There is increasing experimental evidence that the attitudes of teachers to their pupils affect the performance of the pupils. In other words, teacher expectations are to some extent self-fulfilling. It is thus important that the teacher should think well of her pupils and set standards of work which are high for them. There will, of course, be considerable variation in pupil achievement and understanding, these variations being determined by many influences: the child's intellectual development, cultural background, emotional stability, the attitudes of home and school, and the quality of teaching he has experienced. Nevertheless the approach suggested in this book will allow for these individual differences.

# Bibliography

Almy, M. (1966). *Young Children's Thinking.* New York: Teachers College Press.

Almy, M. (1969). *Logical Thinking in Second Grade.* Unpublished Report. New York: Teachers College.

Ames, L. B. (1946). The Development of the Sense of Time in the Young Child. *Journal of Genetic Psychology,* 68: 97–125.

Apostel, L., W. Mays, A. Morf, and J. Piaget (1957). Les Liaisons Analytiques et Synthetiques dans Les Comportements du Sujet. *Etudes D'Épistémologie Génétique,* Vol. 4. Paris: Presses Universitaires de France.

Ausubel, D. P. (1964). Some Psychological and Educational Limitations of Learning by Discovery. *The Arithmetic Teacher,* May: 290–302.

Beilin, H., J. Kagan, and R. Rabinowitz (1966). Effects of Verbal and Perceptual Training on Water Level Representation. *Child Development,* 37: 317–29.

Boring, E. G., (1936). Temporal Perception and Operationism. *American Journal of Psychology,* 48: 519–22.

Bradley, N. D. (1948). The Growth of the Knowledge of Time in Children of School Age. *British Journal of Psychology,* 38: 67–78.

Brown, P. G. (1969). Tests of Development in Children's Understanding of the Laws of Natural Numbers. M. Ed. Thesis, University of Manchester.

Cremin, L. A. (1961). *The Transformation of the School.* New York: Knopf.

Dienes, Z. P. (1960). *Building up Mathematics.* London: Hutchinson.

Dienes, Z. P. (ed.) (1965). *Current Work on Problems of Mathematics Learning.* Hamburg: UNESCO.

Dodwell, P. C. (1969). Instructional Factors in Number Concept Understanding and Arithmetic Learning. In *Programmed Learning Research: Major Trends* (eds. F. Bresson and M. de Montmollin). Paris: Dunod.

Duckworth, E. (1964). Piaget Rediscovered. In *Piaget Rediscovered* (eds. R. E. Ripple and V. N. Rockcastle). Ithaca, N.Y.: Cornell University Press.

Fehr, H. F. (1966). The Teaching of Mathematics in the Elementary School. In *Analysis of Concept Learning* (eds. H. J. Klausmeier and C. W. Harris). New York: Academic Press.

Flavell, J. H. (1963). *The Developmental Psychology of Jean Piaget.* New York: Van Nostrand.

Inhelder, B., M. Bovet, H. Sinclair, and C. D. Smock (1966). On Cognitive Development. *American Psychologist,* 21, 160–64.

Inhelder, B., and J. Piaget (1958). *The Growth of Logical Thinking from Childhood to Adolescence.* New York: Basic Books.

Inhelder, B., and J. Piaget (1964). *The Early Growth of Logic in the Child.* London: Routledge & Kegan Paul.

Kersh, B. Y. (1964). Learning by Discovery: What Is Learned? *The Arithmetic Teacher,* April, 226–32.

Lovell, K. (1966). *The Growth of Basic Mathematical and Scientific Concepts in Children.* London: University of London Press. Fifth Edition.

Lovell, K., and I. B. Butterworth (1966). Abilities Underlying the Understanding of Proportionality. *Mathematics Teaching,* 37, 5–9.

Lovell, K., B. Mitchell, and I. R. Everett (1962). An Experimental Study of the Growth of Some Logical Structures. *British Journal of Psychology*, 53, 175–88.

Lovell, K., and E. Ogilvie (1961). A Study of the Conservation of Weight in the Junior School Child. *British Journal of Educational Psychology*, 31, 138–44.

Lovell, K., and A. Slater (1960). The Growth of the Concept of Time: A Comparative Study. *Journal of Child Psychology and Psychiatry*, 1, 179–190.

Lunzer, E. A. (1965). Problems of Formal Reasoning in Test Situations. In *Monographs of the Society for Research in Child Development, European Research in Cognitive Development*, 30, No. 2.

Lunzer, E. A. (1968). Formal Reasoning. In *Development in Human Learning 2* (eds. E. A. Lunzer and J. F. Morris). London: Staples.

Piaget, J. (1950). *The Psychology of Intelligence.* New York: Harcourt Brace.

Piaget, J, and A. Szeminska (1952). *The Child's Conception of Number.* New York: Humanities Press.

Piaget, J. (1954–55). Le Développement De La Perception De L'Enfant à L'Adulte. *Bull. Psychol., Paris*, 183–8, 489–92, 553–63, 643–71.

Piaget, J., and B. Inhelder (1956). *The Child's Conception of Space.* London: Routledge and Kegan Paul.

Piaget, J., B. Inhelder, and A. Szeminska (1960). *The Child's Conception of Geometry.* New York: Basic Books.

Piaget, J. (1964). In *Piaget Rediscovered* (eds R. E. Ripple and V. N. Rockcastle). Ithaca, N.Y.: Cornell University Press.

Piaget, J., and others (1968). *Epistemologie et Psychologie De La Fonction.* Paris: Presses Universitaires de France.

Piaget, J., and others (1969a). *L'Identité.* Paris: Presses Universitaires de France.

Piaget, J. (1969b). *The Child's Conception of Time.* London: Routledge and Kegan Paul.

Ripple, R. E., and V. N. Rockcastle (eds.) (1964). *Piaget Rediscovered.* Ithaca, N.Y.: Cornell University Press

Siegel, I. E. (1968). Reflections. In *Logical Thinking in Children* (eds. I. E. Siegel and F. H. Hooper). New York: Holt, Rinehart and Winston.

Sinclair, H. (1969). Developmental Psycholinguistics. In *Studies in Cognitive Development* (eds. D. Elkind and J. H. Flavell). New York: Oxford University Press.

Smedslund, J. (1963). The Effect of Observation on Children's Representation of the Spatial Orientation of a Water Surface. *Journal of Genetic Psychology*, 102, 195–201.

Steffe, L. P., and R. B. Parr (1968). *The Development of the Concepts of Ratio and Fraction in the Fourth, Fifth, and Sixth Years of the Elementary School.* Madison: University of Wisconsin Center for Cognitive Learning, Technical Report No. 49.

Sturt, M. (1925). *The Psychology of Time.* London: Routledge and Kegan Paul.

Taback, S. F. (1969). The Child's Concept of Limit. Unpublished doctoral dissertation, Teachers College, Columbia University.

# Bibliography

Thomas, H. L. (1969). *An Analysis of Stages in the Attainment of a Concept of a Function*. Unpublished doctoral dissertation, Teachers College, Columbia University.

Van den Bogaerts, N. (1966). In *L'Épistémologie Du Temps*. Paris: Presses Universitaires de France.

Wagman, H. G. (1968). *A Study of the Child's Conception of Area Measure*. Unpublished doctoral dissertation, Teachers College, Columbia University.

Whitrow, G. J. (1961). *The Natural Philosophy of Time*. London: Nelson.

The publications suggested below are in addition to those listed in the Bibliography.

### For Chapter 1

Beard, R. M. (1969). *An Outline of Piaget's Developmental Psychology for Students and Teachers*. New York: Basic Books.

Boyle, D. G. (1969). *A Student's Guide to Piaget*. New York: Pergamon.

Piaget, J. and B. Inhelder (1969). *The Psychology of the Child*. New York: Basic Books.

### For Chapters 2–10 inclusive

When only certain chapters are relevant to the work covered in this book, these have been indicated.

Association of Teachers of Mathematics (1967). *Notes on Mathematics in Primary Schools*. Cambridge: Cambridge University Press.

Braswell, J. S., and T. A. Romberg (1969). *Objectives of Patterns in Arithmetic and Evaluation of the Telecourse for Grades 1 and 3*. Madison: University of Wisconsin Center for Cognitive Learning, Technical Report 67.

Churchill, E. (1962). *Counting and Measuring*. London: Routledge & Kegan Paul.

D'Augustine, C. H. (1968). *Multiple Methods of Teaching Mathematics in The Elementary School*. New York: Harper & Row. Chapters 3–8 inclusive, 11, 14, 15, 16.

Dienes, Z. P. (1966). *Modern Mathematics for Young Children: A Teachers' Guide to the Introduction of Modern Mathematics to Children from 5 to 8*. London: Educational Supply Association.

Dodwell, P. C. (1960). Children's Understanding of Number and Related Concepts. *Canadian Journal of Psychology*, 14, 191–205.

Dodwell, P. C. (1961). Relations Between the Understanding of the Logic of Classes and of Cardinal Numbers in Children. *Canadian Journal of Psychology*, 16, 152–160.

Dwight, L. A. (1967). *Modern Mathematics for the Elementary Teacher*. New York: Holt, Rinehart and Winston. Chapters 1–10 inclusive, 12, 16, 17.

Grossnickle, F. E., L. J. Brueckener, and J. Reckzel (1968). *Discovering Mean-*

*ings in Elementary School Mathematics.* New York: Holt, Rinehart and Winston. Fifth Edition. Chapters 1-12 inclusive, 17, 18, 19, 20.

Harper, E. H. and L. P. Steffe (1968). *The Effects of Selected Experiences on the Ability of Kindergarten and First-Grade Children to Conserve Numerousness.* Madison: University of Wisconsin Center for Cognitive Learning, Technical Report 38.

Isaacs, N. (1960). *New Light on Children's Ideas of Number.* London: Educational Supply Association.

Mathematical Association (1970). *Primary Mathematics: A Further Report.* London: Mathematical Association.

Minnesota Mathematics and Science Teaching Project (1967/68). Minneapolis: Minnemast.

1. *Watching and Wondering*
2. *Curves and Shapes*
3. *Describing and Classifying*
5. *Introducing Measurement*
6. *Numeration*
7. *Introducing Symmetry*
8. *Observing Properties*
9. *Numbers and Counting*
10. *Describing Locations*
11. *Introducing Addition and Subtraction*
12. *Measurement with Reference Units*
13. *Interpretations of Addition and Subtraction*
14. *Exploring Symmetrical Patterns*

Nufield and The Schools Council Project (1969). New York: Wiley.

*I Do and I Understand*
*Mathematics Begins*
*Beginning Mathematics*
*Computation and Structure 2*
*Computation and Structure 3*
*Shape and Size 2*
*Shape and Size 3*
*Pictorial Representation 1*

Piaget, J. (1969). *The Child's Conception of Movement and Speed.* New York: Basic Books.

The Schools Council (1966). *Mathematics in Primary School.* London: Her Majesty's Stationery Office.

Scott, J. A. (1969). *The Effect of Selected Training Experiences on Performance on a Test of Conservation of Numerousness.* Madison: University of Wisconsin Center for Cognitive Learning, Technical Report 92.

Steffe, L. P. (1966). *The Performance of First Grade Children in Four Levels of Conservation of Numerousness and Three IQ Groups When Solving*

*Arithmetic Addition Problems.* Madison: University of Wisconsin Center for Cognitive Learning, Technical Report 14.

Swenson, E. J. (1964). *Teaching Arithmetic to Children.* New York: Macmillan. Chapters 1–14 inclusive, 19, 20.

The National Council of Teachers of Mathematics (1964). *Topics in Mathematics for Elementary School Teachers.* The Twenty-Ninth Year Book. Washington: The National Council of Teachers of Mathematics.

Van Engen, H., M. L. Hartung, and J. E. Stockl (1965). *Foundations of Elementary School Arithmetic.* Chicago: Scott Foresman. Chapters 1–8 inclusive, 10, 14, 15.

Williams, J. D. (ed.) (1967). *Mathematics Reform in the Primary School.* Hamburg: UNESCO.

# Index

## A

Abstraction
　description of, 20
　levels of, 4, 7, 14, 21
Addition, introduction to, 50–54
Almy, M., 19, 20, 193
Ames, L. P., 172, 193
Analytic thinking, 22
Angles, 99–101
Apostel, L., Mays, W., and Piaget, J., 28, 193
Apparatus, 184–188
Area, 107–114
Assessment of progress, 189
Association of Teachers of Mathematics, 195
Ausubel, D. P., 185, 193

## B

Beard, R. M., 195
Beilin, H., Kagan, J., and Rabinowitz, R., 83, 193
Binary operation, definition of, 45
Boring, E. G., 171, 193

Boyle, D. G., 195
Bradley, N. D., 172, 193
Braswell, J. S., and Romberg, T. A., 195
Brown, P. G., 144, 193

## C

Churchill, E., 195
Classification, 7–8, 23
Classroom organization
　changing the nature of, 183–184
　varieties of, 181–183
Clock arithmetic, 138–140
Concepts, definition of, 21
Counting, 34–35
Cremin, L. A., 190, 193
Curves, 95–99

## D

D'Augustine, C. H., 195
Dienes, Z. P., 43, 181, 186, 193, 195
Discovery learning, 184–186
Distance, 101

Division, introduction to, 62–63
Dodwell, P. C., 20, 193, 195
Duckworth, E., 19
Dwight, L. A., 195

## E

Euclidean concepts
    axes of reference, 80–83

## F

Fehr, H. F., 44, 50, 193
Flavell, J., 2, 193
Fractions, 144–147

## G

Games, function of, 186–187
Geometrical loci, 114–116
Geometry, 95–120
    classroom activities, 116–120
Graphs (*see* Pictorial representation)
Grossnickle, F. E., Brueckener, L. J., and Reckzel, J., 195

## H

Harper, E. H., and Steffe, L. P., 196

## I

Inhelder, B., Bovet, M., Sinclair, H., and Smock, C. D., 16, 193
Inhelder, B., and Piaget, J., 7, 12, 15, 193
Integers, 137–138
Intuitive thinking, 22
Isaacs, N., 196

## K

Kersh, B. Y., 193

## L

Language, role of, 16–17
Length, 101
Location of point in space, 153–154
Logical-mathematical experience, 11
Lovell, K., 27, 193
Lovell, K., and Butterworth, I. B., 14, 193
Lovell, K., Mitchell, B., and Everett, I. R., 7, 194
Lovell, K., and Ogilvie, E., 177, 194
Lovell, K., and Slater, A., 173, 194
Lunzer, E. A., 14, 112, 194

## M

Mappings, 125–129
    and graphs, 129–130
Mass and weight, 167–170
Mathematical association, 196
Mathematical concepts, definition of, 21
Mathematical sentences, 63–67
Mathematics, how children regard, 17–18
Measurement
    of area, 108–112
    of length, 102–105
Minnesota Mathematics and Science Teaching Project, 196
Multiplication, introduction, 56–61

## N

National Council of Teachers of Mathematics, 197

# Index

Nuffield and the Schools Council Project, 51, 196
Number
  bases other than ten, 43–44
  development of the concept of, 36–40
  line, 133–137
  patterns, 148–151
  from the Piagetian standpoint, 25–28
  properties of the set of natural numbers, 140–144
  strip, 40

## P

Pairing, 36
Parents, 189
Physical experience, 10
Piaget, J., 1, 70, 77, 173, 194, 196
  and education, 18–20
  and intellectual growth, 1–14
    views on factors influencing, 14
Piaget, J., and Inhelder, B., 10, 16, 70, 72, 73, 76, 79, 81, 163, 194, 195
Piaget, J., Inhelder, B., and Szeminska, A., 101, 107, 111, 153, 177, 194
Piaget, J., and Szeminska, A., 25, 26, 194
Pictorial representation, 153–166
  interpretation of, 162
  mathematical value of, 157–159
  stages in the construction of, 159–162
Place value, 40–43
Point, 71–73
Projective concepts, 73–80
  geometrical sections, 79–80
  perspectives and their coordination, 74–79

Proportions in geometrical form, 162–166

## R

Rational numbers, 147–148
Recording work done, ways of, 188–189
Recursive argument, 28
Relationships, 121–123
  equivalence, 52
  and mappings, 125–129
  properties of, 123–125
Ripple, R. E., and Rockcastle, V. N., 19, 194

## S

Schools Council, 196
Scott, J. A., 196
Seriation, 24–25
  of sets in terms of number of members, 34
Sets, 25–34
  conservation of number of members of, 32–33
  empty, 33
  intersection of, 47–48
  union of, 48–49
Siegel, I. E., 19, 194
Similarities in geometric form, 162–166
Sinclair, H., 16, 83, 194
Smedslund, J., 83, 194
Space
  classroom activities, 83–86
  perceptual and representational, 70–71
  related activities in numerical field, 92–94
  simple transformations in, 90–92

Spatial work, importance of, 69
Steffe, L. P., 196
Steffe, L. P., and Parr, R. B., 14, 194
Straight line
　projective, 74–75
　special instance of curve, 97
　subdividing, 105–107
Sturt, M., 172, 194
Subset, 30–31
Subtraction, introduction to, 54–56
Swenson, E. J., 196
Symbols, 49–50
Symmetry, 86–90

### T

Taback, S. F., 14, 194
Teachers' knowledge of mathematics, 189–190
Temporal operations, 173–175
Thomas, H. L., 14, 131, 195
Time, 170–177
　activities, 175–177

Time (*cont.*)
　perception of, 177
　some notions of, 171–173

### V

Van den Bogaerts, N., 5, 195
Van Engen, H., Hartung, M. L., and Stockl, J. E., 197
Venn diagram, 45–47
Volume, 177–179

### W

Wagman, H. G., 111, 195
Weight and mass, 167–170
Whitrow, G. J., 195
Williams, J. E., 197

### Z

Zero, 40